RISK CONTROL

Second Edition

by

Shaun Wilkinson

Witherby & Co. Ltd.
32-36 Aylesbury Street,
London EC1R 0ET

OTHER BOOKS IN THE SERIES

Business Finance for Risk Management
Business Organisation and Finance
Corporate Risk Management
Insurance, Non Marine – An Introduction
Liability Exposures
Liability Risk and the Law
Local Government a Text for Risk Managers
Risk and the Business Environment
Risk Analysis
Risk Financing
Risk Management in Healthcare
Treasury Risk Management

British Library Cataloguing in Publication Data

Wilkinson, Shaun
Risk Control
1 Title
ISBN 1 85609 262 3

Notice of Terms of Use

The Institute of Risk Management
6, Lloyd's Avenue
London EC3N 3AX
www.theirm.org
Tel No: 020 7709 9808

1st Edition 1997
2nd Edition 2003

WITHERBYS
PUBLISHING

Shaun Wilkinson

2003

ISBN 1 85609 262 3

Printed and Published by
WITHERBY & CO. LTD
32-36 Aylesbury Street
London EC1R 0ET
Tel No: 020 7251 5341   Fax No: 020 7251 1296
International Tel No: +44 20 7251 5341
International Fax No: +44 20 7251 1296
E-mail: books@witherbys.co.uk
www: witherbys.com

Introduction

Once the type and size of a problem is known the next logical step is to decide how best to respond to that problem and its likely effects. So it is with exposure to risk; once the scope and nature of an exposure to risk has been assessed the next step involves the determination and implementation of measures that will eliminate or reduce the risk, or reduce any loss that may eventuate, both at an economical cost. By doing so the need for loss financing will be reduced in most instances and any losses that do eventuate will be minimised.

This book looks at the measures that may be used to control the various types of operational exposures to risk. As many of these measures have their genesis in the identification and assessment phase of the Risk Management Process, the early part of the book examines, albeit from the point of view of controlling risk, some fundamental features of risk management.

The basic concepts of controlling risk are explored in terms of how these may be applied to risks other than fire. There are of course a number of control measures that are specific to a particular type of risk and these are also discussed at the appropriate points in the text. Unlike in the earlier edition of this book the chapters on fire risk control have been grouped together towards the back of the book. However, it is not intended that this text should provide the complete up to date answer for every situation, but rather it should provide the reader with a basic framework that may assist in solving risk control problems.

It should also be realised that the risk control measures that are installed may not always work as intended. Regular monitoring and review of the performance of risk control measures is therefore essential, as is taking action to improve any that do not come up to standard and to take advantage of any that perform better than expected.

Whilst this text has been aimed at general readers and students of the Institute of Risk Management in the UK, as far as possible it has not been framed in a country specific form. It is therefore essential that the reader supplement his or her reading of this text with study of the relevant legislation and regulations of the country in which he or she is domiciled. In addition, as there is continual product development of risk control measures, supplementary reading of material of the country of domicile is essential to keep fully up to date.

This edition is a reformatting of the earlier edition with some additional enhancements. The earlier edition was the result of a major rewrite of "Physical Control of Risk" which was based on the Risk Management Study Courses written for the Insurance Institute of New Zealand. This has been supplemented by many detailed discussions with fellow Risk Managers around the world.

I thank the Institute (now part of the Australian and New Zealand Institute of Insurance and Finance) for giving its permission to use material from the Study Courses. Finally I would like to thank my wife for all her work in transcribing my rough notes and word processing the text for me, and Jonathan Cassidy for help with the technical evolution of the book.

Shaun W.L. Wilkinson
Auckland, New Zealand
August 2003

Contents

1

HAZARD IDENTIFICATION

1.1 THE CONTEXT OF RISK CONTROL

1.1.1   Controlling risk is one of the essential steps in the risk management process. However for Risk Control to be successful it is vital that not only are all of the risks to which the organisation is exposed first identified and assessed, but also that the context in which the management of risk is to take place within the organisation is determined and understood. The strategic, organisational and risk management contexts should be established prior to any work starting on applying the risk management process so that risks are managed in accordance with the organisation's overall strategic and organisational objectives. In addition when setting the contexts the scope and boundaries of the risk management process are established, as are the criteria that are to be used in evaluating risk. Unless this is done there is a very real danger that any decisions taken in the management of risk will not be correctly aligned or as effective or as efficient as they could be.

1.1.2   Once the contexts have been established, the risks identified, analysed, evaluated and ranked, treatment (including control) may commence. At the same time the existing risk control techniques that have been used are also identified, analysed and evaluated as are possible improvements. Throughout each of these steps there should be a continuing process of monitoring and review of the process as well as communication and consultation with all of the stakeholders concerning the risks and how they should be managed.

1.1.3   Having evaluated and ranked the risks the acceptability of each risk should be determined before deciding which of the many risk and loss avoidance and reduction techniques should be used to control each risk. Essentially these involve the avoidance, the reduction of the likelihood and/or the consequence of both risk and loss. Risk transfer or risk sharing (including insurance) is the other technique that may be used as part of the risk treatment process. It should be noted that the process is an iterative one, which continues with each risk until the combination of selected treatment options produces an acceptable result. In actual fact the risk management process itself should be ongoing with continual refinement of the selected treatment options to ensure that the risks continue to be managed in the most effective way possible.

1.2   HAZARD AND RISK

1.2.1   A classification of the sources of the hazards to which an organisation may be exposed shows that there are two major groups of sources, inherent hazards and human hazards. Inherent hazards are inherent to the organisation, its buildings, plant, equipment, processes and material used and the environment in which it operates; whilst human hazards relate to the people who are associated with the organisation, the stakeholders, such as its management, employees, customers and competitors. Each of these major source groups may be broken down further as can be seen from Table 1.1 at the end of this chapter.

1.2.2   If we understand both the nature of the hazard and the dimensions of its associate risk we will be in a much better position to efficiently and economically control the risk so as to minimise the need for risk transfer or loss financing.

1.3   THE ROLE OF ENERGY

1.3.1   **Energy** is a major factor in most hazards. As will be realised most hazards, involve an accumulation of energy under controlled circumstances. The hazard arises because of the **threat** that this accumulation of energy may escape from the control mechanism that is usually used to contain it. Once it escapes it may of course cause **injury or damage** or both.

1.3.2   In identifying the possible threats from energy one must examine each source of energy for:-

> (a) **over use** e.g. more fuel stored on the factory floor than is needed for the work to be done
>
> (b) **unnecessary use of that particular type of energy** e.g. use of a hazardous material in place of a less hazardous one

(c) **excessive accumulations** e.g. short steep ramps, no speed regulators

(d) **no provision for preventing its release** e.g. no railings on scaffolding, no insulation on hot surfaces

(e) **no provision for a controlled release** e.g. no safety valves

(f) **no means of channelling the released energy away from injuring a person or damaging property** e.g. no separation of pedestrian and vehicular traffic

(g) **no barriers on its source** e.g. no electrical insulation, guards or enclosures

(h) **no barriers in between the source and the worker or other property** e.g. no shields, safety nets or barriers.

1.3.3   Each of these threats leads logically to one or more possible means of controlling the threat. There are many sources of energy ranging from electrical through nuclear to the various types of kinetic energy both linear and rotational. See Table 1.2 at the end of this chapter. All can and do pose a threat from time to time.

1.4   THE ROLE OF CHANGE

1.4.1   Whilst **change** is an ever present factor of today's world being an essential part of progress, for a variety of reasons it also increases the likelihood that a loss may occur. In addition an increase in human error may often result from a change. Therefore identifying areas of change frequently provides the indication of the likely control measures that could be used.

1.4.2   Change is often inherently unpredictable. As a consequence change can have unwanted and unexpected side effects even where the change has been well planned. Change in any system or process is pervasive, directional in that it rarely turns back and it is ongoing. Most changes have an exponential effect over time that can have a quite devastating effect on any problems that the change engenders particularly where energy is involved. Therefore there is a continuing need for further changes in the systems (or controls) to cope with the new hazards and risks created by the changes. As can be seen from *Figure 1.1* these counter changes invariably lag behind the effect of the primary changes.

Figure 1.1

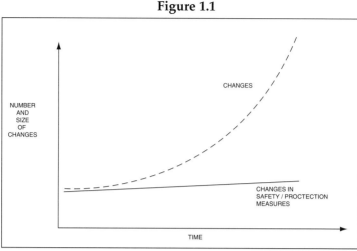

Counter Changes Lag Behind Primary Changes

1.4.3   However, it must be recognised that change is:-

(a) **not synonymous with progress** i.e. change does not always result in progress although progress can only be achieved through change

(b) **unable to be reversed** i.e. once change has been initiated it is impossible to restore things to their previous state

(c) **a traumatic event for most people**

(d) **most powerful when it is least complex**

(e) **successful only when it results in added value**

(f) **frequently the cause of unfamiliarity with the new state** which leads to errors being made and as a consequence losses. For example the increase in fires in textile mills following their conversion from working with natural to man made fibres.

As a consequence change is frequently a major factor in an increase in risk.

1.5   THE CAUSE, RISK AND EFFECT CHAIN

1.5.1   The link between energy and change in relation to accidents is found in the chain linking cause, risk and effect. It is necessary to go through the sequence of this chain to identify the significant hazards in any situation and to measure the risks arising out of those hazards. *Figure 1.2* sets out this chain. It will be seen that the hazard identification and risk management process will probably follow the following sequence:

(a) firstly looking at the major accumulations of energy together with what has changed in recent times or what is new to determine possible causes of future loss

(b) examining the relationship with the major hazards or likely causes that have been discovered and the likelihood that these hazards will lead to a loss. The combination of the hazard in terms of its potential to cause damage and the likelihood that damage will occur provides an indication of the probable common cause of future loss

(c) having determined these, the next step is to assess the likely effects on the business

(d) having done this, then determine the likely consequence of the flow-on effects of risk

(e) finally the optimum mixture of controls is determined

Figure 1.2

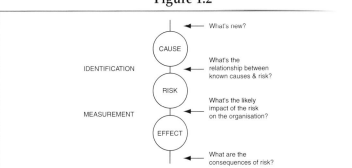

The Chain of Significant Hazards

1.5.2   A study carried out in England proposed that all causes of loss may be classified into one of seven basic categories, and that if any one of these causes leads to a loss producing event, then loss in the form of liability, injury or death, property loss or damage or loss of earnings will result. As can be seen from *Figure 1.3* the categories may be grouped into three generalised groupings, namely:

(a) **natural phenomena,** such as flood, earthquake, storm etc.

(b) **breach of a natural** law, such as design or construction failure and equipment failure.

(c) **man's activities,** for example operating error, maintenance weakness or failure, external interference or insufficient supervision or training.

Figure 1.3

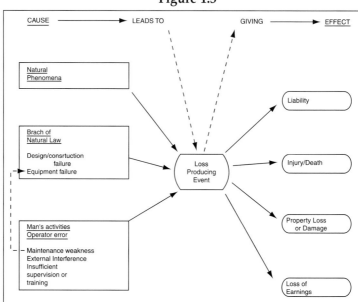

The Three Generalised Groups of Loss of Earnings

1.5.3   Most loss producing events are the end result of a chain of events and as a consequence it is often not possible to identify a single cause, as there are usually a number of different causes each at a different depth varying from immediate to remote.

1.5.4   It is essential when looking at likely causes of loss, ie the sources of hazard and energy, to remember that usually there is some human involvement. This however does not mean to say that when looking at possible causes of accidents or loss that it is assumed that the cause has been found once it is established that a human action or lack of action was involved. It is necessary to probe the reasons for that action or lack of action to determine the true cause. This should be borne in mind when identifying possible hazards. As a rough guide five questions beginning "why" need to be asked before the prime cause of loss is likely to have been determined.

1.6   HAZARD IDENTIFICATION AND RISK ASSESSMENT

1.6.1   There is a need to identify hazards and assess the associated risks so that the actions that should be taken in order to control those risks may be prioritised, and to make the most efficient use of the scarce resources that are available for this. In order that the optimum decisions may be made the identification and assessment should be done in a systematic way so that those making the decision have as complete a picture as is possible. Whilst it is not possible to accurately quantify every risk it should be possible to provide an analysis that clearly identifies the major elements and the extent to which they have been quantified.

1.6.2   When identifying hazards and assessing the risks involved it is not only necessary to discover likely sources of hazards but also to identify their likely area of operation as well as their likely effects. A loss may affect people, property or earnings or a combination of any of these three. Understanding how losses may arise provides an excellent basis for determining the optimum control measures that will eliminate or reduce loss.

The four essential steps in correctly assessing risk are:

(a) identify the hazards

(b) analyse the likely consequences of an event involving the identified hazards

(c) assess the likely frequency of an event involving the identified hazards

(d) compare the results against society's and the business's tolerance of risk.

However it will be readily recognised that in order to correctly identify hazards there needs to be a sound understanding of the type of material, process, situation and activity that may under certain conditions become a hazard.

1.6.3   It is the **probability** of the event occurring that alters the hazard into a risk. The following are a series of questions the answers to which will enable the hazards and their associated risks to be better understood:

(a) what is the source of potential danger, i.e. what is the hazard?

(b) who or what is at risk?

(c) what injury or damage could be caused? i.e. if a loss occurs how large is the loss likely to be?

(d) what can go wrong? i.e. the likely cause of loss

(e) what are the chances that the exposure to the hazard could result in a loss?

(f) what are the chances that injury or damage will be caused if things go wrong?

Associated with these questions are the following questions that will provide a lead into the means of controlling the hazards and the risks that are identified:

(g) how to prevent things going wrong?

(h) how to protect if things go wrong or if exposure to hazard and risk is unavoidable?

As will be seen from the above, assessment and control are closely allied, with the former leading naturally to the latter. It is quite normal for thought to be given to possible control measures whilst the risks are being assessed.

1.6.4 **Why should risk be assessed?** There are a number of reasons for doing so which may be classified under one of the following headings:

(a) **social**

The public has become increasingly aware of the many risks to which they are exposed every day of their lives. There is a widespread feeling that all risk can and should be eliminated, or if this is not possible it should be moved to somewhere else. A totally risk free environment is an impossibility and it follows that it is essential to assess the risk so that rational judgement may be made on how to best manage it.

(b) **legal**

As a result of public pressure following disasters, legislation has been introduced requiring that risks be assessed. In addition there is a public expectation that anyone who is in control of an activity should be held responsible for the consequences of that activity particularly if they earn money from it.

(c) **economic**

Whilst an organisation may substantially reduce its risks by managing them (eliminate, reduce, and control) some residual risk will always remain. The consequences of this residual risk have to be borne by the organisation itself, or they may be transferred to a third party such as an insurer. It is better to do this from a state of understanding rather than from a state of ignorance.

1.6.5 **What are the aims of risk assessment?**

There are four:

(a) **understanding**

(b) **measurement**

(c) **costing**

(d) **control.**

In other words it is the gathering of facts to enable a risk to be **managed**. Decisions have to be taken on whether or not the risk is commercially acceptable, on what risk and loss control measures should be implemented and how these and any losses are to be financed.

1.6.6 There is a very wide variety of methods that may be used to identify the hazards and risks associated with an organisation. Every organisation is different and any one of a number of methods may be used depending on the type of organisation and the activities in which it is involved. To fully identify the hazards associated with a particular article, substance or situation, it is essential that before measuring the degree of risk involved the nature of the hazards and the associated risks themselves are understood. This understanding may be gained from a variety of approaches such as:

(a) Those that relate to the organisational aspects of the business, for example:

(i) **analysis of the organisation's annual accounts** – this will give a broad indication of the types of activities that are involved together with the amount of assets employed and the earnings that are being made

(ii) **organisation chart** – which will reveal the management structure and the extent of any likely controls over the various activities

(iii) **flow chart of operations** – charting the flow of materials into and out of the organisation should enable interdependencies, bottlenecks and duplications to be quickly identified together with any dependencies on suppliers and/or customers. Also charting of the flow within the processes will enable the effects of errors or mishaps at any stage of the process to be identified. There are a number of techniques that may be used for this such as failure modes and effects analysis, event tree analysis, cause and consequence analysis and HAZOP and HAZAN studies.

The last two are Hazard and Operability and Hazard Analysis studies (HAZOP and HAZAN) that can highlight potential deviations from normal operating conditions. Both tools enable hazards to be identified and assessed before a plant is built. HAZOP is an open ended technique that is ideal for identifying new hazards and is qualitative, whereas HAZAN being a quantitative technique is ideal where there is no code of practice in existence *(see Figure 1.4)*. Both however involve using a team of people with different types of expertise and knowledge.

Figure 1.4

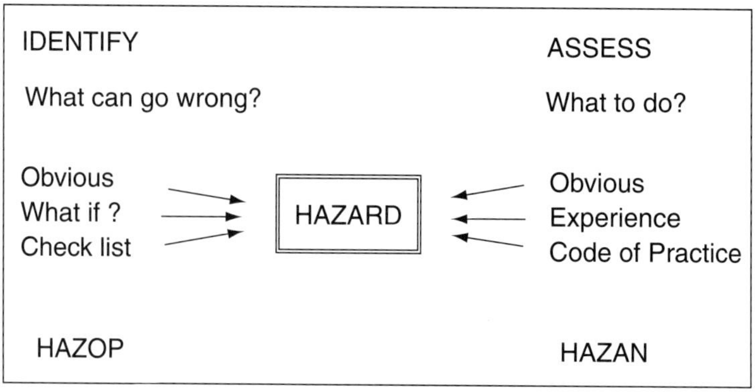

Hazop is Qualitative and Hazan Quantitative

(iv) **analysis of the various contracts entered into by the organisation** such as sales, purchases and leases will determine the degree to which risks are transferred into and out of the organisation.

(v) **the organisation's strategic plans** which will provide an indication of likely future developments and therefore possible new exposures.

(b) those that involve a physical inspection of a site process or machine such as:

(i) **site inspection or physical survey** – apart from walking around the site to get an overall impression of it, there is a need to inspect the more significant areas in more detail. In addition every opportunity should be taken to question the shop floor management and employees as these people invariably have a very good appreciation of the hazards and risks that are involved in their activities.

(ii) **safety audits** such as the International Safety Rating System (commonly known as 5 Star System) that focus primarily on the safety of people both within and outside the organisation.

(iii) **gridcharts** which are used to summarise the major risk areas.

(iv) **environmental audits/operational audits** which focus on those activities that may lead to environmental problems in the future or which are currently impairing the environment.

(c) there are a number of check list based methods including:

(i) a variety of risk check lists such as **risk analysis and asset exposure analysis forms**. These act as an aide memoire as well as the source of exposure charts, threat and event analysis and hazard logic tree as circumstances require.

(ii) **Dow Index** and **Mond Index** that assists in identifying fire and explosion hazards from a chemical point of view. They are usually only used in chemical plants as is CIA Risk Assessment methodology.

(d) those that relate to losses for example:

    (i) **fault tree analysis** that examines the relationship between fault and the ensuing loss.

    (ii) **incident investigation and recall** are techniques for establishing what went wrong and what should be done to prevent problems in the future. It is however, essential that an in-depth analysis is undertaken to overcome the conditioning that many people have which is to only look at the most immediate cause or the point at which an exchange of energy takes place. The analysis should explore the underlying reasons for the immediate cause such as:

- a build up of energy
- deviations from normal
- errors
- unsafe acts
- unsafe conditions.

    (iii) the **loss statistics** of similar organisations, sites and occupations.

1.7   IDENTIFICATION AND MEASUREMENT

1.7.1   Before a risk can be managed effectively it must be examined carefully, identified and measured in terms of:

(a) the **frequency** of its likely occurrence

(b) the **probability** of loss or damage

(c) the **severity** of the effects of a loss

(d) the **perception** of the probability of loss and its effects;

so that it may be assessed in comparison with similar risks.

At best this can only be a soundly based opinion but it should provide a guide of how much better or worse a particular risk is than a normal risk of the same type.

1.7.2   There is a relationship between frequency and severity, which is important in deciding what action should be taken to handle the risk.

(a) **chronic losses** which are small and regular and which are almost inevitable, such as most motor accidents. These should be looked upon as a trade risk and should not be insured as to do so tends to lead to "pound swapping". However the annual aggregate total of this type of loss can often be significant and they therefore should not be ignored. Quality control is one methodology that can help in controlling these losses.

(b) **sporadic losses** which are medium sized and irregular that may happen from time to time and may be able to be controlled to a significant extent.

(c) **catastrophes** which are very large losses which may occur on rare occasions. Such losses will probably have a devastating effect on any organisation that they affect.

1.7.3   The measurements that are able to be made of most risks can be combined so as to provide a sound basis for decision making.

For example often with a risk there are various differing probabilities of loss each of which may have a different consequence or severity. By multiplying these two factors together it may be possible to obtain a series of results that may make a choice on the best method to handle the risk more straightforward to make. For example:

Probability A x Consequence B = Result AB compare then

Probability C x Consequence D = Result CD choose the

Probability E x Consequence F = Result EF optimum result

It is also possible to plot each risk in a table in terms of its probability and consequences as the means of fixing its position in the table, thereby quickly establishing which risks exceed an organisation's tolerance level. Action can then be directed at handling these risks and their effects whilst risks that are tolerated may be ignored. See *Figure 1.5.*

Figure 1.5

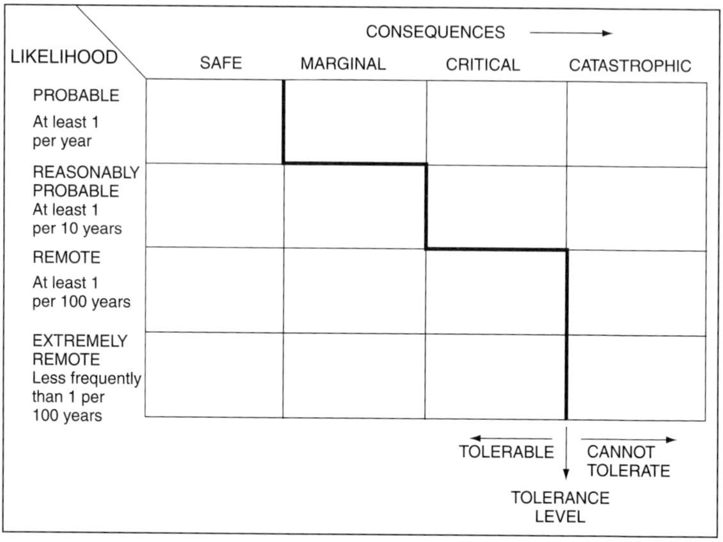

Caption to follow

1.7.4 Perception

Whilst frequency and severity can provide a quantitative measure of the likely effects of a risk the perception of those effects is often quite different. For example if the frequency and severity of motor losses and aircraft losses are compared you will find that the result is very different from that which is perceived by the average man in the street. Statistically the risks associated with car travel are greater than those of air travel.

1.7.5 Costing

From this assessment it should be possible for a Risk Manager to determine which of the methods of handling risk and loss are the most economically viable for the business.

However, for risks that are not associated with an industrial organisation that has a Risk Manager the normal method of handling a particular risk is usually a decision of whether:

(a) to fully insure

(b) to partially insure

(c) not to insure at all

This is based on the cost of the premium that the insurer quotes for the risk and the possible effects on the business of a major loss at some time in the future. In such circumstances little or no attempt is made to control the risks unless the insurer insists that one or more risk control measures should be implemented before quoting.

Without having fully costed the risk and its effects it is not possible for a manager to make a reasoned judgement as to which of the many alternative means of controlling risk are likely to be most effective.

1.7.6 **Control**

Risk reduction and loss control measures cost money to implement and therefore it is essential that the risk be quantified so that the most cost effective methods of handling it may be determined. As insurance is generally more costly and less effective than the other methods, the Risk Manager will try to minimise his use of insurance by the use of control measures. It is interesting to note that insurers use a process very similar to that outlined above to assess risk so that they may determine whether or not to accept, and if so, to set an adequate rate for the risk.

1.8 ASSESSING THE FIRE RISK

1.8.1   Once the nature of fire and the factors leading to its inception have been considered, it is necessary to examine the circumstances which may cause it to be sustained or propagated in the particular circumstances that are being considered.

1.8.2   The inception risk and the propagation risk are entirely disconnected factors in the overall assessment. In a large warehouse the inception risk may be small but the bulk storage or combustible materials over a large area presents a high propagation risk. Conversely, although the inception risk may be high, perhaps because of a process involving high temperatures, there may be little danger of the fire spreading, because combustible materials are kept clear of the hazardous area. Or the danger of fire spread may be low because the particular process is undertaken in a building or compartment that is cut-off, or segregated in a fire sense from the remainder of the site. Again, a process that is clearly hazardous may present a reduced inception risk because of rigorous enforcement of statutory safety requirements, but this does not affect the propagation risk in any way.

Accordingly in assessing the risk:

(a) the **inception risk** may be gauged by how a building is occupied and the services, utilities, processes and hazards associated with such occupation

(b) the **propagation risk** may be gauged by the extent to which the size and layout of the premises and the presence of combustible materials which may facilitate propagation of the fire

(c) the **concentration of values** involved; that is, the extent to which high valued materials subject to risk are concentrated within relatively small areas. Conversely the materials may spread over a large area or may have a relatively low value

(d) the **construction** of the building to assess the degree to which it can resist a fire or arrest its progress.

These are usually assessed in the course of a survey in which the site is inspected in some considerable detail and the results noted down in the form of a plan and report.

1.9 CONSEQUENTIAL LOSS RISK ASSESSMENT

1.9.1   The Consequential Loss (or "Business Interruption") policy cover is based on the Fire policy and therefore the plan and report prepared for the latter is usually used in assessing the Consequential Loss risk. There are, however, some additional features that must be surveyed and reported on so that the risks involved may be assessed in full. These additional features include:

(a) any areas of possible **bottleneck** in the process, for example where all the products have to be worked on by one machine which if destroyed or damaged would stop all production

(b) the possibility of **access** to the site being restricted, for example could a fire in another property block or limit entry to the property being surveyed until the debris is cleared away

(c) the possibility of **supplies** such as power, raw materials used in production being cut or stopped as a result of damage to the property of the supplier

(d) the possibility that **customers** will be unable to take delivery of or purchase the goods or services as a result of their property being damaged

(e) **seasonal factors,** for example a fruit cannery or a ski resort.

1.9.2   From a Risk Manager's point of view perhaps the most important features to be examined are 1.9.1 (a) and (d) above together with the availability of replacement office or other facilities or machinery should they be damaged or destroyed. For example:

(a) can it be obtained?

(b) if so, from where?

(c) how long will it take?

(d) are spare parts or alternatives available?

In addition the increase in the use of the "Just in Time" (JIT) philosophy can greatly accentuate a loss if the ramifications of an interruption to processing have not been thought through. JIT enables a business to makes significant cost savings by enabling it to reduce the amount of raw materials, part-processed goods and fully finished stock that needs to be stored. However if an interruption occurs and the business is not able to quickly and easily supply its customers with the services or goods that they have ordered the resultant loss will quickly escalate.

With some industries such as the petroleum and chemical industries there is a significant degree of interdependence between different plants within the same business. This is another factor that the Risk Manager should take into account when evaluating the risk exposure.

1.10   PERILS RISK ASSESSMENT

1.10.1 Exposure to loss resulting from perils such as explosion, flood and windstorm means that surveyors are often asked to prepare reports dealing with such perils, particularly where there is an exposure to water damage or explosion in trade or industrial risks. The information needed naturally varies, but as a general rule the following features need consideration.

1.10.2 **Aircraft**

Proximity to airports or airfields and the purposes for which the airport is being used (e.g. private, commercial, armed services, and the like) as well as the situation of the property with respect to the airport runways all need to be considered.

1.10.3 **Explosion**

(a) details of:

(i) any process where the explosion risk is abnormal; and/or

(ii) any storage of goods of an explosive or highly reactive nature

(iii) vessels or appurtenances such as pipework which are under pressure or vacuum;

(b) explosion risk (if any) from surrounding properties.

1.10.4 **Windstorm, Storm and Tempest, Hailstorm, Snowstorm and other Climatic exposures**

(a) situation – consider exposure to elements – proximity to coast – elevation

(b) construction and general state of repair (particularly the roof)

(c) maintenance (e.g. chimneys – tall trees near enough to cause damage).

1.10.5 **Flood**

(a) level of premises relative to surrounding land and water courses

(b) distance from sea, river or other water which might cause flooding

(c) the condition of any water courses in the proximity particularly down-stream from the site

(d) basements on the site and their use.

1.10.6 **Burst Pipes**

(a) main stopcocks and their accessibility if they need to be turned off outside working hours

(b) subsidiary stopcocks

(c) details of elevated tanks and if provided with stopcocks and/or overflow pipes

(d) susceptibility of tanks and pipes to frost and whether or not adequate protection has been provided.

1.10.7   In addition, with Storm, Tempest, Flood and Burst Pipes, the following general features should also be reported on:

(a) age and condition of property

(b) details of any previous damage by the perils concerned

(c) the susceptibility of any contents to damage

1.10.8   **Subsidence**

(a) situation of premises, with particular reference to position, e.g. side of hill, bank or river

(b) details of any nearby quarries, mines or underground workings

(c) nature of subsoil

(d) confirmation that the ground on which the building is sited is not 'made-up' or 'fill'.

1.10.9   **Earthquake**

(a) past earthquake experience of the region.

(b) proximity to and alignment with known fault lines.

(c) nature of the subsoil

  (i) type

  (ii) nature of subsoil layers

  (iii) ground water.

(d) materials used in the building's construction

(e) design of the building

(f) standards of the workmanship in the building and plant

(g) sensitivity of machinery and other contents to earthquake forces

(h) likelihood of fire or explosion following earthquake:

    (i) ignition sources

    (ii) combustible materials

    (iii) firefighting capability in adverse conditions

    (iv) fire and explosion prevention measures designed and built into the building and plant.

1.11   BURGLARY OR THEFT RISK ASSESSMENT

1.11.1   The burglary risk is assessed in a similar manner to the assessment of fire risk, though, of course, particular attention must be paid to the features that affect the likelihood of loss from burglary or theft.

The person making the assessment should try to imagine himself as the criminal, armed with the type of equipment that is freely available at the present time. Such equipment includes pinch bars, screwdrivers, heavy hammers, tyre levers, pipe wrenches, tyre jacks, bolt cutters, battery-operated electric drills, oxy-acetylene cutting equipment, or the thermal lance.

1.11.2   It was normal for many companies to ask the police to advise on the security precautions to be installed, though this did not relieve the person assessing the risk of the responsibility for reporting on the standard of security and possible improvements. Whilst the police are still interested in safeguarding property they are normally more concerned with safeguarding life. As a result there has tended to be a reduction in the police involvement in survey work for burglary loss control in recent years. The person undertaking the burglary survey may as a consequence become far more involved in giving advice on burglary loss control.

1.11.3   To identify the exposure to burglary and theft risks:

(a) study details of any previous attempts at burglary and theft at the site before visiting the property

(b) try to tour the property with a senior member of the business which occupies the property

(c) keep in mind the cost of providing good protection throughout the whole time that the survey takes to complete and document

(d) work through the property systematically, paying particular attention to the external features of the property itself and of buildings in the immediate neighbourhood

(e) consider:

(i) the use or uses to which the property is being put

(ii) the attractiveness and portability of the goods and materials that are present in the property

(iii) how entry may be made and how the goods or materials may be removed from the property.

(f) try to cover all aspects of loss prevention, visualising the possible causes of loss

(g) pay particular attention to the following features:

(i) the moral and morale hazard of the people involved in the business

(ii) the neighbourhood – how accessible is the building?

(iii) the boundary walls and fences

(iv) the illumination of yards and enclosed areas

(v) the presence of external fall pipes

(vi) cellars

(vii) the materials used in the construction of the property

(viii) the means of locking doors, windows and other openings in the exterior walls of the property. Also the means of securing internal doors.

(ix) safes and strongrooms

(x) any alarm systems that have been installed.

1.12 LIABILITY RISK ASSESSMENT

1.12.1 The assessment of general liability risks is complex and as a consequence surveys are normally limited to the larger and more complicated risks. The scope of liability exposures is such that it is not possible to adequately cover all the many different types of hazard in a text of this type. However, as a general practice, the person assessing the risk must try to anticipate how injuries may occur and how property may be damaged. In addition, whilst not all people are careless, it is safe to assume that most will be at some time or another and the risk should be assessed accordingly. Furthermore exposure to liability risk involves many different factors all of which should be identified and analysed in order to accurately quantify the exposure. These factors include:

(a) people; for example management, leadership, training, qualifications and other human factors

(b) machinery and equipment; for example design, maintenance, construction and manufacture

(c) systems and procedures; for example quality assurance, operational practices and communication

(d) the environment including:

(i) the physical environment; for example situation, and climatic conditions

(ii) contractual conditions; for example specifications, tenders, and contract terms

(iii) legislation, regulations, standards and codes.

1.12.2 The person examining the risk should pay special attention to:

(a) ensuring that all activities undertaken by the business are known about and understood;

(b) access to the premises by:

(i) customers

(ii) members of the general public.

(c) materials used in any aspect of the occupation, checking for any that are:

(i) toxic

(ii) carcinogenic

(iii) flammable

(iv) explosive

(v) corrosive; or

(vi) otherwise dangerous to person or property;

to ensure that they are handled and stored properly

(d) machinery, lifts, hoists, cranes and the like, used in the building checking to ensure that:

    (i) adequate guards are fitted and used

    (ii) all equipment is regularly inspected and maintained

    (iii) all operators are adequately trained and supervised;

(e) the interior of the premises, checking to ensure that:-

    (i) all floor surfaces

    (ii) all staircases, passageways and public spaces;

are not only well lit but also maintained in a good state of repair and are not slippery even if wet.

(f) the exterior of the premises, checking to ensure that:

    (i) overhead signs

    (ii) parapets, guttering and chimneys

    (iii) trapdoors, cellar flaps, goods chutes, pavement lights, grilles and gratings in the pavement outside the premises

    (iv) stairs, walkways, passageways and public spaces are adequately illuminated and have a non slip surface;

are all maintained in a good state of repair.

(g) trees on the premises to ensure that they are:

    (i) not the type of tree that has a large, hungry rooting system such as willow

    (ii) healthy and not constituting any hazard;

(h) the collection and disposal of waste

(i) the standard of quality control, management and housekeeping

(j) any possible improvements that will reduce the risk and/or the size of any likely loss

(k) compliance with national safety legislation.

1.12.3 Whilst the person identifying and assessing the liability risks arising out of only the ownership or occupation of premises should take many of the points raised in 1.12.2 above into account, the following should also be examined:

(a) the public access into and out of the premises should be clearly marked, free of obstruction, well lit and maintained. In addition, the floors should be covered with a surface that remains non-slip under all conditions.

(b) the possibility of a fire or large amounts of liquids being able to spread from the premises to adjoining property and vice versa

(c) the possibility of site and/or ground water contamination from a previous occupation of the site or an adjoining site. In addition, the possibility that site contamination may spread to adjoining sites or watercourses should be considered.

1.12.4 The assessment of product liability risks involves the examination of additional topics in some depth. It is a different type of liability risk and with the large volume of exports to countries such as those in North America this is now frequently treated as a separate topic – Products Liability. It is often the subject of a special report covering in detail all aspects of each product individually:

(a) **the type of product** – whether edible or not?; whether it is for human use or not?

(b) **where it is to be sold?** – if it is to be sold overseas (particularly Canada and U.S.A. where different standards of care apply) then the personal injury aspects must be carefully considered

(c) **quality control and hygiene standards** – are these being enforced?

(d) **design and development** – is this adequately controlled and is each new product fully tested before distribution?

(e) **packing and distribution** – is this adequate for the type of product?

(f) **documentation, disclaimers, instructions etc.** – are these clear enough for all likely users?

(g) **any possible improvements** that will reduce the risk and size of loss

In all of this it must be remembered that the technical specifications against which any product is measured are constrained to a significant extent by the legal standards that will apply. It is therefore essential that the producer of the product understands the legal risks to which the product will be exposed whenever it is sold. Even if the producer takes the greatest possible care they may still be held liable in the event of injury or damage. In addition it should be remembered that the law is in a state of constant change and that it is therefore prudent to retain legal advice throughout the life of the product.

There are a number of checklists available covering the safety and quality of products that can be usefully used in assessing and improving products risks.

1.12.5 The identification and assessment of professional indemnity risks is not easy, because of the rapid expansion of the boundaries of liability for the consequences of advice given, or specialist work undertaken. Increasingly, giving any kind of advice may be viewed as acting in a professional capacity and can lead to the advice giver being sued. The person assessing the risk must identify:

(a) the extent and scope of services provided in the business

(b) the extent and scope of technical advice and support given to customers or third parties.

1.13 MOTOR AND MOBILE PLANT RISK ASSESSMENT

1.13.1 The assessment of a Motor or Mobile Plant risk does not involve a survey as such but may on occasions involve:

(a) as the major hazard in Motor risk is the driver, a special report on him, such as a certificate from a doctor certifying that he is fit to drive

(b) a report on the roadworthiness of the vehicle or item of plant. This may be because of its age or because it had been involved in an accident. Such a report would normally be a certificate from a qualified motor engineer.

(c) an investigation of the use of the vehicle, for example in a hazardous situation such as a quarry face.

1.13.2   The Risk Manager of motor fleets makes frequent assessments of the experience of the fleets with which they are involved. The survey in these cases is concerned with:

(a) the loss experience of the fleet

(b) possible alternatives for improving that loss experience

(c) other ways of reducing the cost of the risk and loss involved.

1.14   ENGINEERING RISK ASSESSMENT

1.14.1   In most countries Engineering risks (e.g. Boilers, Lifts, Hoists and Pressure Vessels) have to be surveyed and certified as being safe by an approved engineering authority or a government department before they may be used. In addition these risks have to be inspected and certified at regular intervals (normally 12 months) thereafter.

1.14.2   Therefore the need for an independent survey is limited and would tend to be restricted to the:

(a) moral hazards. Is the housekeeping as well as the servicing and maintenance regular and adequate?

(b) public liability aspects.

1.15   CONTRACTORS AND ERECTION RISKS

1.15.1   This is a composite type of risk that can contain elements of:

(a) Fire and Special Perils.

(b) Consequential Loss.

(c) All Risks.

(d) Public Liability.

(e) Engineering.

In addition many risks are not situated within the confines of a building and therefore the possibility and likely effects of an occurrence of natural events must be considered.

1.15.2 Some of the following aspects which are particular to these types of risks that must be considered by the person assessing the risk are:

> (a) whether the project will be completed as a whole or whether it will be completed and handed over in sections.
>
> (b) whether the project involves extending an existing building or machine or whether it is completely new.
>
> (c) the length of the maintenance period (if any) after completion.

The plans, drawings and bill of materials plus a copy of conditions of contract should also be made available to the person who is assessing the risk.

1.15.3 Construction sites are amongst the most hazardous in terms of worker injury. As a consequence it is essential that the identification of all hazards and their associated risks be carried out on an ongoing basis so as to ensure that the continual changing state of the site and its hazards are able to be properly managed.

1.16   EMPLOYEE FRAUD RISK ASSESSMENT

1.16.1 As employee fraud (sometimes known as "Fidelity Guarantee") risk is primarily concerned with moral hazard, every attempt is made to gain details concerning the person who is being guaranteed. The normal means of doing this is by obtaining:

> (a) former employer's reports
>
> (b) referee's reports
>
> (c) credit checks

which are concerned with moral hazards, and

(d) employer's report that deals with the physical hazards as well as the moral hazards.

1.17 WORKER INJURY RISK ASSESSMENT

1.17.1   The safety of workers or employees is a major preoccupation of most Risk Managers because accidents to workers or employees represent a significant proportion of the total losses suffered by many employers. Therefore the identification and assessment of such exposures is often extremely important for the Risk Manager and his employer.

1.17.2   The investigation of an accident usually shows that there is more than one cause involved. The human element whether in the form of management controls, training, operating procedures or similar is often found to be a major factor in the cause of accidents. Therefore in the assessment of the risk of worker injury it is essential that each step of the human element of each task undertaken in the business be examined in some depth.

1.17.3   Analysis of compliance with Health and Safety regulations is a feature of risk assessment and sets the agenda for risk reduction and control.

1.18 MARINE RISK ASSESSMENT

1.18.1   Marine Hulls and Cargoes are exposed to many of the same perils as are buildings and plant which are situated on land plus the perils associated with the sea. In addition as the vessels travel in the open seas they are often well away from the many loss prevention and reduction facilities that are readily available for land based assets and personnel in the event of a loss happening. Marine Hulls and Cargoes therefore need to be able to cope with most losses without having to invoke outside help.

1.18.2   Therefore apart from water damage, fire is of significance as is explosion, mechanical breakdown and human error. As a consequence the survey of the hull is concerned with the general condition of the hull itself the machinery in it particularly the engines and the equipment carried. The Lloyd's Survey is an example of such surveys.

1.18.3   The use of a well-trained crew, particularly for the critical positions in the larger vessels is extremely important. Many countries therefore, not only register vessels sailing under their flag, but have, and enforce, regulations to ensure that the critical positions such as the Captain, Mate and Chief Engineer are held by people who have a specific qualification that is appropriate to that particular position.

1.18.4 In excess of 75% of all cargo losses are preventable. It is therefore important that those risks associated with a particular type of cargo that may be reduced or prevented are identified and assessed so that the appropriate action may be taken.

TABLE 1.1

INHERENT HAZARDS

CHEMICAL
Corrosive
Toxicity
Flammability
Pyrophoricity
Explosive
Oxidising
Photoreactive
Hydroreactive
Carcinogenic
Shock sensitive
Stored energy

MECHANICAL
Weight
Speed or acceleration
Stability
Vibration
Rotation
Translations
Reciprocation
Pinch or nip points
Punching or shearing
Sharp edges
Entrapment
Impact

ELECTRICAL
Shock
Short circuit
Sparking
Arcing
Explosion
Radiation
Fire
Insulation failure
Overheating
Emissions

MISCELLANEOUS
Noise
Light intensity
Stroboscopic effect
Temperature effect
Pressure, suction
Ventilation
Ignition sources
Decomposition
Slipperiness
Moisture
Aging

RADIATION
Alpha, gamma and beta
X Ray
Infrared and ultraviolet
Radio and microwave

HUMAN HAZARDS

PERSONAL
Ignorance
Boredom and loafing
Negligence
Carelessness
Horseplay
Smoking
Alcohol or drugs
Sickness
Exhaustion
Disorientation
Stress
Physical limitations
Cultural background
Warnings

HUMAN ERRORS
Failure to perform
Incorrect performance
Incorrect supervision
Incorrect training
Over qualification
Poor Judgment

ENVIRONMENTAL
Weather
Noise
Temperature
Light
Floor texture
Ventilation
Complexity
Comfort conditions
Social factors
Psychological factors

TABLE 1.2

SOURCES OF ENERGY

ELECTRICAL
Battery banks
Diesel units
High lines
Transformers
Wiring
Switchgear
Underground wiring
Cable runs
Service outlets and fittings
Pumps
Motors
Heaters
Power tools
Small equipment

NUCLEAR (OUT OF REACTOR)
Faults
Temporary storage areas
Receiving areas
Shipping areas
Casks
Burial grounds
Storage ranks
Canals and basins
Reactor in-tank storage area
Dollies
Trucks
Hand carry
Cranes
Lifts
Shops
Hot cells
Assembly areas
Inspection areas
Laboratories
Pilot plants

KINETIC/LINEAR (VEHICLE)
Car
Trucks
Buses

KINETIC/ROTATIONAL
Centrifuges
Motors
Pumps
Cafeteria equipment
Laundry equipment
Gears
Shop equipment (grinders, saws, brushes etc)
Floor polishers

KINETIC/ROTATIONAL (PRESSURE, TENSION)
Boilers
Heated surge tanks
Autoclaves
Test loops and facilities
Gas bottles
Pressure vessels
Coiled springs
Stressed members
Gas receivers

KINETIC/LINEAR (IN-PLANT)

Forklifts
Carts
Dollies
Railroad
Surfaces
Obstructions
Shear Presses
Presses
Crane loads in motion
PV Blowdown
Power assisted

KINETIC/ROTATIONAL (FALLS AND DROPS)

Human effort
Stairs
Bucket and ladder
Trucks
Elevators
Jacks
Scaffold and ladders
Crane cabs
Pits
Excavators
Elevated doors
Canals
Vessels

KINETIC/ROTATIONAL (CRANES AND LIFTS)

Lifts
Cranes
Slings
Hoists

2

RISK CONTROL

2.1 INTRODUCTION

2.1.1   Preventing and minimising loss are the most effective means of reducing the cost of risk apart from eliminating or reducing the risk itself.

Risk and loss reduction is an area that should be of vital concern to:

(a) **the management of each individual organisation**

(b) **other stakeholders, including the organisation's insurers**

(c) **the community as a whole.**

2.1.2   This has been recognised by the existence of a large number of organisations, part of whose function is the reduction of risk and minimising the effects of loss on the community such as:

(a) Health and Safety Executive

(b) Fire Protection Association

(c) Fire Brigades

(d) Police Force

(e) Consumer Institute or the organisation representing the interests of the consumer

(f) Emergency response teams or similar

(g) Financial Reporting Council.

2.1.3   The following are seen as being essential for the effective management of both hazards and risks:

(a) management must be aware of the hazards and how serious their impact could be in the event of an incident as well how such incidents may occur and may be prevented

(b) the organisation must be willing to spend the money necessary to effectively control the hazards and risks

(c) the appropriate facilities and equipment must be in place

(d) the appropriate systems and procedures including systems for monitoring and auditing performance must be in place

(e) there must be an adequate risk management organisation, a sufficient level and competence of staffing as well the appropriate communication and training arrangements

(f) the appropriate means of detecting the occurrence of emergency situations and the handling of such situations

(g) risk management must be promoted actively throughout the business and must be built into its culture.

2.1.4   There are a number of different means by which loss may be prevented or minimised:

(a) **prior to a loss happening**

These are means that aim at reducing the chance of loss occurring by:

(i) eliminating the possibility of its occurrence – avoiding the risk, e.g. using non-flammable liquid in place of a flammable liquid

(ii) reducing the probability of its occurrence – improving the risk, e.g. ensuring effective financial controls are established.

(b) **upon a loss happening**

These are concerned with:

(i) detecting the occurrence and raising an alarm

(ii) minimising the effect and size of loss.

(c) **following the happening of a loss**

These are concerned with limiting the effects of loss by:

(i) minimising the extent of loss

(ii) maximising the salvage recovery

(iii) effecting rehabilitation as soon as possible after the occurrence.

2.1.5   The purpose of risk control is to minimise the total cost of risk to an organisation whilst at the same time ensuring the long term economic survival of the organisation. To determine the **total cost of risk** the following should be taken into account:

(a) the cost of the injury or damage

(b) the cost of handling and settling the loss

(c) the cost of any risk control measures

(d) the cost of any loss financing measures

(e) the costs recovered from any loss financing measures, such as insurance, that have been put in place by the organisation.

Another cost that should be taken into account is the **opportunity cost**. In other words, how else could the money have been spent if it had not been used to meet the costs listed above?

2.1.6   All risk control and financing measures cost money but some are more cost effective at minimising the total cost of risk than others. The risk control measures can be divided into those that:

(a) **eliminate or reduce the risk**

(b) **prevent loss** i.e. the risk exists but no loss occurs

(c) **detect and reduce the extent of the loss**

(d) **rehabilitate, restore and recover.**

The amount of money spent can be kept to a minimum by providing for the measures whenever possible during the early stages of the creation of a hazard and by implementing measures that change the level of risk.

2.1.7   During the assessment of a risk the person assessing should be constantly aware of the need to reduce risk and to prevent and minimise loss. They should therefore actively promote ways and means of reducing risk and preventing and reducing loss. All risk control measures involve taking action before the loss can occur so that it may be prevented or controlled. Therefore, in essence all risk control measures involve planning if they are to be successful in that the likelihood of loss is foreseen and the risk measures that are implemented are expected to prevent or control the loss. Risk control measures cannot be implemented successfully after the loss has occurred.

2.1.8   There is usually a sequence of events leading up to the loss that result from the exposure to hazard but invariably the final event in the sequence – **the event** – is not only unexpected but also it is not planned nor is it intended. However this does not mean that there should not be planning undertaken to reduce the likelihood of an event occurring, or to reduce the extent of the severity of that event. There are a wide range of measures which can be successfully implemented:

(a) **prior to the accident or loss in the workplace**

Establishing a safe workplace by:

(i) ensuring that the building in which the work area is located is soundly constructed for the use to which the building is being put, and that it is correctly maintained

(ii) only using machinery and equipment, materials and processes that are safe or that are able to be used in a safe manner

(iii) implementing safe systems of work

(iv) ensuring that employees are both competent and trained in all aspects of their assigned work

(v) providing adequate supervision

(vi) enabling the organisation to cope with any major accident and to recover quickly from its effects. This will involve having a disaster plan for each of the likely major events;

(b) **during the accident or loss**

Establishing systems and procedures that:

(i) detect the happening of the accident or loss

(ii) avoid, eliminate or minimise the immediate effects of the accident or loss;

(c) **following the accident or loss**

Implementing systems that:

(i) assist in minimising the long term effects of the accident and which help in returning to the pre-accident position as quickly as possible

(ii) enable everything that is possible to be learnt from the events that led up to the accident so that strategies to avoid similar accidents in the future can be devised and implemented.

Designing inherently safe plants, processes and systems is the most cost effective means of avoiding loss and dealing with hazards that exist. Adding on protective and other safety equipment as well as new procedures to an existing operation is not the most effective solution – they control, but do not avoid the likely loss.

2.2   LOSS CONTROL MANAGEMENT

2.2.1   The purpose of Loss Control Management is to limit the total cost of losses to the lowest possible level by implementing measures which:

(a) prevent losses from occurring i.e. eliminating the cause of loss

(b) protect people and/or property from loss

(c) limit the extent of any loss that may occur

(d) maximise the recovery from any loss that has occurred.

To be fully effective an overall co-ordinated approach should be used so that the measures that are implemented are fully integrated one with the other, as well as with the organisation's normal operating systems and procedures. As can be seen from *Figure 2.1* Loss Control Management is part of Risk Management. It is not however Risk Management.

Figure 2.1

"Risk Management is the logical and systematic means of minimising the causes and adverse effects of accidental loss or destruction, so as to conserve the assets and earning power of an organisation, all at the least possible cost."

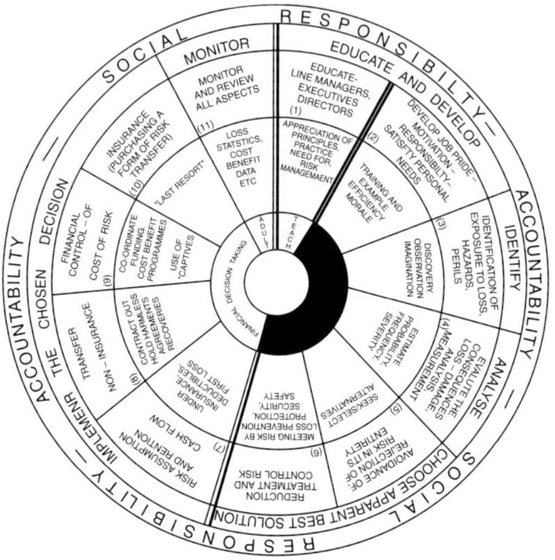

SOCIAL — RESPONSIBILITY — ACCOUNTABILITY — IDENTIFY — ANALYSE — SOCIAL — RESPONSIBILITY — IMPLEMENT — ACCOUNTABILITY — DECISION

MONITOR
MONITOR AND REVIEW ALL ASPECTS (11)

EDUCATE AND DEVELOP
EDUCATE-LINE MANAGERS, EXECUTIVES DIRECTORS (1)

INSURANCE (PURCHASING A FORM OF RISK TRANSFER) (10)

LOSS STATISTICS, COST BENEFIT DATA ETC

"LAST RESORT"

APPRECIATION OF PRINCIPLES, PRACTICE NEED FOR RISK MANAGEMENT (2)

DEVELOP JOB PRIDE, MOTIVATION, RESPONSIBILITY, SATISFY PERSONAL NEEDS

FINANCIAL CONTROL - OF COST OF RISK (9)

CO-ORDINATE FUNDING, COST BEING, PROGRAMMES

USE OF CAPTIVES

TRAINING AND EXAMPLE EFFICIENCY MORALE

IDENTIFICATION OF EXPOSURE TO LOSS, HAZARDS, PERILS (3)

TRANSFER NON - INSURANCE (8)

CONTRACT OUTS ASSESSMENTS AGREEMENTS RECOVERIES

DISCOVERY OBSERVATION IMAGINATION

ESTIMATE PROBABILITY FREQUENCY SEVERITY

IDENTIFICATION OF LOSS OVER THE 4 MEASUREMENTS (4)

RISK ASSUMPTION AND RETENTION (7)

CASH FLOW

PRINCE PROACTIVE, RE-ACTIVE FIRST LOSS

MEETING RISK BY PROTECTION SECURITY, LOSS PREVENTION SAFETY

REVENUE/SELECT ALTERNATIVES

REJECTION OF RISK IN ITS ENTIRETY

AVOIDANCE OF (5)

CHOOSE APPARENT BEST SOLUTION
REDUCTION TREATMENT AND CONTROL RISK (6)

FINANCIAL DECISION

DECISION DAMAGE

LOSS CONTROL MANAGEMENT MAY BE SEEN AS COMPRISING SEGMENTS TWO TO SIX

Footnote: Emphasis and order or importance will vary from time to time, according to individual needs and corporate philosophy

Compiled and arranged by: B.W. Haines

A Total Approach to Managing Risk

2.2.2   The measures to limit the extent of any loss and to maximise the recovery from loss are of two basic types:

(a) **passive,** i.e. the nature of the measure itself limits the loss or facilitates recovery without any change in state e.g. walls, automatic fire doors, curtain boards and the contingency or business continuity plan.

(b) **proactive** i.e. the measure involves taking steps to limit the loss or maximise the recovery e.g. sprinklers, burglar alarms, and salvage operations.

2.2.3   The measures can also be classified in terms of:

(a) reducing the **probability** of loss such as fitting safety guards to machines and removing possible sources of ignition

(b) reducing the **severity** of loss such as sprinklers, storage of goods susceptible to water damage above the ground floor level and providing first aid facilities

(c) reducing both the **probability** and the **severity** of loss such as education and training of management and employees and the use of fire resistant building materials.

2.3 THE IMPORTANCE OF ACCIDENTS AND NEAR-LOSS ACCIDENTS

2.3.1   A combination of factors or causes comes together under just the right circumstances to bring about loss. Rarely in the case of a loss that involves safety, production or quality will a single cause be found. It is however generally accepted that:

(a) **losses are caused; they just don't happen.**

(b) **the causes of loss can be determined and controlled.**

2.3.2   There are four major elements in any business activity and each can play a part in the causes of loss or near-loss incidents. All four of these elements should relate or interact properly with each other, or problems may be created that could result in loss or near loss. These four elements are:

(a) **people**

This element includes both management and employees. It is recognised that the human element is involved in most causes of incidents. However, we must be very mindful that the responsibility of management in setting the optimum situation and conditions in which the work may be safely carried out. What employees receive or fail to receive by way of education, motivation, job tools, workplace facilities and layout depends on their relationship with management people. This is critically important because the employee is usually the human element directly involved in most losses or near-losses, since what they, the employees, do or fail to do is seen as being the immediate cause of the loss. Usually, however, a lack of training, education, motivation or suitable job conditions may greatly influence the actions of the employee and may well be the true cause of the loss.

(b) **equipment**

By equipment we mean the tools and machinery with

which the employee works. In recent times bad design of controls, displays on machinery and equipment and other types of man – machine interface is often found to be a major source or cause of many losses or near-losses.

(c) **material**

The materials that people use, work with or make provide another major source of the causes of incidents. Material can be sharp, heavy, hot, acid, alkali or toxic. In all cases this element of the business system provides a major source of losses or near-losses. However it must be remembered that materials often also play a major role in the profit made by the business.

(d) **environment**

The physical surroundings that include the buildings used by the business and its employees, the area in which the business is situated and the air breathed by the employees are all part of the environment, as are lighting, noise levels and atmospheric conditions.

2.3.3   An Updated Domino Sequence

H. W. Heinrich developed a domino sequence as a means of teaching people about accidents and their prevention. It proposed that accidents were the end result of a chain of events and if one of the events was to be removed the accident would not happen. His original sequence is shown in *Figure 2.2.*

Figure 2.2

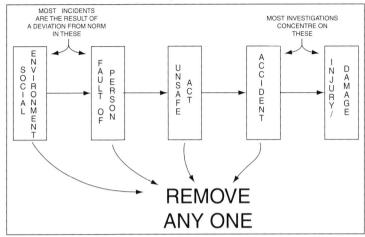

The Domino Sequence

An updated version of this domino sequence is shown in *Figure 2.3*. This highlights the direct management relationship involved with the causes and effects of all losses and near losses as described below:

Figure 2.3

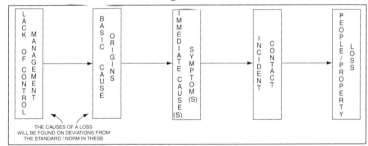

The Updated Domino Sequence

(a) **lack of control – management**

The first domino in the sequence of events that could lead to an accident is the lack of control by management. Control in this context refers to one of the four functions of every manager:

(i) **Planning**

(ii) **Organizing**

(iii) **Leading**

(iv) **Controlling**

Whatever position the manager may hold, planning, organizing, leading and controlling are essential if the work is to be done properly. However, to do any work properly a manager needs to know what work is required so that he or she can manage its performance. This may be detailed in the form of a job description. However, the job description on its own is not enough, there must also be a standard against which performance in that job can be measured. If either of these is not adequate then there is a deviation from normal and the first domino could fall.

(b) **basic cause(s) – origin(s)**

A lack of management control allows the existence of certain basic causes of incidents that can lead to accident or loss. These causes have also been referred to as root causes or indirect causes since the substandard practices and conditions (immediate causes) which are most closely associated with the incident originate directly from them. Basic causes are frequently classified into two groups:

(i) **Personal Factors**

Inadequate Physical or Physiological Capability
Inadequate Mental or Psychological Capability
Lack of Knowledge or Skill or Training
Improper Motivation
Physical or Physiological Stress
Mental or Psychological Stress.

(ii) **Job Factors**

Inadequate Work Standards
Inadequate Design or Maintenance
Inadequate Purchasing Standards
Normal Wear and Tear
Abuse or Misuse
Inadequate Leadership and/or Supervision
Inadequate Engineering
Inadequate Tools and Equipment.

(c) **immediate cause(s) – symptoms**

When the basic causes of incidents exist, they provide the opportunity for the occurrence of substandard practices and conditions (called errors) that could cause this domino to fall and lead directly to loss.

(i) A substandard practice or condition (error) is any deviation from an accepted standard or practice. The practice could involve both acts of people and conditions related to physical things.

(ii) The unsafe act or practice is a violation of an accepted safe procedure which could allow an accident to occur

(iii) The unsafe condition is a hazardous physical condition or circumstance that could directly permit the occurrence of an accident.

Whether these deviations from normal are referred to as substandard practices and conditions or unsafe acts and conditions every one is a symptom of the basic cause that allowed the practices or conditions to exist.

(d) **incident – contact**

Whenever substandard practices and conditions exist there is always a chance that an incident may occur that may or may not result in a loss. The incident is "undesired", since the final results of its occurrence may produce damage or injury.

(e) **people – property -loss**

Once the entire sequence has taken place and there is a loss involving people or property, the results are usually chance events. The element of chance is involved in quality and production losses as well as those involved with safety, health and security.

2.3.4   Whilst it may be argued that there are an infinite number of causes of accidents there is always an involvement of the human factor although it is rarely the principal cause of an accident. The principal causes of accidents particularly those involving injury include:

(a) inadequate supervision and control

(b) inadequate training

(c) inadequate work procedures and instructions

(d) poor housekeeping

(e) poor design or layout of the workplace

(f) bad ergonomic design of the individual work areas

(g) mechanical failure

(h) inadequate protective equipment and clothing, e.g. machine guards, ear muffs

(i) badly maintained working surfaces particularly floors

(j) selecting a person who is not physically or mentally suited to the task that has to be done.

2.3.5   There are many incidents that are sometimes referred to as near-miss accidents. Under slightly different circumstances a near-miss accident could have resulted in personal injury and/or property damage. Several scientific studies have proved conclusively that information obtained from analysing near-miss accidents (incidents) can be used effectively to prevent or control future personal injury or property damage type accidents. The proportion of incidents that occur that could have resulted in injury or damage compared to those that actually do give management many opportunities to take preventative action before the same incidents occur again – resulting in loss.

2.3.6   The importance of the near-miss accidents can be seen from the result of a detailed study, undertaken by Frank Bird in the USA, into the frequency and severity relationship of the various types of accident. As will be seen from *Figure 2.4* for many near-miss accidents there are a number of accidents that involve property damage, a smaller number that result in minor injuries and very few that result in death or a serious injury. One conclusion that may be drawn from the results of this particular study is that if the number of near-miss accidents is reduced then the number of the other types of accident will also be reduced. Another conclusion is that there is a very definite relationship between the number of accidents involving property damage and those involving death or injury. It is therefore essential that all incidents which resulted in, or could have resulted in, loss or injury are monitored on a continuing basis.

Figure 2.4

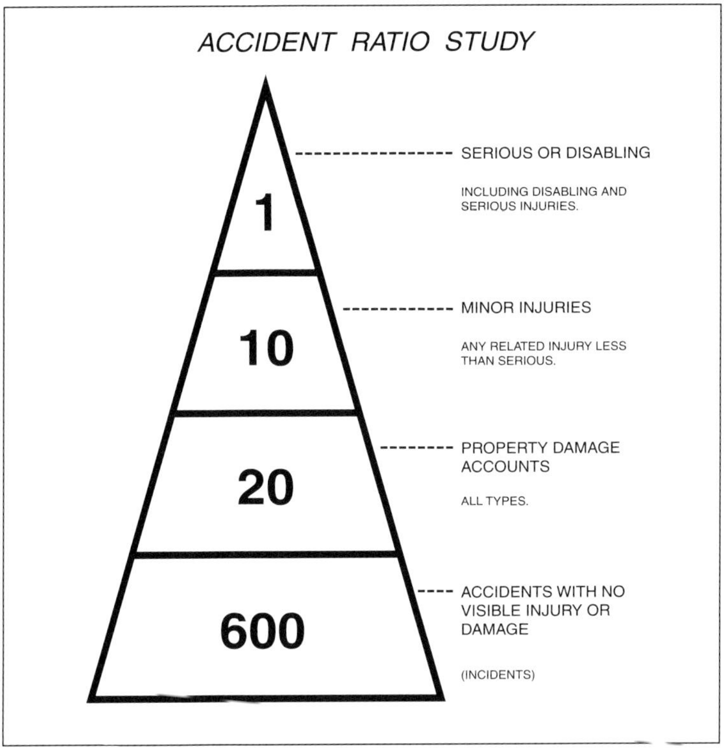

ACCIDENT RATIO STUDY

1 — SERIOUS OR DISABLING
INCLUDING DISABLING AND SERIOUS INJURIES.

10 — MINOR INJURIES
ANY RELATED INJURY LESS THAN SERIOUS.

20 — PROPERTY DAMAGE ACCOUNTS
ALL TYPES.

600 — ACCIDENTS WITH NO VISIBLE INJURY OR DAMAGE
(INCIDENTS)

A Comparison of Near-miss to Fatal Accidents

2.3.7   A study of past incidents can often provide a clue as to what action will be most effective in controlling risk and preventing loss. This is particularly true of those incidents that do not actually lead to loss – the near-miss accidents. When studying any incident it is important to look past the incident itself to identify the deviation or deviations from normal which set in motion the chain of events that culminated in the incident. Correcting the deviation or deviations will avoid future incidents and therefore control risk.

2.3.8   Whilst the prudent organisation will strive to avoid loss it is not possible to eliminate all accidents no matter what precautions may be taken. Nor is it possible to provide total reimbursement for the total cost of the loss. This is because the total cost of an accident is made of the following components:

(a) **direct costs** of the loss or injury, which are usually provided for financially.

(b) **indirect costs** which are associated with repairing the damage or rehabilitating the injured person, the administrative processes that accidents inevitably involve, compensation for pain and suffering, lost production, downtime disruption, wasted labour costs, lost opportunities, and the time spent on investigating the accident.

(c) **the long term effects** of diverting money and/or resources from other more productive uses to repair, or rehabilitate the results of the accident. In addition there is often the likelihood of the organisation suffering a loss of reputation and/or market share as a result of the accident.

A number of studies have been done on the relative size of these three components of the total cost of accidents and the results are often displayed in the form of the "iceberg" diagram. A typical example of this is given in *Figure 2.5*. It shows that whilst part of the total cost is visible much of the cost is hidden and as a consequence usually will not be taken into account when assessing the cost of an accident.

Figure 2.5

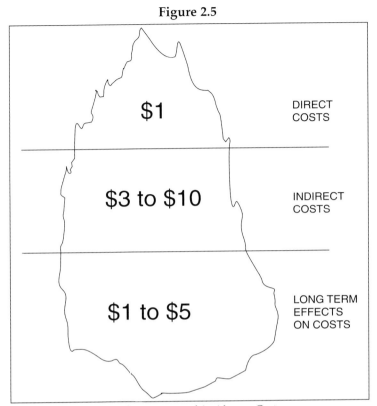

The Consequence of Accident to Cost

2.4.   RISK REDUCTION

2.4.1   Money spent on implementing risk reduction measures will invariably be the most cost effective because the likelihood or the severity of loss will be reduced by such measures.

2.4.2   **Risk Avoidance**

   (a) Obviously if there is no exposure to risk there is no likelihood of loss. However, the situations where this type of measure may be taken are fairly rare because such measures are only effective when there is no exposure to hazard. This means that in most cases the decision to avoid a risk must be taken in the planning stages of a project. For example the construction of a nuclear power plant; or the takeover of a company that has extensive liability exposures.

(b) It is perhaps unfortunate that rarely are the possible risks recognized before completion of the planning stage of a project. Even if they are recognized, only in exceptional cases is full consideration given to the hazards and risks of the proposed project when making the decision to proceed or not. All too often the failure to appreciate fully the hazards and risk will lead to the project, when implemented, being less successful than expected.

(c) Taking the decision to stop doing something after it has been implemented thereby avoiding the risks that are involved is usually a very expensive decision to make. The cost is often such that the decision to abort is deferred or not taken until after the inevitable major loss occurs or the cost of the losses exceeds the profits being made.

2.4.3 Risk Reduction

There are two general approaches that may be taken to reduce risk:

(a) **reduce the frequency of losses** or in other words try to prevent the loss from occurring; and

(b) **limit the loss** when it does occur or in other words restrict its severity.

Figure 2.6 gives another view of these approaches and highlights these two major groups of risk reduction techniques.

Figure 2.6

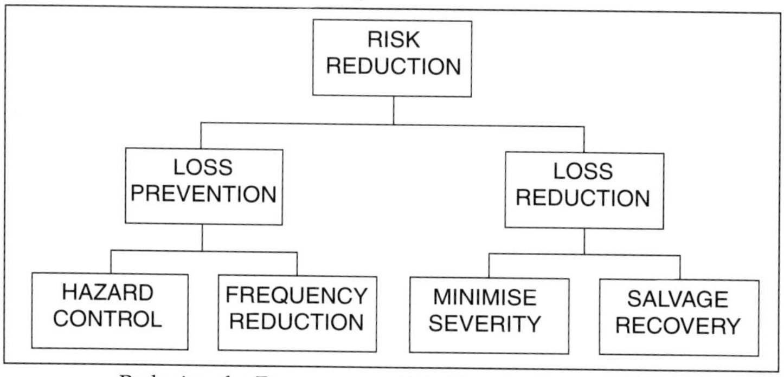

Reducing the Frequency and Limiting the Loss of Risk

2.4.4   Loss Prevention

By the use of one of a number of different techniques it is possible to change the risk so that the likelihood of a loss occurring is reduced either by lessening the hazard and therefore its associated risk of loss or by reducing the frequency of losses itself.

There are a wide variety of techniques that may be used to reduce risk. The following are some strategies that deal with risk in terms of the energy that is involved by working to either prevent a loss from occurring or by controlling its impact. All are important in preventing injuries:

(a) **limit energy**

Use minimum necessary for the task. At the input side of every operation seek ways to reduce actual or potential input. Smaller weights for manual handling. Small containers for hazardous material. When necessary, stop the operation, e.g., manufacture of extremely hazardous substances, or vehicle operation in selected areas. Remove unneeded objects from overhead surfaces. Use slower or smaller machines such as grinders.

(b) **use safer substitutes**

Use less hazardous chemicals. Use designs needing less maintenance or which are easier to maintain. Use remote or automatic oilers. Use material handling equipment. Look for cheaper, better ways to do tasks. Use of carbon dioxide instead of carbontetrachloride in fire extinguishers.

(c) **prevent build-up**

Use regulators, governors, and limit controls. Provide signals and controls such as gas or humidity detectors. Maintain housekeeping and minimize storage to prevent fuel build-up. Control floor loadings. Reduce speed. Lengthen steep grades. (A process control that does not provide redundancy for a failed sensor will continue to feed material thereby adding to the problem).

(d) **prevent release**

Design for unexposed hazards. Use factors of safety in structure design. Protect stores energy from anticipated shocks, e.g. in collisions. Contain energy for conservation, e.g. thermal insulation on pipes, interlock and goof-proof valves, doors and release mechanisms, insulation of electrical equipment and wiring. Improve error-provocative situations. Provide toe boards and railings on elevated walkways or working platforms. Use safety chains and lifelines. Eliminate energy intersections, e.g., one-way traffic or overpasses, or remote storage of flammables. These, together with the strategies listed below, enable loss producing events to be tackled at every stage.

2.4.5 Loss Reduction

The following are some strategies that handle the loss in terms of the energy that is released:

(a) **Provide slow release**

Rupture disks, safety valves and bleed offs. Reduce potential energies at ends of operations. Provide error-forgiving road margins. Use seat belts.

(b) **channel release away**

Separate in space or time or combination. Ventilate.

(i) Separate in space. Eliminate two-way traffic, and separate vehicle and pedestrian traffic. Use aisle and lane markings. Separation distances for explosives, oxygen storage, or incompatible materials. Use exhaust systems for waste etc. Grounding (earthing). Rope off areas. Use "Keep Out" signs or locked doors, vents and curtain boards. Remote control of hazardous operations.

(ii) Separate in time. Delay mechanisms. Alarms and exits. Maintenance or explosives work off-shift.

(c) **barrier on source**

Electrical insulation and double insulation. Electrical cabinets. Guards, enclosures, filters and fences. Noise reduction.

(d) **barrier in between source and people or property**

Energy is released, keep it from travelling far. Walls and

shields. Acoustical ceilings. Safety nets and rails. Firedoors and shutters; Flood Banks.

(e) **barrier on human or object**

Personal protective equipment such as shoes, hats, gloves, eye shields and respirators. Bumpers and Buffers etc.

(f) **raise injury threshold**

Proper staff selection: Physical conditioning and acclimatization. Damage resistant materials.

(g) **ameliorate** (The accident has now occurred.)

(i) Prevent the second accident. Shut off energy flow, stop traffic. Isolate dangerous areas.

(ii) Rescue persons and objects.

(iii) Contain the loss such as extinguish the fire, clean up, dry out etc.

(iv) Provide emergency services such as emergency showers, eye washers etc.

(v) Change person's job to one with a lower risk.

(h) **rehabilitate**

Return persons to health and restore capabilities, repair objects or property.

Using one of the number of different techniques listed above it is possible to minimise the extent of any loss when it occurs.

Figure 2.7

LOSS CONTROL MEASURES			
	PHYSICAL DEVICES	PROCEDURAL DEVICES	EDUCATIONAL & TRAINING DEVICES
PRE-CONDITIONS FOR LOSS (PRE-OPERATION)	VENTING CURTAIN BOARDS	MAINTENANCE & SERVICING	EDUCATION
PREVENTION OF LOSS (DURING OPERATION)	AUTOMATIC CUT-OFF FIRE DOORS	NOTIFICATION & INSPECTION	CLEAR INSTRUCTIONS ON FAULTS CORRECTION
EARLY DISCOVERY OF LOSS (POST LOSS)	ALARMS	SECURITY PATROLS	TRAINING
LIMITATION OF LOSS (POST LOSS)	SPRINKLERS DRENCHERS	FIRST AID OFFICERS INTERNAL FIRE BRIGADE	DISASTER PLAN CONTINGENCY PLAN EVACUATION PROCEDURE

Categories and Stages of Loss

As can be seen from *Figure 2.7* these measures can be applied at different stages of the loss and they can be categorised by their nature into physical, procedural and educational training measures.

2.4.6   To summarise looking at risk from the perspective of energy; energy is an essential ingredient in all forms of work. Risk only becomes a problem when energy is transferred other than to produce some form of work. Risk reduction consequently is largely a matter of controlling and channelling energy. (See *Figure 2.8*).

Figure 2.8

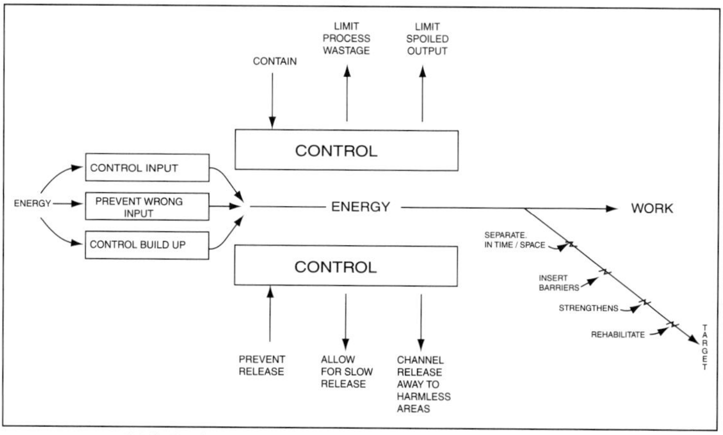

Risk Reduction, Controlling and Channelling Energy

2.4.7   Another way of approaching the reduction of risk is to break the approaches down into two basic types:

(a) those that involve physical measures; and

(b) those that involve financial measures.

Figure 2.9 gives a breakdown of each type of measure and provides examples of each. It also stresses the importance of top management commitment to risk reduction for it to be fully effective.

Figure 2.9

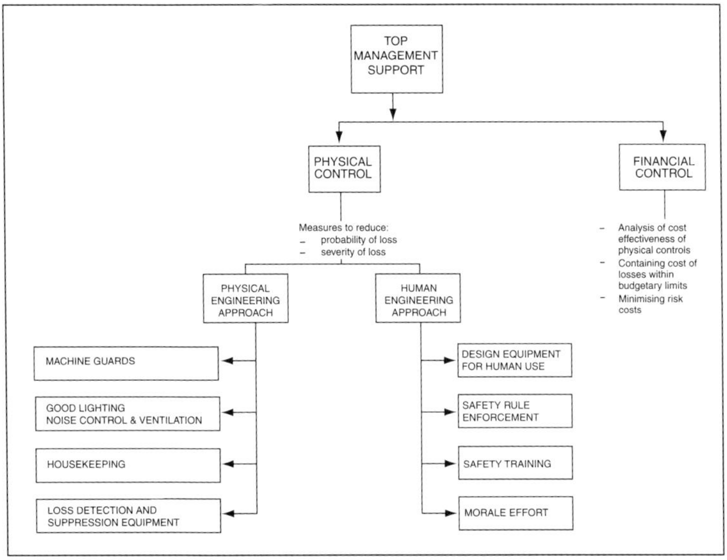

Physical and Financial Measures towards Risk Reduction

2.5 RISK SPREADING

2.5.1   Spreading the exposure by breaking the exposure into a number of smaller separate entities and distributing these over a wide area on the same site or by placing each entity on a separate site will spread the risk. The effect of this is that if a loss does occur, the amount that may be lost is limited to the amount of the exposure at one of the sites, rather than the whole amount if all of the exposures were to be on the same site.

2.5.2   However, it must be noted that although the maximum amount that may be lost has been reduced, in fact the likelihood of loss has been increased to some extent because additional opportunities for loss to happen have been provided. Each new site provides extra chances for a loss to occur.

2.5.3   Where dangerous goods such as toxic chemicals and explosives have to be stored in bulk it is normal for these to be stored:

(a) in areas away from other property and people

(b) in separate specially built storage facilities such as bunkers for explosives or Dangerous Goods Stores

55

(c) each type of chemical and explosive is often stored in its own separate facility to avoid contamination and to reduce the risk of different substances acting as fuels or accelerant for each other.

This is risk spreading in action.

2.6   LOSS COMPENSATION AND COMBINATION

2.6.1   Loss Compensation and Combination are two techniques that may be used to even out the effects of loss. For both techniques to work effectively a large number of risks exposures is needed and as a consequence both are used by insurance companies as well as many other types of financial institution to:

(a) offset their losses in one class or subclass with surpluses in another class or subclass

(b) improve their prediction of the likely loss experience of individual classes or subclasses.

2.7   ACCEPTABLE RISK

2.7.1   The primary objective of risk control is the avoidance of loss. However, it will be realised that all too often it is not possible to avoid all loss and as a consequence a secondary objective of risk control is loss reduction. Here again it will be realised that it is rarely possible to reduce loss to zero in financial terms. Thus there remains the prospect that despite all of the risk control efforts there may be an exposure to the risk of loss. Whether any further action is taken will depend on whether or not the exposure to the risk of loss that remains at that stage is acceptable to the organisation. In fact, it would also be normal to apply the same measure to the decision to implement a risk control measure. An acceptable risk is one where the exposure to loss is such that if a loss should occur the organisation's survival would not be threatened.

2.7.2   What is an acceptable risk for an organisation depends on a number of different factors such as:

(a) the financial strength of the organisation

(b) the attitude of the board and management of the organisation ie. are they risk takers or risk averse?

(c) the nature of the risk exposure itself in terms of the organisation's activities, i.e. if a loss occurred whatever its size would it severely damage the organisation's future trading performance

(d) the measure necessary to handle the risk of loss and its consequences so as to minimise its effects on the organisation.

The correct identification and assessment of the risk of loss is the essential first step in determining whether a risk is acceptable or it requires further treatment in order to improve the risk so that it becomes acceptable. In this, care must be taken to ensure all aspects of the risk and all of its consequences are taken into account in its evaluation.

2.7.3   In addition to correctly evaluating the risk it is also necessary to take stock of the organisation's own resources as ultimately it is these that will cushion the impact of any loss. One common measure is the organisation's loss retention level for which there is a wide range of techniques that may be used. Listed below are some of those that are often used by risk managers.

(a) **annual aggregate limits**

   (i)   1%–5% of Working Capital

   (ii) 1%–5% of pre-tax Earnings. This is sometimes expressed as 1%–3% of current Earnings plus 1% of the average of the previous five years pre-tax Earnings.

   (iii) Up to 10% of Earnings Per Share. This is also sometimes expressed as 3% to 5% of Earnings Per Share plus 0.1% to 0.5% of Sales.

   (iv) 1% – 3% of Total Assets

   (v) 1% of Net Worth plus 1% of average of last five years pre tax Earnings

   (vi) The Basket Method brings together a range of different elements and was postulated by Robert J Hansman in Risk Management July 1982 covering:

Liquidity Elements		Weighting Factor		Result
Working Capital	x	0.03	=	
Non Dedicated Cash	x	0.25	=	
Financial Strength				
Net Worth	x	0.02	=	
Total Assets	x	0.02	=	
Gross Sales	x	0.01	=	
Earnings				
Projected Earnings	x	0.05	=	
Historical Earnings	x	0.05	=	
(last 3 years)				

Total of Results

Total of Results

Mean = 7

$$\frac{\text{Standard Deviations of Factors}}{2} = \textbf{Adjustment}$$

Risk Retention Level = **Mean less Adjustment**

(b) **Limit any one occurrence**

 (i) Up to 0.1% of Turnover

 (ii) Up to 0.1% of Shareholders Funds.

These are only guides to the maximum value of loss retention and they should, therefore, be modified to take into account the current circumstances and attitude to risk of the business.

When assessing whether or not a risk is acceptable any loss financing should be taken into account as an extension of the organisation's financial resources. It therefore should not be treated as being a measure that reduces the exposure to the risk of loss or of improving the acceptability of risk.

2.7.4 There are basically only two ways by which an unacceptable risk may be handled:

(a) **reduction of the risk** so as to lower the residual risk to an acceptable level. Reducing the frequency of loss or its severity or both would do this.

(b) **avoidance or elimination of the risk** This may be the only viable option if it is not feasible to reduce the risk to an acceptable level, or the costs of doing so are excessively high in comparison to the loss exposure itself.

Transfer of the risk of loss does nothing to reduce or avoid the risk. However, it may limit the loss for the organisation to some extent. However loss financing and risk or loss transfer cannot be regarded as measures by which an unacceptable risk may be improved. They are simply measures that extend the financial resources of the organisation.

3

THE MAJOR CAUSES OF PROPERTY LOSS PRINCIPLES OF IGNITION, COMBUSTION, FIRE GROWTH, EXPLOSION

3.1   THE MAJOR CAUSES OF LOSS

3.1.1   The major causes of loss are predominantly associated with natural events such as flood, extreme climatic conditions, earthquake and volcanic eruption, together with fire and explosion. All of these can result in a catastrophic loss being experienced not only because of the destruction or damage that they can cause to assets, but also because of the interruption to an organisation's ability to earn income.

3.1.2   Another related group of causes of major loss is that involving the destruction or corruption of the essential information of an organisation or the loss of its ability to access and process that information where the organisation is totally dependent on that information or processing capability. Increasingly the computer system and the information that it contains are becoming the heart of modern business.

3.1.3   Liability in all of its forms is a rapidly growing area of causes of major loss for many industrial organisations as well as most professionally based ones. One of the major difficulties with liability losses is the long delay between the time of occurrence of the incident giving rise to the loss, its manifestation and eventual settlement. This often leads to the final settlement being influenced by:

(a) inflation

(b) changes in legal interpretation.

3.1.4   Whilst the causes that have been described so far can and do result in major losses most are not a major cause of loss. For these we must look at the chronic losses -the frequent but small value losses – which collectively frequently erode an organisation's 'bottom line' to a significant extent. However, few organisations ever quantify this type of loss so the full extent of the loss from chronic losses is rarely seen and action to control them is as a consequence rarely more than piecemeal.

3.2 HOW THINGS BURN

3.2.1   There is a principle in nature known as the Law of Conservation of Energy, which says that energy is neither created nor destroyed – it is simply turned from one form to another. The Law provides basic explanations of fire and the means by which fire grows or is prevented or extinguished.

3.2.2   The car engine provides a simple example of the Law. Petrol, the car's fuel, contains a great deal of stored energy, some of which is converted by the car engine into motion. The rest is converted into heat and noise. The heat in turn is transferred into the water of the cooling system and the radiator transfers it to the air.

What happens inside the cylinder of the car is in fact a fire – a very quick fire, but a fire nevertheless. Thus the example above gives a clue to what fire is.

Fire is an extremely rapid self-sustaining energy conversion system in which oxygen is combined with another substance (the fuel) such as carbon or hydrogen whereby the energy stored in the fuel is released as heat and usually visible light.

In addition, besides the heat and light, products of the combustion such as smoke (soot), gases (carbon dioxide and water vapour) and sometimes (as in coal fire) tars are also released.

3.2.3   Therefore a fuel, by definition, is a substance which contains a great deal of stored energy and the products of combustion of the fuel, have by definition, low amounts of energy. This can be simply shown in a diagram as in *Figure 3.1*.

Figure 3.1

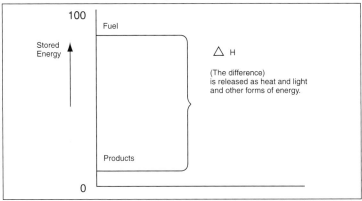

Defining Energy in Fuel

3.2.4   How then is this energy actually stored in the fuel? The answer lies in the chemical structure of the substance and in particular how tightly the atoms that make up the molecules of the substance are bonded together. In the combustion process these bonds (which themselves are a form of energy) break down and new arrangements of atoms (the products) which do not involve such high energy bonds are formed. The pathway by which this happens is known as a "chemical reaction".

The distinctive thing about the chemical reactions that we call "fire", is the very high release of energy in the form of heat and light.

3.2.5   For the most part, fuels tend to be fairly stable compounds, which need the addition of another substance to provide the reaction path. The most common "combustion supporter" is the oxygen in the air around us. You will see vast quantities of fuel living happily in contact with oxygen every day without burning.

The reason for this is that the fire reaction needs an input of energy **(the "activation energy")** to get things moving. Indeed this is exactly what happens when the heat from the arsonist's match has the effect of increasing the kinetic energy **(energy of motion)** of the fuel molecules and the oxygen molecules, until eventually they are colliding with one other with sufficient force as to cause the chemical reaction to commence. *Figure 3.2* illustrates this.

Figure 3.2

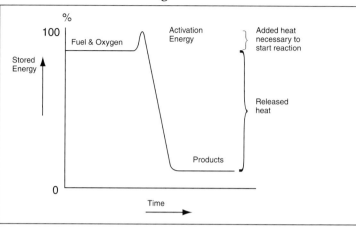

Activation Energy increasing the "Energy of Motion"

3.2.6   Along the reaction path, the molecules of the fuel reduce the molecules of oxygen to form new molecules of the products of combustion. These have a much lower energy state. Of course, nothing is quite as simple as it seems and the reaction path is no exception. What actually happens is that there is a sort of chain reaction in which some intermediate substances are (very briefly) formed. These are called "chain carriers" and generally they also have high levels of stored energy. It is important to understand this because chain carriers are significant in the problem of ensuring effective fire extinguishment. Hence, our fire reaction is more accurately shown in this way in *Figure 3.3.*

Figure 3.3.

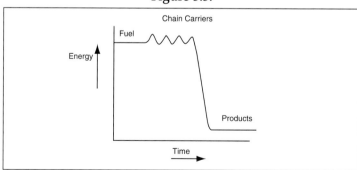

Fire Reaction in Relation to Chain Carriers

In the case of burning hydrogen this is simplistically expressed in Figure 3.4.

Figure 3.4

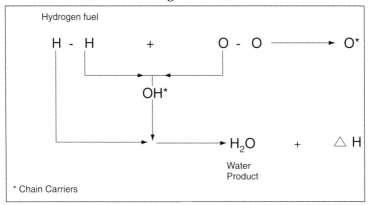

3.2.7   The usual visible evidence that this reaction has reached completion is the flame, although it is possible to have surface combustion (as occurs in the charcoal coals of the barbecue) without flame. The flame really defines the outer limits of the chain reaction zone and is mainly visible because carbon is often released and makes it glow orange. As it cools, it becomes visible as black smoke. Actually, orange flame and soot is a mark of inefficient combustion because it is possible to burn carbon – i.e. it is itself a fuel. The fact that it is produced shows that there was a shortage of oxygen available to the chain reaction. A domestic gas stove or a primus is designed to ensure that there is plenty of oxygen available to the reaction zone and, as a result, you see a clean burning bluish flame without any soot and you feel a much greater release of heat. Of course, there are substances other than carbonaceous materials which can be fuels (for example, metals such as magnesium) and there are other substances which fill the role of the supporter of combustion (for example: chlorine) with certain special fuels.

3.2.8   However, it is important to appreciate that, whereas fuels and oxidisers can live in close association with each other, the introduced factor of the activation heat is the trigger that starts the fire.

Figure 3.5 is a four sided figure that represents the ingredients of any fire (the "Tetrahedron of Fire"). All must be present for a fire to start and continue burning.

Figure 3.5

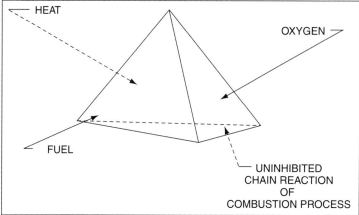

The Tetrahedron of Fire

Fuel-Oxygen-Heat   Suitable chain reaction conditions.

3.2.9   Energy released by a fire in the form of heat is transferred by the following three methods – convection, conduction, radiation.

(a) **Convection** is the mass movement of hotter, less dense gas through its cooler, denser surroundings ('hot air rises'). It also applies to liquids e.g.: when boiling a pot of water.

Convected heat is the primary agent of fire spread within an enclosed space. Usually about 75 per cent of the combustion products of a fire are dissipated in rising convection currents of hot gases at temperatures of 800-1000 Degrees Centigrade which heat anything in their path. When the upward movement of a convection current is blocked, e.g. by a ceiling, the hot gases spread laterally along the underside of the ceiling (the 'mushroom effect'). See *Figure 3.6.*

Figure 3.6

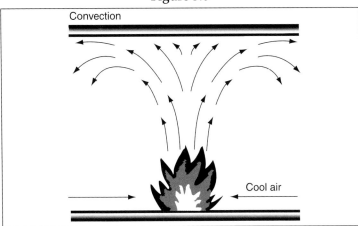

The Mushrooming of Fire when Contacting an Obstruction

Convected air currents can carry smoke and toxic gases long distances and can smokelog escape routes. Also they often carry burning brands, which can ignite combustible materials at some distance from the seat of the fire.

(b) **Conduction** occurs along and through solid materials. Hence, whilst a steel door won't burn, it will very easily conduct heat from one side of the door to the other.

(c) **Radiation** is a "pure" form of energy transfer across space from a hot body. Radiant energy travels in straight lines but decreases as the square root of the distance. Even so, it is quite possible for radiation from a big fire to ignite buildings on the opposite side of the street.

Energy can be converted from one form to another – it is never lost – and in a fire the released heat is likely to spread in each of these forms simultaneously.

3.3.   SOME IGNITION SCENARIOS

3.3.1   Most fires will occur because activation heat energy is introduced into an otherwise perfectly normal situation in which combustibles are sitting waiting, in contact with the oxygen in the air (incidentally, about 21% of the air is oxygen).

3.3.2   Anyone looking at an industrial or commercial concern needs to develop an instinctive ability to spot these situations with a view to either:

(a) **Moving the heat source away from the combustibles** (e.g.: fixing radiant heaters high up on a wall), or

(b) **Moving the combustibles well back from the heat source** (e.g.: clearing back stored goods before commencing cutting and welding).

3.3.3   The following account for up to 80% of industrial fires:

Electrical ignition
Smoking
Arson
Flammable liquids
Cutting and Welding – Hot work
Malfunctions of safety equipment and interlocks on hazardous processes

Housekeeping is often an aggravating factor in a fire loss.

3.3.4   The question of whether it is better to control the fuel or the heat, is sometimes determined by the state (or phase) of the fuel. Liquid fuels and gaseous fuels are much more mobile than solid fuels (although loose paper that is able to be blown about has caused a few fires) and these will tend to "seek out" the energy source.

Most fuels (whatever their usual state) actually burn in the gaseous phase. When the activation or ignition heat is applied to a block of wood, it first causes the wood to release volatile combustible vapours and it is these that actually burn. Similarly, liquid fuels actually burn in the gas phase and they must first be heated to convert them from liquid to vapour.

It is more difficult to do this with some liquids than others. Liquid fuels with a high flashpoint are those that need considerable ignition heat in order to commence burning. (Heavy fuel oils are an example). Low flashpoint liquids (such as petrol) will generally release sufficient vapour for ignition when warmed by normal air temperatures. Obviously these are more dangerous and precautions to keep them away from heat sources need to be more stringent. (see *Figure 3.7*).

Figure 3.7

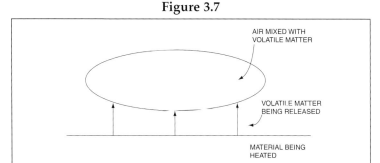

Dangerous Liquids must be kept away from Heat Sources

Generally there is a minimum and a maximum proportion of fuel to air that will allow the combustion reaction to be sustained. These are known as the upper and lower flammability points. The wider the spread of these points are for a fuel, the potentially more hazardous it is.

3.3.5   (a) **flammability limits** are defined as the lowest and highest percentages by volume of fuel gas to air at 1 atmosphere that will burn. The difference between the two limits is the **flammability range**. When the amount of fuel present is too little to permit a self-sustaining reaction, the mixture is said to be "too lean." It is below the **lower flammability limit (LFL)**. When the fuel is so plentiful, there is not sufficient oxidizer, the mixture is "too rich": above the **upper flammability limit (UFL)**.

In addition to the flammability limits many substances also have explosive limits namely the **lower explosive limit (LEL)**, and the **upper explosive limit (UEL)**. For example hydrogen in the air will burn when it reaches at least 4.0 per cent of the mixture by volume; but it will only explode when the percentage is between 18.3 and 59. Whilst methane, propane and butane are burned as fuels for cooking and heating with few problems, these gases have generated disasters when concentrations exceeding their lower explosive limits were ignited.

From a safety standpoint, lower flammability limits are of much greater interest than upper limits since they indicate the lowest concentrations at which combustion will begin.

(b) **Flash point** is the lowest temperature at which liquid will give off enough vapour to form a momentarily ignitable mixture with air. A fuel will not burn as liquid. In the presence of its liquid, the vapour pressure of a gas is governed by its temperature. There is a definite temperature for any liquid at which it will provide enough gas by vaporisation to approach the lower flammability limit in air. If an outside source of ignition is then used these vapours will burn in a momentary flame and then die out. The temperature at which this occurs is the **"flash point"**. Vapour concentration at this temperature is inadequate to sustain continuous burning after ignition, so the reaction stops as soon as the available combustion gas is consumed.

(c) **Fire point**

If the liquid is heated higher than the flashpoint, the higher temperature will cause vapours to be produced rapidly enough to permit continuous burning after ignition by an open flame or spark. The lowest temperature at which continuous burning occurs is **the fire or ignition point**. (With solids, this is also known as the **kindling temperature**.) The fire point is always higher than the flash point; but the difference between the two varies, since vapour pressure depends on the substance in question.

(d) **Flash point versus fire point**

The flash point is safer than the fire point since it indicates that the lower limit of flammability is being approached, and the level of hazard is approaching danger point. Both are approximations determined under stipulated conditions in a laboratory. Actual field conditions may and will differ. Also, a high-flash-point liquid heated until its vapour pressure is equal to that of a more volatile liquid at a lower temperature constitutes an equal hazard.

(e) **Auto-ignition or spontaneous ignition temperature**

The auto-ignition temperature is the lowest at which a flammable mixture will burn without application of an outside spark or flame, and continue to burn without further application of heat. (Fire point is the lowest temperature at which a liquid produces enough gas to sustain continuous combustion after being ignited by a spark or open flame.)

3.4 FIRE GROWTH SPEED

3.4.1 What turns a good fire (e.g. the open fire) into a bad fire is when it starts to grow by consuming fuels which it was not intended to burn, e.g. the building structure and its contents. As a fire within a compartment progresses from ignition to and beyond the fully developed stage it is possible to identify four distinct phases of its progress. These are indicated below in *Figure 3.8.*

Figure 3.8

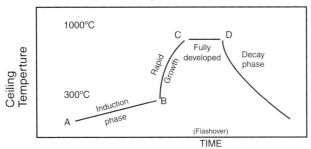

The Four Distinct Stages of Fire Growth

The fire probably starts from a very small igniting source (A on the diagram) and as the area affected gradually increases it becomes more sizeable, but still small, and will reach stage B (on the diagram). At that stage the rate of increase of fire suddenly changes and the phase of rapid growth occurs. This normally occurs soon after ceiling temperatures exceed 300 degrees centigrade and this point is known as **flashover**. In this second stage the fire will continue to grow until it reaches a maximum intensity (C on the diagram), usually when all available fuel is completely involved. Then there will be a period of burning in the fully developed state until the fuel starts to become consumed (D on the diagram), and the fire enters its decaying stage until all the fuel is exhausted and the fire is finished.

Experience of fire incidents shows that the induction stage (A and B) can be very variable in length of time; it can last for hours or it can be over in minutes. In this initial stage the fire is small and can probably be dealt with by any available fire aid appliance but when B on the diagram is passed and rapid growth starts, the fire will certainly be too large to control by a fire aid appliance.

3.4.2 Flashover is preceded by the released heat from the growing fire gradually heating up all combustibles until their ignition

71

temperature is reached. At that time, widespread ignition occurs and literally, the entire compartment is burning. After flashover it is inevitable there will be a major or total loss within the compartment.

As a fire is increasing in size there are two factors at work:

(1) The fire spreads to adjacent combustible items and so there is progressive increase in the fire area. This part of the fire process is referred to as **"fire spread"**

(2) The fire grows in heat output. This is to say the heat output of unit area of the fire is small at the start and increases with time until a final value is reached. After this the heat output decays as the fuel on that particular unit area is consumed.

3.4.3   Obviously anything that facilitates heat transfer to fuels (i.e. any combustibles) enhances the speed of fire growth. Furthermore, some combustibles contain greater amounts of stored heat (which can be expressed as kilocalories/gram) than others and the presence of these also facilitates faster growth. The principal factors of fast growth in a compartment are:

(a) **The type of materials** such as combustibles which:

   (i) have a high calorific value

   (ii) are in liquid or gaseous form

   (iii) are in a finely divided (e.g. dust) or sheet (e.g. paper) form.

(b) **Method of storage** such as combustibles that are stored vertically – particularly in racks.

(c) **The surface area of combustible materials**. In the case of solids and liquids fire can only occur at or near the surface. Materials such as textiles or foam plastic with large surface areas in relation to their volume ignite readily and burn more rapidly.

(d) **The adequacy of the oxygen supply**. Combustible materials burn freely in normal air that contains 21 per cent oxygen. But a fire consumes oxygen, and if the oxygen content of the air is reduced to 16 percent or less it will not normally sustain further combustion. If the air supply is not sufficient to replace the oxygen as it is consumed then the fire growth will be slowed.

(e) **The amount of combustible materials.**

3.4.4   Other factors that influence the speed of the fire growth are:

(a) spacing of the combustible materials

(b) size and area of the ignition source

(c) wind or draught direction and velocity

(d) shape and dimensions of the enclosure or compartment.

3.5.   SPREAD OF FIRE BETWEEN BUILDINGS

3.5.1   Methods by which fire spreads between buildings are:

(a) **Sparks**

Whilst it is possible for fire to be spread by sparks it is unlikely to spread from one building to another because the sparks will usually settle on cold surfaces and do not have sufficient energy to raise that surface to ignition point

(b) **Brands**

Burning brands often spreads fire. These are small pieces of burning wood that are light enough to be carried by the wind or convection currents from one building to another. Forest fires are spread mainly from brands.

(c) **Flame**

If the spacing between buildings is small enough the flames from a burning building may leap across the intervening space to set fire to adjacent buildings

(d) **Radiation**

This is the most important method by which fire spreads between buildings. If the heat transferred from a fire onto a surface close to the fire is sufficient the surface will, after a certain time, ignite. The higher the heat, the shorter the exposure time for ignition. If flying brands are also present the amount of heat required for ignition to occur is reduced. The following factors affecting the ignitability of a building by radiation are:

(i) the length of time of exposure

73

(ii) intensity of radiation

(iii) the surface of material.

(e) **Flammable liquid/gas**

These will enable fire to spread from one building to another by the liquid or gas escaping from its container in one building and flowing to another.

3.6　CLASSES OF FIRE

3.6.1　The reason for classification of fires is to provide an easy way of defining the suitability of various extinguishing agents. Hence the story goes, Class A extinguishers can be used on Class A fires and so on.

An example of the Classifications

(a) **Class A Fires**

Those involving solid common fuels such as wood, paper and textiles, which are easily extinguished by water.

(b) **Class B Fires**

Those involving liquid fuels, liquifiable solids (e.g. fats), which generally have a flashpoint below the boiling point of water and thus, are not so easily extinguished by water. Most are also less dense than water and will therefore float on top of water flowing wherever the water flows.

(c) **Class C Fires**

Those involving live electrical equipment where safety of the operator necessitates use of electrical non-conductive extinguishing agents. However, once the equipment has been de-energised Class A or B extinguishing agents may be more suitable for putting out the fire.

(d) **Class D Fires**

Those involving combustible metals, e.g. Magnesium, Aluminium, Zirconium (Metals).

Class B fires requires a great deal of caution because whilst the flame can usually be easily extinguished, the end result may be a large gas leak with a resultant explosion danger. Sometimes it is safer to let the gas burn off and to simply protect the surrounding property from the effects of the fire.

3.7 FIRE LOAD

3.7.1 The Fire Load is defined as being the *amount of the heat generated in BTU/ft sq (KJ/m sq) by the complete combustion of the combustible products in a compartment.*

There are two fire loads:

(1) Fire-Load of Contents – **Occupancy** fire load

(2) Fire-Load of Building – **Gross** fire load.

3.7.2 The fire load in a compartment varies with:

(a) its **occupancy** i.e. the materials, their quantity and position within the compartment

(b) its **location** within the building i.e. gives an indication of likely ventilation rate – the higher the rate of ventilation the hotter the fire

(c) **time.**

3.7.3 Occupancy may be classified according to the fire load:

(a) **Low Fire-Load** – less than 100,000 BTU/ft sq (1 million KJ/m sq) e.g. domestic buildings offices, hotels

(b) **Moderate Fire-Load** – (1 to 2) x 100,000 BTU/ft sq (1 million KJ/m sq) e.g. trade and factory buildings

(c) **High Fire-Load** – (2 to 4) x 100,000 BTU/ft sq (1 million KJ/m sq) e.g. bulk storage

(d) the **'abnormal'** risks such as those in which the processes used involve:

(i) the application of heat, especially to combustible materials e.g. ironing, drying rooms and compartments, heat treatment, creosoting

(ii) the production of flammable waste or dust, particularly when the latter arises through the use of disintegrators, grinders and similar reducing machines

(iii) spray painting with flammable or explosive liquids

(iv) the use of flammable solvents.

3.8   SPONTANEOUS COMBUSTION

3.8.1   Where certain materials are stored in air or are brought into contact with other materials, they may commence to undergo a chemical reaction, which produces heat **without the application of an external heat source.** If only heat is developed the material is said to undergo spontaneous heating. Many animal and vegetable materials, e.g. hides and skins, palm kernels, may undergo spontaneous heating, thereby suffering damage. The spontaneous heating may be due to bacterial action or the oxidation of some constituent, or a combination of both.

3.8.2   If conditions are favourable for the conservation of heat, the temperature will rise, thereby accelerating the reaction and the rate of heat production until light is produced also, i.e. the material is set on fire and is said to ignite spontaneously and to **undergo spontaneous combustion.** Spontaneous combustion is thus the process of the generation of heat and light in a material by chemical changes, which occur without application of external heat.

3.8.3   Spontaneous ignition will occur in some substances, such as:

(a) **Yellow Phosphorus,** which if exposed to air at ordinary room temperature will spontaneously burst into flame, but its spontaneous ignition temperature is not quite as low as this. The phosphorus oxidises slowly, giving out heat, and this raises the temperature of the outer layers to the spontaneous ignition temperature of phosphorous, namely 66 degrees centigrade, and then the material catches fire.

(b) **Iron** can be prepared in a specially active, finely divided form (pyrophoric iron) so that it burns immediately on contact with air

(c) **Haystacks**

Here it is believed that the temperature is raised to about 50 degrees Centigrade by the growth of bacteria, germination of seeds, and the continued growth of thermophylic bacteria. At this temperature vegetable matter is decomposed, giving active carbon that oxidises rapidly, possibly causing spontaneous ignition. Spontaneous ignition is aided if the hay is damp and ventilation is poor.

(d) **Coal**

With coal its composition is the most important factor, e.g. the presence of finely divided coal is more liable to spontaneous heating and ignition than coarser material, if air is able to easily come into contact with the coal dust, and hence the formation of dust in handling coal should be avoided. Fresh coal is more likely to heat than old, and anthracite is safer than lignite or soft coal.

3.9 CONDITIONS FAVOURABLE TO SPONTANEOUS IGNITION

3.9.1 The spontaneous ignition and combustion of a material in air are likely when:

(a) it has a **large surface area** in relation to its mass in contact with the air. This is the case with finely divided solids, e.g. the carbon deposits in stills or an oil film spread on textile waste

(b) for some reason or other the material is in a **special reactive** form as in the case of linen charred by contact with hot water pipes or freshly made charcoal, or the material contains a reactive constituent, e.g. a drying oil

(c) the physical condition of the material is such that it is sufficiently **porous** to allow good access to air, as with textile waste

(d) the conditions are such that **heat is conserved,** as with haystacks

(e) some secondary internal chemical process, such as bacterial action raises the temperature, as with haystacks. Microbiological action can raise the temperature up to as high as 75 degrees centigrade.

3.10 EXPLOSION, DEFLAGRATION AND DETONATION

3.10.1 **An explosion is a sudden and violent release of large amounts of gas and/or vapour**.

This may arise from:

(a) the bursting of a cylinder of compressed gas

(b) a very rapid exothermic reaction i.e. involving a heat reaction which produces large volumes of gases and/or vapours

(c) a very rapid exothermic reaction which produces the heat to warm and expand the atmosphere.

Both (b) and (c) are effectively an extremely rapid propagating fire.

An explosion may arise out of dust suspension in air, a gaseous/vapour air mixture or an explosive substance as well as a mechanical failure such as that outlined above.

3.10.2 It is an essential feature for the reaction to be exothermic – otherwise, it would not be rapid and, moreover, the heat increases the volume of any gas produced. The oldest explosive is a mixture of sulphur and carbon (substances oxidisable to gases) with potassium nitrate (an oxidiser). The third type of explosion described in paragraph 3.10.1 occurs with metallic dusts in air. Note however an explosion may be a deflagration or a detonation:

(a) *Detonation is an explosion in which the speed of reaction through the reacting material is equal to or exceeds the speed of sound. A* shock wave is produced even if not contained.

(b) *Deflagration is an explosion in which the speed of reaction through the reacting material is less than the speed of sound. A* shock wave is only produced if the deflagration occurs within a confined space.

3.10.3 Another form of explosion is the implosion in which the vessel collapses in on itself – which may occur when the pressure inside the vessel is considerably below the external pressure.

3.11   DUST AND DUST EXPLOSIONS

3.11.1   How Dust Explosions Occur

Dusts have a larger surface area than the solid materials from which they are formed, and when the dust is in the form of a cloud the individual particles are surrounded by air. As a consequence their rate of burning is much greater than that of bulk solids. Provided that the particles are neither too far apart nor too close together, ignition will be followed by a spread of flame through the dust cloud as successive zones are heated to ignition temperature. The spread of flame results in a build-up of pressure by the expanding hot gases creating pressure waves. These travel ahead of the flame. Any dust lying on surfaces in the path of the explosion will be thrown into the air and could cause a secondary explosion that will be more violent and extensive than the first.

3.11.2   To assess whether it is likely that a dust explosion will occur on its premises and the possible extent of an explosion a firm needs to know:

(a) if it is producing a dust that may explode. Here both the composition and size of the dust particles are important.

(b) the minimum concentration of dust that will support an explosion

(c) the temperature at which the dust will ignite

(d) the minimum "spark ignition energy" that will ignite an explosion.

3.11.3   The **composition** of the dust is very important. Readily combustible materials, such as sugar, starch, cereals and sulphur, which burn quickly and give gaseous reaction products – water vapour, carbon dioxide – are most dangerous. Proteins such as dried blood, which burn less readily because they contain a high percentage of nitrogen, are not so dangerous. Metallic dust such as those of aluminium and magnesium, give less violent explosions because they do not generate gaseous combustion products or the sudden pressurization of a large volume of gas that comes from the sudden heating of the air. Dusts that contain a high proportion of mineral matter are comparatively safe.

3.11.4   The **size** of the dust particles is important because it governs:

(a) **The rate of settling**

The smaller the size the lower the density, then the more easily the material is dispersed and the slower the particles settle with consequently greater danger.

(b) **The rate of oxidation**

The smaller the particles, the greater the surface area per given weight and hence the more rapid is the combustion.

3.11.5   The **percentage of dust in the air** is also important, just as it is with mixtures of flammable gases and vapours with air. An explosion will only propagate through a dust cloud if the concentration of dust lies between certain limits. The minimum explosive concentration is fairly well defined and is usually in the range 2% – 4% in air, whereas the upper limits are not so clearly defined. Although this concentration of dusts may seem low it is similar to the values for minimum explosive concentrations of hydrocarbons, vapours and mists. Dust at this concentration appears as a very dense cloud. The concentrations of dust which give the most rapid rate of rise of pressure is about three times greater than the stoichiometric concentration (at which fuel and oxygen are exactly balanced).

An important point about dust explosions is that the explosion itself, though powerful, usually gives rise to very small fires, but the main fire risk is that any burning dust will ignite the wood or fabric upon which it is resting.

3.11.6   **Ignition Temperature**

The composition of the dust determines the ignition temperature; for example, the ignition temperature of sugar dust/air mixture is 540 degrees centigrade and of leather dust/air is 740 degrees centigrade. The dust has to be heated to a minimum temperature before ignition occurs. The ignition temperature indicates the allowable temperature for exposed surfaces in an atmosphere likely to be contaminated by dusts. As most dust clouds are ignited in the range of 400-500 degrees centigrade, "black heat" surfaces can cause ignition. However some dusts such as zirconium and sulphur ignite at much lower temperatures.

3.11.7   **Ignition Energy**

For any given dust the minimum spark ignition energy is that required to initiate an explosion at the most explosive concentration of the dust. The energy required is of the order of 10-15 millijoules, which is many times greater than for flammable gases and vapours. Thus mixing powders with flammable solvents can be hazardous as the solvents can be ignited by a spark having only a fraction of a millijoule of energy, which can easily be produced in handling powders.

3.12 EARTHQUAKE

3.12.1 Earthquakes can cause widespread and often extensive damage to property whilst at the same time disrupting lines of communication, services and transport. They can also cause injury or death.

Earthquakes are essentially oscillating forces having horizontal and vertical components, induced by sudden shifting of adjacent strained rock masses.

Geological knowledge and understanding of earthquakes has improved considerably during recent years with major developments in the concepts of continental drift and plate tectonics.

3.12.2 It is now generally accepted that the continents are part of a number of large plates (sources vary between seven and twelve), which are moving relative to each other. In this movement one plate moves beneath another, sometimes creating new land ridges or deep oceanic trenches. This process of subduction is thus the cause of earthquakes such as the 1964 Alaskan earthquake. Along the plate boundaries and elsewhere are fault lines with rocks subject to movement in several different patterns such as horizontal sliding, upward or downward displacement, etc. The major fault lines are relatively well known and many minor fault lines have now been plotted. Perhaps the most famous fault is the San Andreas fault in California, which runs through San Francisco down towards Los Angeles and up past Vancouver. Movement since 1851 shows that the Pacific Plate (on the sea side of the fault) has been moving northwards at about two inches a year – in the 1906 earthquake there was 21 feet of horizontal displacement.

3.12.3 Earthquakes are the release of energy when the stress contained with the fault line becomes excessive. The point of release is called the focus of the earthquake with the point of the Earth's surface immediately above the focus called the **epicentre**. The focus may be deep seated or shallow. Earthquakes produce several different types of **waves:**

(a) **Primary** waves spread out from the focus with a series of compressions followed by dilations as the waves flow through the interior of the Earth.

(b) **Secondary** waves which are sideways moving (at right angles to the primary waves) and slower than the primary waves.

(c) **'L'** waves (named after A. E. H. Love) which are surface waves vibrating horizontally resulting from the primary wave striking the Earth's surface. There is a second kind of surface wave (**Rayleigh** waves) which is described as being retrograde elliptical in which the motion is similar to a light object moving up and down and backward along an ocean wave on the shore.

Primary waves travel about 5.6 kilometres per second, secondary waves about 3.2 kilometres per second gradually decreasing in intensity. The surface waves are slower but can still cause substantial vibration at considerable distances (over 80 kilometres) from the epicentre.

3.12.4 Two main scales are used to measure earthquakes:

(a) **Richter** scale, which relates to the displacement of the ground surface as on a seismograph situated at 100 km from the epicentre of an earthquake and thus measures energy released in quantitative terms. Each increase in number represents a 10-times increase in energy eg Richter 8 is 10 times Richter 7.

(b) **Modified Mercalli** scale, which measures the intensity of the earthquake by considering its observed effects on buildings and people. It is a qualitative measure.

San Francisco (1906) was Richter 8.3, Napier (1931) Richter 7.7, Tokyo (1923) Richter 7.9, Anchorage (1964) Richter 8.4, with the highest recorded figure Assam (1950) at 8.7 (the 1755 Lisbon earthquake has also been estimated at 8.7). One source has related the Modified Mercalli to Richter as follows (but the correlation depends on geography):

Richter	Modified Mercalli
7	MMIX to X
8	MMXI
8.5	MMXII

3.12.5   The distribution of serious earthquakes has been concentrated in the following regions:

(a) **Circum Pacific Belt** – west coasts of North and South America, all of Central America, Japan, Taiwan, Philippines, New Zealand

(b) **Alpine-Himalayan** – North Africa, Southern Europe, Near East, Iran, India, Burma, China

(c) **Caribbean**

(d) **Azores**

An examination of fault maps will show that the potential for earthquakes exists in many countries. As an illustration, in England, the Colchester earthquake of 1884 is estimated now at 6.9 and the 1896 Hereford earthquake at Richter 7.2. No country is totally free of earthquakes.

It is becoming common for earthquake scientists to also measure earthquakes in terms of Moment Magnitude, which provides a more accurate quantification of the amount of energy released. For example Kobe which rated 7.2 on the Richter scale rated 6.9 in terms of Moment Magnitude. By contrast Northridge was rated at 6.7 on the Moment Magnitude scale that showed that it only released half as much energy as the Kobe earthquake.

3.12.6   There is a correlation between frequency and size and as can be seen from the following worldwide average for a recent twelve year period:

6-6.9 Richter	-	195 earthquakes
7-7.9 Richter	-	15.5 earthquakes
8 & over	-	0.7 earthquakes

It is not really possible to estimate, even very roughly, a return period for a major earthquake in different geographical locations based on past experience as geological activity varies in intensity – although obviously earthquake-prone areas are generally known. In many parts of the world fault movement is now measured on a continuous basis – it is assumed that the risk increases when visible fault movement stops. The Chinese were able to predict four of the five major earthquakes in the 1970's but the fifth, which was not predicted, was the most severe.

3.12.7 Damage caused by earthquake is related to soil type and building construction. Many of the major cities of the world are situated in alluvial areas made up of material deposited by water flow such as rivers. Mud, silt, clay, sand and gravel are unconsolidated and present the worst earthquake risk. When nearly full or saturated with water, the soil can "liquify" with buildings sinking or toppling. Some insurers rate soils in terms of earthquake resistance as follows:

Mud	-	Worst
Silt	–	Poor
Sand	-	Poor to Fair
Gravel	-	Fair
Stiff Clay	-	Fair to Good
Rock	-	Good

and suggest that the modified Mercalli scale can be adapted to produce deviation for different types of soil with the same intensity, earthquakes varying in effect by three points (e.g: MMVI to MMIX). Another factor that influences the amount of damage is the depth at which the earthquake's energy is released. Shallow earthquakes tend to be very much more destructive than those in which the energy is released at depths that are greater than 50 kms.

3.12.8 Any seismic risk evaluation must include not only the building and its services but also its contents. With these the effects of being vigorously shaken in any plane and the resultant toppling, sliding, snapping and settling motions must be taken into account so as to determine the most suitable protection measures.

3.12.9 Volcanic activity is often allied with earthquakes particularly when there is an upsurge in volcanic activity. In geologically young countries the likelihood of eruption is an ever present risk albeit a very remote one in many parts of the world.

3.13   FLOOD

3.13.1 Many areas in the world sometimes experience exceptionally high rainfall within a short period of time and this, if coupled with a comparative young geology, can lead to significant flood exposure.

This has been recognised by many local authorities that have implemented flood protection measures where appropriate. However, in some instances these have not been fully completed or have not been maintained with the result that under certain conditions the degree of exposure is increased.

3.13.2 Location of the building is the most important factor in identifying and assessing the flood exposure. Certain areas of a country are more prone to flooding than others and where possible premises should be situated outside these particular areas. Even though historical records are sometimes comparatively short the local histories and local newspapers in many places are able to provide some information on past floods. In addition, an examination of the top and subsoils by drilling a core sample in the area in which it is proposed to place the building will often reveal information as to the frequency and extent of past flooding. If as is frequently likely it is not possible to avoid situating a building in a flood zone, the position of the building becomes of importance. Proximity of the site to water courses both existing and previous as well as its ground floor height above the general level of the land around the site must be considered.

3.13.3　Other factors that need to be taken into account when assessing the flood exposure and determining how best to manage the associated risk include the natural variation in climatic conditions of each of the seasons. In addition the possibility of a general warming of the world's climate as a result of the 'greenhouse effect' with its consequential increase in climatic extremes should also be included in the decision making.

4

WORKPLACE SAFETY AND HEALTH

4.1   INTRODUCTION

4.1.1   There are many hazards to which human beings can be exposed during their lifetime and in addition to the risk exposures that these produce human beings often subject themselves to a wide range of physical risks in their everyday lives. People learn to live and automatically cope with all sorts of risk exposures. However statistics show that generally:

    (a) the home is the most hazardous place; followed by

    (b) the motor vehicle; and then

    (c) leisure pursuits; with

    (d) the work place actually being the least hazardous place for people to be.

As the workplace provides a more controlled environment than any of the other places or activities on the list we can learn more from controlling its risk exposures than the other places or activities. The knowledge gained can be applied with considerable success to the home, driving a motor vehicle and undertaking leisure pursuits.

4.1.2   There are two major sources of hazard at work that affect the health and safety of both employers and employees, namely the people themselves and the particular working environment. Each of these can be broken down further into:

    (a) **Human**

        (i)   Moral and Morale

        (ii) Human Errors;

    (b) **Working Environment**

        (i)   Working Conditions

(ii) Machinery

(iii) Processes

(iv) Materials

(v) Social.

4.1.3   The workplace is a complex structure being made up of elements of four different working environments:

(a) the **Physical Work** environment

(b) the **Chemical Work** environment

(c) the **Biological Work** environment

(d) the **Social Work** environment.

The mix of the elements varies not only from industry to industry but also from workplace to workplace within the same industry.

4.1.4   Whilst certain industries involve exposure to specific unique hazards there are many hazards which are common to many or all industries. A text such as this however is not suitable for a detailed explanation of either the unique or the general hazards to which people are exposed at work, at home or at play. For such an explanation the reader should refer to the many specialised texts on the subject.

4.1.5   Most countries have legislation in force covering the safety of people in the workplace and elsewhere. In addition safety legislation is subject to regular updating and change in most countries. The safety legislation in every country differs and the reader is advised to regularly refer to the legislation of the country in which he or she is working in order to ascertain the detailed conditions that apply in that particular country.

4.2   HUMAN SOURCE OF HAZARD

4.2.1   **Moral and morale hazards** are intangible and are extremely difficult to quantify. However, they are of vital importance in the assessment and control of any risk. As opposed to the physical characteristics of property, moral hazard is related to the human element – the people associated with the organisation, the character, outlook, management skills, supervisory competence, work involvement and employee relationships of the managers, as well as their attitude towards insurance and the management of risk.

4.2.2   Although moral hazards are not readily quantifiable, the upper and lower limits can be easily recognised. At one extreme is the person who deliberately sets fire to his premises, perhaps in times of recession or bad trade, in order to obtain a payout under insurance cover, or he may act in collusion with another to stage a theft of his own property with a similar aim. A shopkeeper or manufacturer who is unable to weather a period of bad trade and who perhaps has an excessive amount of some goods which, through change of fashion, are worth much less than their original cost, is sometimes tempted to use a fire or a theft to solve this problem. As it is seldom possible to anticipate such criminal acts the risk can never be assessed. At the other extreme is the highly efficient manager who is aware of the need for efficiency, tidiness, cleanliness and good labour relations in the factory or business premises, and who adheres to the requirements of safety regulations. Somewhere in between is the type of person who for example would never deliberately set fire to their premises but who would regard an accidental fire as a stroke of good fortune and do little to minimise its results. A poor moral hazard is also shown by the person who, having a legitimate claim, proves uncooperative and avaricious in the negotiation of the claim settlement.

4.2.3   Moral hazard is totally associated with the actions of the people of an organisation, its management, its employees, the contractors and sub contractors that the organisation uses, its suppliers and its customers. Therefore, management performance, labour relations, housekeeping, control of waste, and control of smoking are all important in determining what action should be taken to minimise loss.

4.2.4   **Human errors** whether they result from commission or omission are an integral part of most losses.

    (a) whatever the accident situation, it is almost certain that there will be some form of human cause even though there will always be a number of other causes. People are unpredictable; they make mistakes; they sometimes indulge in dangerous behaviour or horseplay; their attitude to safety varies and they forget things. Poor management and supervision will also play a significant part in errors in the workplace.

(b) individuals vary in their perception of danger because each one has a different range of past experiences, training and general attitude to safety. In addition, individual perception varies according to behavioural factors such as the arousal of the person prior to the hazard occurring, motivation, memory, personality and attitude.

(c) working conditions can also play a major part in ensuring error free work. They however can be the cause of increased human error.

4.2.5   Moral hazard may arise not only from the activities of the management but also from the actions of employees and third parties. It may, for example, arise from:

(a) the acts of discontented or disinterested employees in carelessly or even criminally causing fire damage to the property of their employer. Good relationships between employer and employee are essential at all times. An unpopular employer may be instrumental in producing a bad safety or fire risk.

(b) the acts of such persons as vagrants, who will often set fire to such property as hay in stacks belonging to farmers against whom they have a grudge.

4.3   HOUSEKEEPING

4.3.1   Good housekeeping is one of the most important elements in managing moral risk as well as the other types of risk, and in particular, in preventing fire and other types of loss. It costs little or nothing to effect but is very easily overlooked and frequently neglected. There are many forms of poor moral hazard ranging from carelessness, untidiness, to the ineffective enforcement of rules or regulations such as those concerning smoking or the routine inspection and maintenance of fire extinguishing appliances, or the closing of fire-break doors outside working hours. Moral hazard may also arise from thoughtless actions or a lack of appreciation of the possible results of an act that is thought to be a matter of minor importance, such as the replacement of a burnt-out fuse by one of incorrect rating. There is also an ever present tendency in workplaces to take short cuts and cut corners particularly where the tasks being performed are boring or the staff involved have been doing the task for a considerable period of time, or where there is pressure to produce more quickly. Taking short cuts or cutting corners invariably leads to loss and often is the result of poor supervision.

4.3.2   The following are some of the major forms of bad housekeeping:

(a) failure to maintain a high standard of order and cleanliness both inside and outside premises. This is particularly important in any premises where processes produce flammable dusts or fluff and the risk of fire and explosion is magnified by the danger of disturbance of these dusts. It is also vitally important in any premises that produce or process food or pharmaceuticals

(b) the presence of defective windows, pavement lights, trap doors and the like

(c) disregard of situations where combustible litter or trade waste can accumulate and into which cigarette ends, lighted matches or other sources of ignition can be dropped

(d) congestion by reason of the premises being unsuited to the purpose for which they are used, insufficient floor space or faulty arrangement in layout of stock, plant, machinery, fixtures and fittings

(e) the failure to maintain clear passageways between machinery and processes and the failure to clear waste regularly even though this may be a requirement of a government regulation or an insurance policy

(f) failure to provide the appropriate safeguards in the storage, use and disposal of hazardous material

(g) the installation of unsuitable types of heating and lighting arrangements

(h) failure to safeguard all supplies of power, lighting and heating when the premises are left unattended or the storage and use of hazardous material

(i) fire-extinguishing appliances either not provided, or if provided being insufficient in number, hidden, not properly distributed and maintained, or of a type unsuited to the hazard present in the area in which they are situated

(j) the presence of poorly maintained or lit floor, work or stair surfaces, which may result in trips, slips or falls

(k) buildings, boundary walls, fences and gates being allowed to fall into a poor state of repair. This may render the premises more vulnerable to fire, burglary or vandalism from external causes.

4.3.3   Good housekeeping in business premises is dependent upon good management. Efficient conduct of the work processes and effective control of the labour force are essential if the business is to prosper. The responsibility for managing the risks of the business rests solely with its management, they are ultimately responsible for overall work operations and for the prosperity of the undertaking, even though the day-to-day work depends upon the competence and capacity of the individual employees. Efficient management means effective direction and supervision of the work force so that productivity and profitability are maintained if not improved. In time inadequate management control will lead to financial difficulties because, whilst the costs of production necessarily remain static or more probably rise in an inflationary climate, the output falls below that which should be obtained to sustain a reasonable growth for the business. The resultant financial cut backs, the shortage of capital and liquid funds invariably leads to a climate in which unfavourable moral hazard will flourish.

4.3.4   Good management is seen in the cleanliness and tidiness of premises, as well as in the arrangement of the machinery and processes so that the work is able to proceed smoothly and efficiently. It is also seen in the regular maintenance and adjustment of the machinery, in strict adherence to all statutory rules, regulations and expressed requirements, and in the steady activity of the employees. Both good housekeeping standards and good staff relations have a significant role to play in helping prevent loss. The signs of a well managed factory have been described as follows:

(a) good layout whereby the raw material enters at one end of the factory, travels straight through the factory during the course of its conversion by machinery or trade processes into the finished product, and emerges at the other end ready for packing and conveniently placed for dispatch and conveyance. A good layout saves time and expense. Work will flow smoothly and costs of carrying work in progress to and fro will be minimised. Employees do not have to make unnecessary journeys about the factory.

(b) discipline and control of workpeople and good labour relations

(c) good lubricating and maintenance methods

(d) a high standard of cleanliness, maintenance, tidiness and supervision

(e) sound procedures for handling, storing and disposing of:

   (i) materials

   (ii) waste and rubbish spaces so as to avoid pollution

   (iii) partially finished and finished work.

(f) good safety procedures for handling:

   (i) hazardous materials and processes

   (ii) an outbreak of fire or other emergency

(g) strong security of premises and hazardous areas

(h) regular instructions and training of staff in:

   (i) hazardous processes and materials

   (ii) observing general fire prevention measures

   (iii) fire-fighting

   (iv) evacuating buildings

(i) the provision of adequate first aid and fire-fighting equipment such as hose reels, buckets, hand pumps and portable fire extinguishers

(j) the existence of workable contingency plans.

A considerable impact can be made on the likelihood and size of loss, at a minimum cost by improving the standard of management and housekeeping.

4.4   PEOPLE

4.4.1   Although the actions or lack of actions of people play a significant part in virtually all losses, people hazards are extremely difficult to control. There are many factors that can and do influence human behaviour. A significant percentage of a manager's time is spent in trying to understand these factors and their effects on his or her staff.

4.4.2 Education and Training

The human factor is rarely absent from the work situation. Frequently carelessness, incompetence or lack of technical knowledge is either an initiating or at least a contributory cause of a loss producing event. Furthermore, the failure of an individual or group to respond in the correct way to a possible loss situation may contribute to the size of any ensuing loss. Consequently education and training have a major role to play in both risk and loss reduction programs, and should cover everyone employed by, or associated with the work of, the organisation.

4.4.3 Management

The aim should be to create in management awareness of the risks to which the organisation is exposed and of the ways in which they may be controlled. The lead in managing risk and therefore risk control must come from the board and top management. Although only a few members of the board and the top management team will need to have a detailed technical knowledge of the various risks and hazards, all should understand and have a commitment to the principal of total risk control. Also, the organisational structure and the division of responsibilities should be geared as far as possible to total risk control. **Risk control is essential at every stage of an organisation's activities,** in other words:

(a) at the planning stage

(b) at the production stage

(c) after sales, usage and service.

4.4.4 Employees

There are several fundamentals in the training of employees, notably:

(a) employees need to be aware of the hazards to which they may be exposed in the course of their work and what steps they can take to minimise the risk of injury to themselves and fellow employees

(b) training may be required regarding the use of special clothing and equipment provided for their safety

(c) instruction for all employees as to what to do in emergencies, for example, upon the outbreak of fire, breakdown of plant and especially the breakdown of safety devices

(d) training of some employees to deal with emergencies until expert help arrives, for example, the training of first-aid and fire-fighting teams

(e) instilling a sense of safety-consciousness in all employees, both in relation to the way they carry out their duties and in the avoidance of defects in the firm's products. The aim should be to instil in each employee a sense of responsibility towards fellow employees, customers and the general public

(f) providing all of the protective clothing and equipment that is necessary to enable the employees to do their work safely and efficiently. In addition such clothing and equipment will need to be inspected regularly and if damaged, repaired or replaced. It will also be necessary for regular check to be made to ensure that both are being used

(g) having all employees medically examined prior to their employment to ensure that they are medically suitable for the job for which they are being employed. There should also be regular medical checks of the employees to pick up any developing occupational health problems.

4.4.5   Contractors, Suppliers and Servicing Agents

Sometimes the organisation can be jeopardised by people other than its own employees, notably:

(a) sub-contractors who undertake work on its behalf

(b) suppliers of components

(c) contractors who may perform work on its premises and plant.

All these people should be made aware of such risks that may affect the organisation, and their co-operation should be sought to control those risks.

4.4.6 **Size**

The number in the workforce provides a good indication of the amount of work being done and the quantity of materials passing through the factory. As a consequence the size of the workforce will provide a measure of the exposure to risk in terms of the quantity of plant and machinery, materials, work in progress and stock present at any one time. The human factor is also important. The risk of loss caused by carelessness, disobedience, neglect or some other form of human failure increases with each additional person working on the premises. Ten woodworkers are more hazardous from a fire point of view than a single woodworker because they handle more wood, make more litter and produce more goods. There is also a greater exposure to the risk of injury and accident with the larger workforce. In sales-shops assistants may be considered as a substitute for cubic capacity in assessing the risk. A sales-shop employing a hundred assistants is more hazardous than one employing less than thirty because the sales-shop premises are necessarily larger and contain a greater amount of stock. The number of employees is also a useful measure for helping assess the exposure to liability risks.

4.5 INJURY AND ILLNESS LOSS CONTROL

4.5.1 Risk prevention measures include:

(a) developing a high level of understanding and skill before undertaking any hazardous activity

(b) wearing the correct well-fitting, protective clothing

(c) using the correct equipment and following proper procedures

(d) undertaking regular exercise and avoiding excessive eating and drinking etc.

(e) avoiding smoking

(f) only drinking in moderation and only in a social situation. Never drinking before or whilst driving

(g) avoidance of hazardous activities such as mountaineering, caving, body contact sports and extreme sport

(h) ensuring that one is fit and adequately trained before undertaking any hazardous activity

4.6 WORKING CONDITIONS

4.6.1   The conditions in which employees have to work play an important part in preventing and minimising accidents whether these result in injury to a person or in damage to property. It will be realised that there are many factors involved in the make up of the working conditions. Some of the more obvious ones are:

(a) atmosphere including:

(i) temperature

(ii) humidity.

(b) lighting including the general colour scheme

(c) noise and vibration

(d) layout

(e) the man – machine interface – ergonomics

(f) cleanliness and tidiness.

All of these factors play a role in helping to form the attitude of the employees to their work and their workplace. It is therefore essential if accidents are to be avoided for the working conditions to be maintained at as close to the optimum for the work involved as is possible.

4.6.2   **Atmosphere**

The provision of clean fresh air at a reasonable temperature and humidity for the type of work being undertaken is the right of every employee. The ventilation (or air conditioning) system should be designed to provide a minimum of 30 cubic metres of fresh air per person per hour. Where toxic or other dangerous substances are in use the ventilation system should be designed so as to contain any of the substance that may escape and to provide for its safe collection.

The temperature and humidity in the work place may vary with the type of work being done. For example if the work is heavy manual then the temperature and humidity may be lower than if the work is clerical.

Whilst people can function in extremes of both heat and cold there are limits in terms of heat and cold with which the human body is unable to cope even if:

(a) the person has been properly and fully acclimatised

(b) the correct clothing has been provided and is being worn

(c) the correct work patterns are being followed with appropriate rest periods

(d) in the case of heat, suitable liquids are freely available for drinking.

4.6.3 Lighting and Colour

Lighting in the workplace is extremely important in ensuring the safety of the employees who work in it. Eyesight deteriorates with increasing age and at the same time the accident rate tends to increase. Therefore whilst the optimum level of lighting needed will vary with the type of work being done it is true to say that the level should be higher than the minimum particularly if the workforce contains a number of older people.

The quality of the light is also important and in particular:

(a) glare should be minimised by the use of non reflective surfaces, indirect lighting and minimising the contrast between the working surface and its surroundings

(b) brightness should be controlled by use of surfaces with an appropriate reflectance value and by the regular maintenance of those surfaces

(c) as much natural light as possible should be used in the work place

(d) the lighting should be designed so as to distribute and diffuse the light without creating shadows or extreme concentrations of light.

Colour of the walls, ceiling and floors is also important and to ensure the maximum distribution of light within in the workplace they should be covered in pale rather than darker colours.

4.6.4 Noise and Vibration

Noise and vibration in the workplace are a form of waste

energy and any reduction in the level of either can result in some cost saving. In addition the presence of either in the workplace can lead to an increase in the number and severity of accidents as well as causing injury to any employee who may be exposed to either for long periods. This is particularly true if the exposure is at a high intensity such as that which often exists on building sites or in heavy engineering shops.

With proper planning the effects of both noise and vibration can be significantly reduced if not virtually eliminated.

These are some of the ways in which this may be done:

(a) incorporate protective measures into the design of the machine or building so as to isolate, control, or insulate the noise or vibration

(b) reduce the noise or vibration at source by such measures as:

    (i) better maintenance

    (ii) substituting softer materials on impact surfaces

    (iii) using belts in place of cogs

    (iv) stiffening vibrating plates

    (v) using more resilient mounts and connectors

    (vi) changing the process such as welding instead of riveting;

(c) reducing the transmission of the noise or vibration by enclosing the source in sound or vibration absorbing materials, fitting silencers on air or gas flows, fitting isolating mounts on machines, and limiting the number and size of openings in any enclosure

(d) providing suitable personal protection such as earplugs and earmuffs. There obviously needs to be a system in place that regularly checks that the protective equipment is being worn, that it is being correctly maintained and that is still doing the job that it is supposed to do.

4.6.5   **The Layout of the Workplace**

The layout of the workplace and in particular the individual work station can influence the incidence of accidents and mistakes. Not only should both be laid out in a sound way from an ergonomic point of view but they should also not be overcrowded or congested. The flow of work through the workplace should be logical, orderly and sequential. In addition all passageways, stairways, corridors and doorways in the workplace should be kept clear of any obstructions, and any openings in floors and walls or uneven floor levels should be properly fenced.

Where the work being undertaken involves a wet process such as in an abattoir or the use of grease or oil such as in a garage care needs to be taken to ensure not only that the water or grease is able to easily drain away so that it may be collected and disposed of in a safe manner, but also that the floor surface does not become slippery.

4.6.6   Ergonomics

Many accidents result from problems in the man – machine interface. A layout of the workplace, the equipment and machinery (particularly its controls) that is adapted to the strengths and the limitations of the individual workers will produce a much safer and more productive working environment. Therefore ergonomics that is concerned with optimising the workplace in human terms is extremely important in helping reduce both risk and loss.

4.6.7.   Sick Building Syndrome

In recent times, following the increasing use of air conditioning and the fully enclosed internal working environment, the working environment in some buildings has deteriorated to such an extent that the health and productivity of many employees who work in them has been significantly disadvantaged. Whilst in many instances the cause of the sick building syndrome can be attributed solely to the air conditioning system and its maintenance or cleanliness, sometimes there are other factors that can play a significant role in creating the syndrome. Examples of these include the use of plastic or formaldehyde based building materials and surface coverings.

The existence of the sick building syndrome in a particular building will be detected not only by the obvious such as a breakdown of the air conditioning plant but also the less obvious. Examples of this are a workforce which continually suffers from minor health problems such as headaches, sore or dry eyes or dry scratchy throats, or who take increased time off work or suffers an otherwise unexplainable drop in performance levels.

The effects of sick building syndrome may be eliminated by:

(a) ensuring that the air conditioning system is:

   (i)   properly and regularly maintained

   (ii) kept scrupulously clean – particularly any cooling water that may be used

   (iii) in full operation whilst any employee is working in the building

(b) installing adequate venting systems to quickly exhaust any chemical fumes produced within the building

(c) limiting the use of plastic or formaldehyde based products in the construction and furnishing of the building or by completely sealing them with a material that has an impervious surface

In effect, the use of good housekeeping practices in a building will ensure that the sick building syndrome is unlikely to occur within that building.

4.7 MACHINERY, PROCESSES AND MATERIALS IN THE WORKPLACE

4.7.1   The machinery, processes and materials present in the workplace be it in industry or the home are a major source of property damage, injuries and industrial illness. It is therefore essential that:

(a) the machinery and processes are properly designed, correctly assembled, fully tested before use, fully maintained, appropriately guarded and are only used for their designed purpose. In the case of materials their purity specification should be as required for the processes, and their storage, movement and disposal properly controlled.

(b) every person who has to operate any piece of machinery, any process or any material:

   (i)   is fully trained in all aspect of the use of that item

   (ii) is aware of the possible problems that may arise from its use and what to do to correct the situation if things do go wrong

(iii) knows how to handle any breakdown or failure of machinery or process.

(c) every machine and process is as inherently safe as it is possible to make them. Protective equipment cannot make an unsafe machine or process safe.

4.7.2 Machinery and Processes

Most industrial processes use machinery and as will be seen in *Chapter 5* accidental contact by a person with any moving part of a machine can lead to injury or even death of that person. Guarding of the moving parts of machinery is essential.

Most industrial processes use energy in one or more of its different forms (e.g. heat, pressure, friction etc.). As we have seen energy that is not applied to work is lost and may in fact be the cause of injury or damage to property. The control of the energy used in a process by one or more of the strategies outlined in *Chapters 5 and 12* is essential if loss in the form of injury, damage or waste is to be avoided.

4.7.3 Materials

A wide variety of materials is used in industry (and the home) which take a number of different forms such as solid, liquid, gas, dust, fume, metal, non metal, solvent or plastic. In the case of the agricultural, horticultural and silvicultural industries materials such as pesticides, fungicides, weedkillers and fertilisers are used extensively. All of these create risk exposures for people and property.

Many of the materials used or produced by industrial processes are:

(a) toxic

(b) carcinogenic

(c) narcotic

(d) an irritant

(e) corrosive

(f) otherwise harmful to people;

and can be inhaled, ingested or otherwise absorbed into the body.

It is therefore essential for management not only to be aware of the hazards of each of the materials used by the organisation but also to ensure that all employees are aware of how each of these materials is to be handled and stored in a safe manner. All employees should also be aware of the safety limits for each of the materials and what to do if the limit is breached at any time. In addition the appropriate equipment and clothing for handling the materials should be provided and used.

4.8 THE SOCIAL WORK ENVIRONMENT

4.8.1 All workplaces are fundamentally human institutions as, without human involvement they will be largely unproductive. This is also true of those workplaces that have been largely automated. Thus a major part of the manager's role is involved in managing people, ensuring that employees are able to get and to maintain job satisfaction. There are many indications of a possible lack of job satisfaction such as work injuries, strikes, labour turnover, plant damage and absenteeism. A lack of job satisfaction tends to lead to loss and therefore specific measures to reduce the likelihood and the extent of any loss of job satisfaction should be an essential part of every manager's armoury.

Quite apart from the problems that give rise to these indications of a lack of job satisfaction are the problems that will occur in the social work environment as a result of absenteeism, labour turnover, employing young or aging workers, fatigue and drug dependency.

4.8.2 Absenteeism

Often when a worker is absent the work that he or she normally does is spread around the other workers. This can put a considerable strain on the other workers and the likelihood of accident or error increases for a number of reasons, such as:

(a) inexperience

(b) stress

(c) overloading

A similar result will often occur when temporary staff are employed to cover for the absentee worker.

4.8.3 Smoking and Other Drugs

Smoking is a widespread form of drug dependency throughout

the world and is a most significant cause of death. It is the main cause of lung cancer and is a major risk factor contributing to the development of coronary heart disease and cerebrovascular disease as well as a number of other life threatening diseases. Research is now citing smoking as being significant in aggravating the risk of certain industrial illnesses when workers smoke whilst handling or working with a number of substances used by industry. Passive smoking is also now being seen as a significant exposure for non-smokers. Quite apart from the health problems created by smoking it is directly or indirectly the cause of many fires. Smokers often dispose of lighted matches or cigarette ends or smouldering pipe tobacco in a careless manner. Whilst it is probable that many fires are attributed to this cause in the absence of any other cause, it is nevertheless obvious from fire brigade reports that careless smoking is a major cause of fires. It is impractical to prohibit smoking at all times in all parts of the factory or business premises. In many people the habit is so deeply ingrained that such a ban would undoubtedly lead to greater hazards from illicit smoking that may consequently take place in situations away from supervision or management control. This may result in increased danger to combustibles such as stores or packing materials, as well as the possibility that a fire from a smouldering cigarette stub might develop to a dangerous degree before it is observed.

Smoking should, of course, be strictly prohibited in workrooms or factories where combustible waste or dusts are produced, where flammable vapours are present, and where combustible materials are stored. Where ashtrays and similar receptacles are provided, arrangements should be made for their contents to be safely disposed of each night. No smoking regulations for hazardous areas should be strictly enforced and management's attitude towards this should be well publicised. The employees will appreciate the reason for the ban, but in all premises it is desirable that smoking should be permitted at certain specified times (for example during morning and afternoon breaks) in suitable places, such as mess rooms or canteens or in clearly defined 'smoking areas'. An adequate number of suitable deep receptacles for spent matches and cigarette ends should be provided. In places of public gathering or entertainment where smoking is permitted it is essential to provide an adequate number of ashtrays or similar receptacles, unless smoking is strictly prohibited, as is now the case in an increasing number of places. On the other hand, where smoking is prohibited it is essential that all ashtrays etc should be removed.

4.8.4 **Alcohol**

Alcoholism is not only a public health hazard in many countries but it is also a significant contributing cause in injuries and property damage. When a person is under the influence of alcohol his or her judgement is impaired, reaction time slower and tolerance level is often lowered. As a consequence there is a much greater propensity for errors and accidents to occur.

Some occupations such as those in the catering and drink trades, the fishing industry, the Services, the medical profession and journalism, seem to have an above average incidence of alcohol problems. As a consequence the detrimental effects on those industries in the form of absenteeism and accidents as well as the consequent risk to health are far more severe than for many other industries. Alcohol is a mind-altering drug that does cause significant health problems and its consumption in other than modest quantities in a social situation does create major problems for industry. Regrettably, because of its general social acceptability the problems created by alcohol for industry are largely ignored or hidden. As with alcohol and driving, alcohol and work should not be mixed.

4.8.5 **Labour Relations**

A good employer/employee relationship is essential for the efficient working of a business. When good management controls the staff, and rules are applied in a sensible way, it is fairly certain that the desirable routine duties will be carried out. Packing material should be kept in its proper bins, not left strewn about the floor overnight. Supplies of flammable materials should be kept in their proper stores and not left in the workshops overnight. Oily rags should be placed in the metal bins provided and not left lying where they were last used or thrown. Everything depends on the works manager, if there is one, or the principal of the firm. The class of labour is important. The employment of skilled high-class labour implies an intelligent and reliable workman or woman. However, it is essential that the type of employee is matched to the work that is to be done. If the more highly skilled people are employed in a job that is routine and which does not require them to exercise their skills, boredom will inevitably set in and mistakes will follow. Where cheap, unskilled or casual labour is all that is needed for the work, then it is more likely that the type of person employed is lower in intelligence and reliability, prone to carelessness or disobedience of rules and disinclined to observe precautions. The hazard is thus increased.

Good working conditions together with a carefully selected and contented labour force are major factors in loss reduction in every sphere of activity. The comfort and welfare of employees is an essential feature of good management. Facilities such as staff sports and social clubs, canteens, rest rooms and even the provision of trained nurses, all help to produce a loyal and contented workforce. Such a staff will normally recognise the value of good amenities and respond by submitting willingly to the rules and disciplines of the factory that they realise to be for the good of all. A well-disciplined staff means that care will be taken to prevent losses.

Under the heading of staff comfort would come adequate lighting, heating and ventilation, reasonable noise levels and a lack of vibration in the workplace, all of which make for good work and careful operations by the employees. An uncomfortable and dissatisfied workforce tends not to care much about anything in the place where they work. This may lead to neglect of precautions, carelessness or even deliberate acts of arson or sabotage.

4.8.6   Workplace Stress

There is good and bad stress. However it often causes problems in the workplace and it can lead to significant levels of loss for not only the individuals affected but also their employers and society as a whole. The medical profession indicts stress as a major factor in many of the main causes of death in modern society (e.g. heart disease).

There are many causes of stress including feelings of job insecurity, a poor working environment, inadequate job definitions and minimal interpersonal skills.

Stress may also arise from the person's

(a) job

(b) role and responsibilities

(c) relations with other people

(d) career

(e) employing organisation

(f) home environment

Measurement of the stress level of individuals within an organisation should be done on a proactive basis and is the essential precursor to its management.

4.8.7   Stress is far easier to prevent than to control and once the presence of stress or its contributing factors has been recognised and assessed one or more of the many alternative ways of managing it should be implemented. These fall into the following major categories:

(a) organisational

(i)   job or task redesign

(ii) redesign of the workplace

(iii) management approach

(b) individual

(i)   raising the level of coping, interpersonal and social skills as well as developing appropriate assertiveness skills

(ii) time management and the effective use of time

(iii) training in relaxation

(iv) managing a healthy and sensible lifestyle

With stress, as with other types of exposure to loss or injury, it must always be remembered that 'prevention is better than cure'.

4.8.8   **Night Work**

Night work is usually defined as work done at any time between 9 pm at night and 5 am in the morning. It is considered a hazard because the normal risks of production such as those in corn mills, namely lighting, heating, use of grinding machinery and cleaning machinery are doubled, if not tripled because of the increase in work period. Machines in use day and night have no time to cool off and the hazards of friction and overheated bearings are increased. Breakdowns tend to become more frequent. Repairs are likely to be postponed or hurriedly done when day and night shifts are worked. Moreover, the alertness and discipline of workpeople are often affected because they are working at times when nature dictates that they should be asleep.

The absence or falling off of alertness or discipline tends to produce conditions in which accidents may occur or fires may occur or develop unnoticed. Overtime does not increase the risk to the same extent as nightwork because it is usually only partial or irregular. Nevertheless when it is the normal practice of a factory to work late the hazards associated with the employees are probably more severe compared to those of nightwork where at least the employees work for a normal period of 7 – 8 hours. Employees, who work overtime, however willingly, are probably already tired after a full day's work and so are less alive to risks and possibly less amenable to discipline.

4.8.9   **Multiple or Plural Tenure**

Where several firms occupy parts of the same building the hazard of each may be affected by the presence of the others. This applies in varying degrees to all forms of risk but is especially so where fire risks are concerned. If a building is of fully fire resisting construction then each fire resisting floor, section or compartment constitutes a separate fire risk and the property it contains may be rated strictly on its own merits without reference to other parts of the building. A tenant who is the sole occupant of a fire-resisting floor or section in theory cannot be affected by the presence or activities of tenants in other fire resisting floors or sections. Difficulties can arise however when premises forming one fire risk are occupied by more than one tenant and each portion has varying hazards. Each tenant is now subject not only to the risk arising from his own occupation, but also to the risk of fire arising from the activities of his co-tenant. The factors involved in assessing accumulation of fire risk are less important where non-hazardous occupations or those in the same class of trade are concerned. Where, however, more hazardous occupations such as those associated with the clothing trade are concerned, or if a variety of manufacturing trades such as printing, plastics fabrication, woodworking and the like are carried on in the same building, the hazard resulting from accumulation of risk becomes a matter of importance to the fire underwriter.

An adverse feature of multiple tenure risks is that it is usually difficult to obtain all the facts necessary to fully assess the whole risk. In addition, whilst many buildings in multiple tenure are occupied by firms of the highest standing, there are other buildings, often old and of poor construction which are occupied by many tenants, some of whom may be of dubious standing. In such cases the standard of management for the whole risk must be considered equivalent to that of the least.

Unless the landlord of the building provides adequate supervision, it is sometimes found that waste and rubbish are allowed to accumulate in the common parts of the building, such as staircases and corridors. The tenants in multiple tenure buildings are by no means invariably undesirable, but there is always an element of doubt. One poor tenant can create a hazard for the entire building. Experience has shown that multiple tenure buildings in certain areas and in certain trades tend to attract a large proportion of undesirable tenants.

In addition, multiple tenure risks need extra care when examining the security of the premises. Other businesses in the same building might prove especially attractive to thieves, whereas if the building had been occupied solely by one firm it might have been ignored. The manner in which each tenant is separated from the other tenancies and the possibility of access to the one part through parts occupied by others are points of importance. It is not unknown for separation to be by the most unsatisfactory method of a partition of timber or plaster-board on a timber frame.

4.8.10 Unoccupied Buildings and "Silent" Factories

These differ because the former are entirely devoid of contents, whereas the latter still contain machinery though it is not in operation. The hazards in connection with empty buildings depend largely upon their condition, usually their supervision is spasmodic and thus unauthorised persons may easily force an entry and perhaps cause damage or a fire, maliciously or through carelessness. In addition, deterioration of the fabric and plant of the building tends to be faster in unused buildings compared with those that are constantly being used.

In the case of silent works or factories, the machinery and/or stock are temporarily not in use and this may be because of unsuccessful trading or because of seasonal operations. A caretaker or watchman is usually appointed, but this person's appointment may not require him to be present in the premises concerned and thus any small outbreak of fire may develop without notice. Power and light are usually cut off, but sometimes arrangements are made for the occasional running of machinery and the opportunity is also sometimes taken to undertake the overhaul of plant. In the case of seasonal business the opportunity is often taken during the quiet season to carry out plant and/or building maintenance. This introduces new hazards into the property, such as welding, which often are the cause of serious major loss.

4.8.11 Arson

Complete automatic sprinkler protection is the principal preventative safeguard against arson. Adequate security is also of prime importance. Well maintained fencing; good exterior and interior lighting; intrusion alarms, guard service and well secured access openings (doors, windows etc) can all help minimise the chances of an incendiary fire. Visitor and employee access to travel within a property should also be controlled. Properly installed, maintained and supervised fire detection and fire protection equipment will also assist in reducing the damage caused by arson.

5

MACHINERY AND INDUSTRIAL SAFETY

5.1   THE HAZARDS AND RISKS ASSOCIATED WITH MACHINERY

5.1.1   Some of the hazards associated with machinery are discussed later in Chapters (8 onwards) that discuss fire and explosion. However, apart from the specific hazards that are discussed later, machines have a number of hazards all of which arise out of the mechanical energy that is created by the operations of the machine or by the machine being operated in an unstable or unsafe situation.

5.1.2   There is a wide variety of hazards and risks associated with machinery, all of which can result in injury or death, as well as in some instances, damage of property The following are broad groupings of these hazards:

(a) traps

(b) entanglements

(c) ejection of particles

(d) contact.

Each of these can lead to a person being injured or killed. For example, a person may become trapped and drawn into the machine, or they may be struck by a part or material ejected by the machine, or may be burnt by coming into contact with a hot surface. Some of the hazards arise not only from the moving parts of the machine itself but also the materials being worked upon by the machine or a fixed structure in close proximity to the machine.

In addition, a part or a component of the machine may fail as a result of fatigue, stress, wear or a defect leading to a breakdown of the machine.

5.1.3   A machine has been defined as an **'apparatus for applying**

power, having fixed and moving parts, each with a definite function'.
The component parts of every machine can be classified as being either
those that perform the output functions of the particular machine, or
those that provide and carry power or motion to those parts that
perform the output functions.

5.1.4   The areas of special hazard in machinery include:

    (a) revolving parts such as shafts and spindles, beaters, drums,
cutting tools such as saws, as well as those enclosed in
casings such as mixer arms, spirals, worms and centrifuges

    (b) discontinuous revolving parts such as fan blades and
spoked wheels

    (c) abrasive wheels

    (d) reciprocating parts such as presses, stamps, guillotines and
perforators

    (e) nips and traps such as those between pairs of revolving
parts or a revolving part and a belt or those between platen
motions, connecting rods or links.

5.1.5   The hazards of many machines are inherent to their design, and
in most cases it is not possible to change the design so as to eliminate
the hazards without changing the machine to such an extent that it can
no longer produce the required output. Therefore, guards and
automatic cut-offs to protect the operators are a common feature of
many machines.

5.1.6   The work of some machines involves the use of physical force
to cut, bend, form new shapes using pressure or impact, lift or move
the materials being worked upon. As a consequence there is the
possibility that injuries to people and damage to property may result
from the:

    (a) cutting action

    (b) the application of pressure or impact resulting in the
crushing of the person or property

    (c) rotational forces that exists in virtually every machine
which can lead to the entanglement and trapping of the
operator because of loose clothing, long hair, loose
strapping or similar unsecured appendages.

5.1.7   The design of many machines is ergonomically unsound which makes them difficult and tiring for their operators to use. In addition the layout of not only, individual work areas, but also the whole of the production floor often leaves much to be desired from an ergonomic point of view. As a consequence, working in such conditions can be both tiring and error prone, leading to a higher than normal level of accidents.

5.1.8   Machines do break down from time to time and the exposure to hazard is increased significantly not only whilst the repairs are being carried out, but also whilst the repairs are being tested, once completed. Extra special care and supervision is needed to ensure that the repairs are done properly and the machine is correctly re-assembled.

5.1.9   Recent developments in machines, including the use of robots and of microprocessors not only to control the machine operations, but also to operate all necessary guards, have all worked towards improving safety. Even so:

(a) full and complete training of all machine operators including regular refresher training

(b) maintaining all machinery on a regular basis

(c) a clean and well laid out work place from an ergonomic point of view

(d) a sensible work schedule for all employees

(e) maintaining a good working environment in terms of ventilation, climate, noise, vibration and lighting

(f) the provision and use of protective clothing, equipment such as safety helmets, shoes and boots and eye protection;

all have a significant part to play in helping to eliminate accidents.

5.1.10 Many countries have enacted legislation or regulations governing virtually all aspects of machine safety and reference should be made to these in order to obtain details that apply in a particular country.

5.2   SAFETY GUARDS

5.2.1   It is often a legal requirement that machinery must be fitted with proper safety guards and there are many ways in which this may be done. For example:

(a) by fitting a static guard which may be fixed, adjustable or take the form of a distance guard

(b) by fitting an interlocking guard which is inter-connected with the machine, so that if it moved from its correct position the machine is stopped from operating. The interlocking mechanism maybe mechanical or electrical

(c) by fitting an automatic guard which is so integrated with the machine itself that the guard physically moves the person away from the danger area before the machine will operate

5.2.2   In addition, there are a number of safety devices that may be fitted to machinery such as:

(a) trip device which if a person gets too close to the danger area activates and shuts down the machine

(b) two handed operating mechanism which requires that both hands be used to operate the controls of the machine

(c) overrun device which prevents machine parts from running under their own inertia

(d) mechanical restraint device that applies a braking mechanism to a dangerous machine part that has been set in motion by a failure of a machine control.

5.3   THE HAZARDS AND RISKS ASSOCIATED WITH LIFTING MACHINERY AND EQUIPMENT

5.3.1   Lifting machinery and tackle are a special form of machinery and as such are subject to many of the hazards and risks discussed above, together with a number of hazards and risks that are peculiar to this type of machinery. The hazards and risks relate in the main to the combination of gravity, weight and height, although in some cases, gravity and uneven working surfaces do accentuate both the hazards and risks. As with all types of machinery, most countries have a series of regulations that govern the use of lifting machinery, which should be studied.

5.3.2   Lifting machinery includes such equipment as hoists, teagles, cranes, their associated lifting tackle, elevators and lifts that are used to carry people or goods, or both. Lifting tackle is normally considered to also include slings, rings, hooks, shackles, swivels as well as the ropes, wires and chains.

5.3.3   **The Specific Hazards and Risks**

(a) **Teagle openings and platform edges** are open positions at some height above the ground into which or from which material is loaded. The major hazard here is possibility of an operator falling out of the opening which may be prevented by fitting adequate fencing and hand holds, as well as using good operating procedures.

(b) **Cranes** of which there are a number of different types, for example, fixed, tower, mobile and overhead travelling cranes. The major risks of all cranes are that they may collapse or overturn. This may be the result of any one of a number of factors such as, overloading, incorrect slewing or incorrect construction, erection or dismantling, as well as high winds. One particular area that the crane operator needs to keep an eye on is the 'maximum permitted moment' for the crane and the current load because, if the lift exceeds this, then there is a very real danger that the crane will overturn or collapse. The crane operator should follow the correct operating procedures and ensure that:

(i) all lifts are made vertically

(ii) the load is not dragged sideways on the ground or some other surface

(iii) the load is free to lift

(iv) all movements are slow and steady whether lifting or slewing.

Regular maintenance of all parts of the crane is essential if it is not to fail or collapse with disastrous results.

(c) **hoists and lifts** which include any platform or cage whose movement is restricted by a guide or guides. There are a wide variety of different types of such goods lifts, main hoists, paternoster lifts and passenger lifts. All should be fitted with substantial enclosures gates or doors, which will prevent people falling or coming into contact with the moving parts. Also, all should be fitted with safety interlocks that prevent movement from starting until all doors are properly closed and which prevent doors from being opened until the lift has stopped correctly on the selected floor. Any hoist or lift inside a building should be fully enclosed with fire-resisting material, including any doorways, apart from that at the top of the shaft which should be of a material that will allow any fire in the shaft to escape with relative ease. As with all lifting machinery regular inspection and maintenance have a significant part to play in eliminating accidents.

(d) **powered working platforms** were developed to provide quick and safe access to positions at some height above the ground which otherwise would be difficult to access. They are much safer to use than virtually all other systems that may be used to reach high remote areas in situations in which mobility, reach and height are required. There are a number of factors that require special attention:

(i) **Siting**

The platform should be sited on a firm, level surface before it is operated. It should also be placed so that it does not cause obstruction for any other traffic in the immediate area, and it should be situated so that the platform may be raised without coming into contact with overhead obstructions and power lines etc.

(ii) **Movement**

Care should be taken to firmly secure the platform before being moved. If the platform is being loaded onto or unloaded from a trailer, the operation should be supervised by a skilled person.

(iii) **Stability**

Raising the platform when standing on an uneven surface, overloading of the platform, wind loading impact or shock loading and improper use can all cause the platform to overturn. The manufacturer's maximum load specifications should be strictly adhered to.

(iv) **Maintenance**

As with all machinery, regular maintenance is essential, as is the use of a mechanical locking bar (a form of guard) when the mechanism for raising and lowering the platform is being inspected or maintained

(v) **Personnel**

Only well trained and medically fit operators should be allowed to operate the platforms. Safety harnesses should always be worn by any person whilst working from the platform, and during the raising and lowering operation.

(e) **chains, ropes and lifting tackle** include not only natural and man-made fibre ropes, wire ropes and chains, but also lifting tackle such as slings, hooks, pulley blocks, shackles, spreader bars and eye bolts. It will be realised that the chains, ropes and other lifting tackle are a critical part of most lifting machinery and equipment. By their very nature and use these items are subject to considerable wear and tear as well as some misuse. It is, therefore, essential that these items are well constructed and strong enough for the use they will be put to as well as being well maintained. The items should be regularly examined and tested as required by the regulations. Care should also be taken to ensure that the items are not used at any time to lift loads that are in excess of their safe working load.

5.4 THE HAZARDS AND RISKS ASSOCIATED WITH MECHANICAL HANDLING EQUIPMENT

5.4.1 There is a wide variety of equipment that has been designed to facilitate the handling of goods, which range through conveyors, elevators and internal building transport systems to goods vehicles. The majority of this type of equipment include a number of trap and entanglement situations in their basic design and, as a consequence, extensive use has to be made of guards and emergency cut-offs.

117

Friction, leading to build-up of heat and static electricity is also a constant problem, particularly with conveyors and some designs of elevator. Proper and regular lubrication and maintenance can help reduce friction and proper earthing can virtually eliminate the static electricity problem.

5.4.2 Conveyors

Amongst the many different types of conveyor are belt, rollers, chain, slat and screw conveyors. Because of the many different trap situations in a conveyor system, guarding such as tunnel, interlock and fixed are used extensively as well as emergency stop systems.

Whilst many conveyors operate in fixed positions, some can be moved from one position to another, depending on the position of the goods to be moved. The moveable type of conveyors are not only exposed to the problems mentioned earlier, but also the hazards of improper erection and/or dismantling which can lead to damage and/or injury. Extra care is therefore required in setting up and taking down such conveyors and it is vital that the conveyor is well tested before being used under load or at speed after being re-erected.

5.4.3 Elevators

As with conveyors, most elevators operate in a fixed position, although there are some that can be moved from position to position, as the work requires. Explosion and fire are a problem with elevators because of the materials being handled and the fact that most elevators penetrate from one fire compartment to another. It is essential that adequate measures are taken to reduce the risks involved, such as incorporating explosion vents and using fire resistant materials in the construction of the elevator and the hoistway in which it runs. As with conveyors, a number of trap situations exist and should be guarded against. In common with all machinery, supervision and control over the operations of elevators is a critical factor in preventing injury and other accidents.

5.4.4 Mobile Handling Equipment

Equipment that is both mobile and able to handle goods has made a considerable impact in the storing and handling of many different types of goods. Not only should the mobile equipment be suitable for the work that it is to do, but also the warehouse or store in which the equipment will be used needs to be correctly laid out and lit so as to facilitate safe movement, manoeuvring and lifting of the goods. Also, the storage system installed in the warehouse and the goods should be matched to the handling equipment so that the goods can be handled in the most efficient and safest way possible. As the equipment is mobile its stability is very important. Finally, only properly trained operators should use the equipment, and it should be maintained on a regular basis.

There is a wide variety of mobile mechanical handling equipment, ranging from pedestrian operated stacking trucks, which may be either manually operated or power operated, through the various varieties of forklift trucks, such as reach, counterbalance and narrow aisle forklifts to order pickers. Recent developments in storage handling equipment has seen the development of the fully automated warehouse in which the order picker has reached a very high level of efficiency being totally mobile both horizontally and vertically under the control of a computer. The lack of people in such facilities can result in dangerous circumstances and even loss situations existing for some time before they are spotted.

Most of the goods handled by forklift trucks are stored on pallets and it is essential that the pallets are kept in a good state of repair. In addition, the type of pallet must be suitable for the type of goods stored on them. For example, goods stored in strong sided cardboard boxes may be stacked on open pallets, whereas goods that are not symmetrical in bulk and which are not stored in a firm sided container must be stacked in posted pallets to ensure that the stack is stable. A forklift truck is sometimes fitted with a working platform so that it may be used in place of the powered working platform that was described earlier. Used in this way they are, therefore, not only subject to the same hazards as the powered working platforms but also those of using a piece of equipment in a way for which it was not designed. For example, the platform plus its occupant who is able to move will tend to make the forklift truck unstable. In addition, the platform may not be firmly fixed to the forks and may not be fitted with adequate fencing.

5.4.5 Goods Vehicles

These include both rail and motor vehicles. The hazards that exist with goods vehicles arise mainly because of poor visibility often coupled with confined or awkward working areas. Reversing (and in the case of rail, shunting) are both particularly hazardous operations and should only be undertaken with a great deal of care and supervision. Loading bays must be carefully designed not only to allow the vehicle easy access but also to facilitate the safe loading and unloading of goods. Obviously the loading and unloading areas must be designed to suit the nature of the goods or materials being moved, for example, grain has very different requirements to palletised white goods.

5.5   ENGINEERING LOSS CONTROL

5.5.1   All machinery has a finite life and at some stage during the life a part will break or malfunction. Any risk reduction measures that are implemented should aim at spotting these future failures before they actually happen and interrupt production. In addition the design, construction and use of the machine should be such that the likelihood of accident or breakdown is minimised.

Possible measures that may be used are:

(a) an extensive program of maintenance such as condition assessment, reactive maintenance, predictive or preventative maintenance

(b) a program of replacing critical parts after a fixed period of use

(c) regular shutdown, dismantling and inspection of machinery

(d) inspection using special electronic equipment that identifies developing cracks and hot spots. Other forms of examination techniques include strain gauge testing and vibration monitoring.

In addition the machine should be:

(a) ergonomically well designed as well as being inherently safe as is possible i.e. the safe way of working is designed into the machine rather than added on in the form of guards and safety switches etc.

(b) fitted with adequate well designed guards as appropriate

(c) fitted with safety switches and valves as appropriate

(d) subject to regular inspection and certification by qualified engineers

(e) operated only by people who have had proper training (both initial and refresher).

5.6 THE CONSTRUCTION INDUSTRY

5.6.1   The Construction industry covers a wide variety of activities, many of which are hazardous. This, coupled with an ever-changing work place and a workforce that is largely casual can lead to a high number of accidents. As a consequence the activities of the construction industry are subject to government regulations in many countries. The reader should therefore refer to the regulations that apply to the country in which he or she is domiciled.

5.6.2   **The Major Causes of Accidents in the Construction Industry**

Most building sites involve the use of temporary work places at some height above the ground. The safety barriers erected are often limited in both scope and strength and the structure of the working platform itself may not be as strong as it should be, particularly where there is pressure to finish a job. As a consequence, falls by workers or materials and collapse of construction work figure highly in the accident statistics, as do accidents involving machinery and tools.

5.6.3   **Falls**

Because much of the construction work takes place above the ground there is an ever present possibility that either a person may slip or some building material or equipment may be dropped and fall to the ground, possibly injuring another person or damaging some other material or completed work.

The falls may occur from:

(a) **working platforms or walkways.** It is essential that all working platforms, stairs and gangways including any scaffolding be:

   (i) properly fenced

   (ii) seated on a stable base

   (iii) constructed of robust materials that are subject to regular inspection and maintenance

(iv) kept clear of litter and other obstructions including projecting nails

(v) sanded or otherwise treated to prevent any horizontal surface from becoming slippery

(vi) properly and firmly anchored to a stable and strong part of the building

(vii) erected and dismantled under the supervision of a competent person.

(b) **roofs** as a result of slippery, pitched surfaces, or through the roof because of the fragile material of which it is made. Another situation in which falls are relatively common is where there is an unmarked and (unfenced) hole in either a roof or a floor. Most of this type of accident can be avoided by:

(i) fitting protection to the eaves, roof edges and all openings

(ii) in the case of fragile roofing surfaces, clearly marking them as such

(iii) ensuring that crawl boards or fixed ladders are used when working on any form of pitched roof

(iv) covering all holes with an adequate closure or guardrails and toe boards as well as clearly marking the presence of the hole

(v) not stacking building materials on roof surfaces

(vi) not working on the roof in unsuitable weather, such as high winds, snow or ice

(vii) using firmly anchored safety harnesses and/or safety nets.

(c) **ladders** either because they are not stable or because they are rotten. A ladder should therefore be:

(i) of sound construction

(ii) correctly placed on a stable and firm footing

(iii) should be firmly fixed at a point close to its top

(iv) of sufficient length to project above the upper landing so as to enable using it to safely reach the landing.

(d) **materials** falling from higher up the building. Even small objects falling from a height can be both dangerous and destructive. The problem can be largely overcome by:

(i) proper housekeeping

(ii) providing toe boards and edge barriers

(iii) installing protective platforms to catch any falling objects

(iv) ensuring that all material being lifted is properly secured

(v) ensuring that all those on the site wear a safety helmet and safety footwear at all times.

5.6.4 Collapse of Excavations

Excavations are a feature of many building sites and whilst most are problem free, collapse may occur as a result of inadequate support to the sides of the excavation for its size and the nature of the soil into which the excavation is made. Collapse may be caused or hastened by stacking too much weight close to the edge of the excavation. There are a number of common sense precautions to ensure that accidents are not caused by excavations, such as ensuring that they are properly fenced and lit. In addition, all underground services in the area should be located and clearly marked before any digging starts and every possible precaution should be taken to avoid undermining any adjacent buildings. Care should also be taken to ensure that the excavation does not become flooded with water or gases which are toxic or which could asphyxiate the workers.

5.6.5 Machinery and Tools

(a)   mobile machinery

There is often mobile machinery on a building site such as dump trucks, mobile cranes and bulldozers. All can be involved in accidents often when not being used as designed. There are a number of precautions such as ensuring that:

(i) all such machinery is properly maintained and is only operated by competent trained people

(ii) all site roadways are maintained and kept clear of obstructions

(iii) machinery is only used as intended and not to carry passengers if not designed to do so

(iv) guards of moving parts are fitted and operational.

(b)   powered hand tools

There are usually many different types of hand tools found on a building site, most of which are powered by electricity. As building sites are usually wet such tools must be properly insulated and earthed with either an earth leakage protection, isolation transformer or both. In addition, there are other risk exposures, such as those discussed earlier in this Chapter. Adequate guarding is essential, as is proper and complete training of those likely to use such equipment. Maintenance and repair of powered hand tools should be done on a regular basis.

5.6.6   Fire Risk

The risk of fire whilst a building is being constructed or renovated is much higher than it is once the building is occupied because of the ever-changing workplace and the amount of temporary construction that is present during this phase.

Measures that should be taken include those which will:

(a) minimise the possibility of fire breaking out and causing injury or death and damage to property, such as:

(i)   improving site management supervision

(ii) installing systems to detect fire quickly and to raise the alarm

(iii) ensuring that employees have been trained in the use of extinguishers

(iv) limiting as far as possible the amount of any flammable materials on site at any one time to that which is needed for the day's work and ensuring that these materials are properly stored

(v) enforcing the use of a hot work permit system throughout the site

(vi) ensuring that all electrical and gas supplies to the site are correctly installed and operated.

(b) limit the effects of any fire that may break out as early as possible during the construction/renovation phase, such as:

(i) completing fire compartments and other fire control features

(ii) completing any facilities that will control the spread of smoke through the site

(iii) completing and charging up any sprinkler or fire hydrant systems

(iv) ensuring that up to date information is available for the fire service when they arrive on site to fight a fire.

5.6.7   **Other Hazards**

(a)   building operations can involve many other hazards such as the use of toxic, flammable and explosive substances, excessive noise and vibration as well as involving hazardous operations, such as welding and cutting. In addition, many jobs involve the use of a number of sub-contractors, which complicates site management and substantially increases housekeeping problems.

(b)   one particular activity of the building industry that requires special care to be taken is that of demolition, particularly where the building being demolished is in a poor state of repair. Careful planning of the demolition job is vital, as are regular inspections to pick up new hazards, as they develop in order to avoid unnecessary loss.

5.7   MISCELLANEOUS INDUSTRIES

5.7.1   There are a number of industries that are similar in many respects to the construction industry in that the majority of the work places in those industries are temporary and are often fully exposed to the weather. Because of this such industries as forestry, mining, quarrying, farming and shipbuilding are all exposed to many of the same hazards as the construction industry. These hazards have been described above in paragraphs 5.5 and result mainly from the combination of:

(a) a temporary workplace that may be exposed to the effects of the weather

(b) the use of dangerous materials of many different types

(c) the use of energy in all of its various forms

(d) inadequate supervision

(e) generally poor working conditions; and

(f) constant change

can lead to a set of circumstances in which a person is injured or killed or property is damaged.

5.7.2   As may be expected many of the mechanisms for controlling risk that are described above in paragraphs 5.5 can also be successfully applied in these industries. However particular attention should be paid to:

(a) ensuring that supervision is adequate at all times

(b) fully training every employee in all aspects of the work that she or he is to do including the use of machinery as well as in handling the many different types of emergencies that may arise

(c) ensuring that employees have free access to the correct machinery and equipment for the job that has to be done and that it is maintained in good working order at all times

(d) ensuring that all essential protective equipment and clothing is available, that it is in good condition, ready for immediate use, when and where required and that it is in fact used when it should be

(e) keeping the workplace as clean and as tidy as possible in the circumstances. This will often require that there is a system for removing rubbish and other waste so that it may be disposed of in a safe manner

(f) implementing and enforcing safe working procedures which are appropriate to the work that has to be done.

5.7.3 Catering

(a)   cooking usually involves the use of heat generated by either electricity or gas, although in some instances flammable liquid or coal may be used. Whichever form of power is used the catering process creates additional hazards apart from those associated with the power source itself. These include:

> (i) hot fats or oils which if over-heated may catch fire and which, together with other heated liquids, may injure by scalding if spilt
>
> (ii) very hot surfaces such as hot plates, oven surfaces or utensils which may injure by burning
>
> (iii) exhaust fans and ducting which over a period of time, if not regularly cleaned, may catch fire as the result of a build-up of fats etc.

(b)   quite apart from the considerable fire hazard presented by the kitchen, there are a considerable number of hazards that threaten the well being of those working in the kitchen. These include:

> (i) slips and falls resulting from greasy or uneven floors and obstructions
>
> (ii) heavy weights that have to be lifted and carried
>
> (iii) sharp surfaces such as knives and slicers
>
> (iv) entangling machinery such as grinders and mixers.

There is also the danger of food poisoning resulting from unclean working surfaces, utensils, poor personal hygiene or bad ingredients.

(c)   a high level of cleanliness and housekeeping is an essential prevention measure, as is a good standard of training for the kitchen employees, which not only covers the use of the equipment but also in coping with spills, injuries and fires. In addition the kitchen area should be:

> (i) well laid out so as to facilitate safe movement
>
> (ii) provided with working surfaces that are easy to keep clean and floors that have a non-slip surface and good drainage
>
> (iii) well lit and ventilated
>
> (iv) fitted with sufficient fire extinguishers of the correct type
>
> (v) fitted with adequate storage facilities for not only the materials used but also the equipment and utensils.

All machinery should be inspected regularly for wear and tear. Maintenance is essential and special care needs to be taken to ensure that the guards and other safety devices are not only fully operational but also are being used.

5.7.4 Dry-Cleaning

(a) dry-cleaning involves the use of highly flammable and toxic liquids. The processes involved can result in the vapours leaking into the general work area where, if there is not adequate ventilation may lead to an explosion and fire. It is also essential that all traces of the liquids used in the cleaning process are completely vaporised from the garment before it is handled or pressed.

(b) some dry-cleaning processes produce a significant amount of waste product, which must be removed from the equipment from time to time. This must be done with great care and the waste stored safely in metal containers with fixed lids in a secure area away from the work area to await collection and safe disposal.

5.7.5 The Chemical and Petroleum Industries

The chemical and petroleum industries work with a wide range of volatile and often dangerous substances. The various processes involved in refining, purifying and making the many substances that are produced by the industries involve both pressure and heat. The various processes often produce very unstable or toxic compounds at the intermediate stages of producing the final product. In addition the byproducts and waste of some of the processes may be toxic or otherwise injurious to health or the environment. Both of these industries are continually developing and marketing new materials and it should be noted that in some instances the long-term effects of using these substances may not be fully understood. There may as a consequence be a hidden risk with using such substances.

A common feature of businesses in these industries is a significant degree of interdependence between different plants within the same business. If one of these plants is forced to close down and unless adequate provision has been made to supply the plants that are dependent upon it, they too will be forced to close.

Effective and efficient risk and loss control is therefore an essential part of the operations of any organisation in either of these two industries. Total commitment by management to all aspects of safety together with the full training of all employees in all aspects of the processes, compounds produced and likely problem areas will provide a good basis on which to build. It also follows that the machinery, pressure vessels and other equipment used in the processes must be maintained in a first class condition. The operating procedures to be used must be fully understood by all personnel who may be called upon to operate the plant. Experimentation and the use of short-cuts should be discouraged.

Waste should be disposed of in accordance with the practices agreed when the plant was first commissioned or if improved arrangements are made subsequently according to those. Finally it is essential that all plants have a fully operational up to date contingency plan that is regularly tested for each of the types of major disasters that may arise at the particular plant.

6

LIABILITY RISK REDUCTION AND LOSS CONTROL

6.1   INTRODUCTION

(a)   there are a number of different types of liability risk all of which are able to be managed to a greater or lesser extent. Liability risks, perhaps because a third party suffers the loss, tend not to be subjected to the same degree of rigorous analysis in risk management terms as Fire or Machinery Risks. Also, liability risks are rarely as visible as most physical risks. A firm application of the risk management discipline to liability risks can however produce a significant improvement in the level of risk exposure.

(b)   all liability risks arise out of an act or an omission by one party that leads to the death or injury of or the damage or destruction of the property of another party, both physical and intellectual. Unlike most other types of risk it is almost impossible to contain the exposure to liability risk so that it can be fully identified and, as a consequence, controlled. Liability can arise from virtually anything that is done by or for the business organisation or that it omits to do or have done.

(c)   for the business organisation legal liability may arise in tort through breach of contract or from negligence. The range of the risks arising from legal liability is such that it is impossible to provide more than a brief overview. Legal liability arose in the first place from Common Law but in recent times there been extensive modification effected to many aspects of legal liability by statute throughout the world. Increasingly legislators have seen fit to change or modify the common law in the light of social change. This is a process that is ongoing.

(d)   there are a number of significant problems to be overcome when assessing liability risks in that:

      (i)   the extent of liability is a constantly moving target because of:

- the attitudes of society are continually changing

- the final total cost of a liability exposure is only determined by the legal process running its course.

Each liability risk is, therefore, unique:

(ii) the boundaries of liability exposures are continually being expanded

(iii) considerable time invariably elapses between the assessment of the risk, a claim occurring and it being finally settled. Inflation and trends in court awards often have a significant impact on the final cost

(iv) many liability claims are complex requiring considerable investigation time by highly skilled professionals

(v) it is almost impossible to accurately assess the possible downstream consequential costs of a claim, eg. the need to retool a production line so as to avoid similar incidents in the future.

(vi) there are a wide range of possible sources of liability loss such as:

- people, including their management

- hardware, materials, processes or equipment being used

- procedures and systems being used

- the contractual conditions that are applicable

- the regulatory environment

- the physical environment

All of which need to be examined when determining the extent of the liability exposure.

6.2 LIABILITY RISK REDUCTION

6.2.1 As with the control of other types of risk the reduction of the frequency of loss should be the aim of all liability risk reduction techniques so as to most effectively manage the risks involved.

6.2.2   With the reduction of **Public Liability** risk the majority of means are concerned with accident or loss prevention and they are concentrated on two aspects:

(a) **occupation**

The occupation itself provides most of the risks and the following should be taken into account in determining the risks and how they may best be managed.

(i) If goods are produced, what type are they?

(ii) How large a geographical area do the activities of the organisation cover?

(iii) What access does the public have to the premises?

It may be possible to reduce the risks by, for example, ceasing to produce a product that gives rise to a number of losses or withdrawing from a country that is more claims conscious than others.

(b) **management**

As with many classes of risk, moral and morale hazards have a considerable impact on the risks of Public Liability. The following need to be carefully considered, with a view to improving, where necessary, the general standard:

(i) housekeeping and maintenance

(ii) quality control over goods produced

(iii) adequacy of guards and safety switches on plant and machinery

(iv) the use and storage of inherently dangerous substances

(v) training in use of machinery and in safety.

6.2.3   In the case of **liability arising out of the ownership or occupation of property** the task of controlling risk is somewhat simpler. This is because often the property concerned is occupied by the organisation and it is in a position to directly control the risks in the same way as it controls its property risks.

As with the General Liability risks the emphasis is on risk improvement and accident or loss prevention in terms of the building and its surrounding and its management.

(a) **buildings and its surroundings** ensuring that:

    (i) all passages, rooms, stairways, entrances, external pathways are adequately lit at all times

    (ii) the floor surface of all such areas are maintained in a good state of repair

    (iii) any hazardous areas or drops are clearly marked and barred off from public access as far as possible.

(b) **management** by improving:

    (i) housekeeping and maintenance

    (ii) access control over the public

    (iii) the safety guards and barriers.

6.2.4   Controlling **liability that arises out of products** is difficult because invariably the business does not have any control over the product once it has left the control of the business. The product is made to sell and it will eventually pass into the hands of the third party. The techniques to control the risks and losses that can arise from a product, including the need for its recall or its guarantee, have a different emphasis from those used to control the General or Premises Liability risks. However, once again, occupation and management feature prominently and in addition to those techniques listed above.

(a) in respect of **production**

    (i) the design of the product must ensure that safety is built into the product itself so that it is inherently safe or virtually inherently safe to use

    (ii) the production processes must be such that any faulty materials or assembly is detected and results in the particular product or batch being scrapped

    (iii) the product itself should be designed to withstand the expected effects of environmental conditions over time, transportation and storage, with a good safety margin

    (iv) the packaging and dispatch of the product should be organised to ensure that any faulty products are prevented from being sent out. In addition, controls should be in place to ensure that all parts of the product are sent out and arrive together with any necessary instructions for proper assembly and use

(b) In respect of **Management**

(i) quality control over all aspects of the research, development and manufacturing phases of the product as well as its packaging, dispatch, marketing and after sales service is essential if liability claims are to be avoided. Total Quality Management procedures can play a major part in achieving this with its emphasis on 'doing the job right first time' for everyone in the workforce

(ii) if the product contains components that are manufactured by another organisation it is essential that the same level of quality control be applied to those components

(iii) a system for handling complaints and claims in a prompt and fair way is essential if the business is to:

- minimise the amount of loss

- improve the product

- convert a claimant into a future satisfied customer.

(iv) the documentation that is sent out with the product, such as warning of hazard notices, operating or assembly instructions, must be written in such a way that it is able to be easily understood by the ultimate end user of the product. The importance of the labelling documentation and warnings is increased when the product is exported, particularly if the common language of the country to which the exported goods are sent is other than the language of the country in which the goods were produced.

In addition products liability exposure is an area in which involving a lawyer at an early stage in the identification, reduction and transfer of risk is likely to be of considerable benefit in avoiding future claims arising from the product.

6.2.5   Reducing the **Professional Liability** (advice) risk is achieved primarily by a variety of human engineering techniques, most of which have already been touched upon above. Education, training and control of personnel all play an important part, as does recognition by all concerned that only the people who create the liability can control it.

Organisational systems, such as using standard procedures and forms for giving advice, or making design recommendations that make monitoring of them simpler, can reduce the exposure to some extent. The introduction of Total Quality Management procedures can also have a significant effect on limiting the number and size of claims. Making and retaining a full and accurate record of all decisions and advice will help in minimise the likely fallout from a future claim

6.2.6 **Directors and Officers Liability** exposures are a specialised form of Professional Liability and, whilst many of the techniques outlined above may be utilised, there are a number of specific techniques that should be employed. In today's volatile and complex economic environment commercial organisations become involved in complex relationships with many parties. As a consequence exposure to professional liability risk for both Directors and Officers has expanded rapidly. Most of the legal actions are brought by shareholders (particularly where the organisation is involved in a merger, acquisition or divestiture) or employees, both present and former. However competitors, customers, clients and government agencies are becoming increasingly active in initiating legal action.

The following are some risk control measures which should be considered and where appropriate adopted in order to reduce the likelihood of lawsuit not only against the business itself but also against the individual Directors and Officers:

(a) any disclosure of information to the public must be neither false nor misleading. Directors and Officers should be careful and conscientious when selecting the content and form of public statements.

(b) directors and officers should also be conscientious in considering their obligations to disclose developments which affect previously issued public statements

(c) during any merger, acquisition or divestment activity all possible options should be considered fully and objectively. The procedure used and the decisions taken should be carefully documented.

(d) directors should always be objective in carrying out their duties as a director maintaining a supervisory role that is independent of the organisation's management. In addition they should be responsive to shareholders' concerns. In this members of the Board:

(i) should attend all meetings and should insist on receiving regular reports sufficiently far enough in advance of meetings to enable their content to be fully understood

(ii) should request additional information as appropriate on any unusual or negative events affecting the organisation of the Board of which they are a member

(iii) fully document all decisions and the facts on which they are based

(iv) should regularly self evaluate performance and should seek independent legal and financial advice as appropriate

(v) should ensure that outside Directors are well represented on any audit committee of the Board

(vi) as individuals, must avoid any hint of a conflict of interest in fulfilling their board duties.

(e) with respect to current and former employees proper attention should be paid to all procedures for handling personnel and to any employment contracts. A staff manual may be regarded as an employment contract. A full knowledge and awareness of the circumstances and issues of each possible problem area should be the prerequisite for taking any decisions concerning staff.

A checklist for Directors and Officers is attached at the end of this Chapter.

6.2.7 **Environmental pollution** is not new but in recent years has become increasingly significant as a liability risk for industry in many countries. As a consequence, the control of the environmental pollution risk has become an important issue for most management. In tackling pollution it must be realised that it can occur in many different forms (such as the pollution of air, water or land as well as pollution caused by noise or radiation) all of which can present their own particular problems of control. An Environmental Impairment Checklist is attached at the end of this chapter that may go some way towards helping to reduce Environment Impairment Liability exposures.

One way to understand and control environmental risk exposures is to use a systematic decision making process that breaks the problem down into manageable chunks for a detailed analysis to be done, and then combines the results into a short list of options. Typically in such a process the following steps would be followed:

(a) the sources of possible exposures and their likely impact are identified

(b) the expected impacts and liabilities are modelled in the form of probability event trees

(c) the alternative control options are identified and all necessary supporting data collected

(d) each of those alternatives is evaluated with a view to selecting the most favourable in terms of effectiveness and cost

(e) the likely effects of time on the overall costs are determined

(f) a time sequenced risk management strategy for dealing with the exposures is established.

6.2.8   Whilst the best way to control this type of risk is not to produce, use or store any substance that may cause pollution, this is not always a viable option. Other controls could include:

(a) changing the processes involved to either eliminate or substantially reduce the quantity of potential pollutants

(b) maintaining all plant, pipework and storage containers in a good state of repair

(c) installing bunds and other similar containment mechanisms around the areas in which the potential pollutant is used

(d) implementing procedures to recover and safely dispose of any potential pollutant that is spilt

(e) implementing procedures to safely dispose of or recycle any potential pollutant once it has been used

(f) implementing procedures to reduce if not eliminate waste and to, if possible, recycle any that is produced. If this is not possible then implement procedures to properly control the safe, long term disposal of all waste.

(g) keeping abreast of the extremely rapid developments being made in understanding of the effects of compounds.

6.3 OTHER FORMS OF LIABILITY LOSS CONTROL

6.3.1   A mechanism that is often used to control the incidence of liability losses upon an organisation is to share the risk with or transfer the risk to another party such as a bailor, lessor or purchaser by means of a clause or clauses in a contractual document. These clauses aim to share or transfer the responsibility for bearing any loss that may arise to a third party. Whilst these mechanisms have been viewed as a transfer of risk in the past they are increasingly seen as a sharing of risk.

6.3.2   Whilst in the case of leases and similar types of contract the clauses are normally fully enforceable, in the case of the other types of contract, the clauses are often found to be unenforceable. This is particularly so when the clause wording is basically 'hold harmless' or an attempt to contract out of or exclude liability. However, if the clause restricts liability rather than excluding it, the courts may well uphold it. Furthermore, the Sale of Goods Act (or similar) in most countries restricts people's right to contract out of the provisions of that Act, such as warranting that the product is 'merchantable' and reasonably fit for the purpose supplied.

6.3.3   These forms of controlling risk and loss fall into one of two types:

(a) those that transfer the responsibility for the property or activity that may be subject to the risk or loss to another organisation or person. Examples of this type of transfer is the sales agreement or the subcontract.

(b) those that involve transferring the risk or loss to a third party rather than the property or activity itself. An example of this type of transfer is the hold harmless clause.

It, however, should be noted that with these types of transfers there is a very fine dividing line between them being seen as a risk control measure as opposed to a risk financing measure.

6.3.4   Most contracts involve some element of risk or loss transfer and often this is inherent in the nature of the contract, for example, a contract of sale. However, precisely what this element will be is usually specified in the contract and is therefore limited only by the ingenuity of the person who drafted the contract. It is, therefore, essential that all contract wordings are checked carefully to ensure that the transfer of risks and any losses is done in such a way that the party who is best able to handle those risks and losses, does so.

Common types of contract which incorporate some element of transfer are:

(a) **Guarantee/Warranty** which normally is effective after the sale of a new product and which promises to repair or replace any defective part found during that period.

(b) **Construction Contract** in which responsibility for certain risks and losses associated with the project are transferred to one of the parties involved. The Contractor's Risks and Liability Policies are effected usually by the Principal or by the major contractor on behalf of all of the firms involved in the project.

(c) **Leases.** Most leases contain insurance provisions that specify which of the parties is to be responsible for financing the loss as well as the required extent of that financing.

(d) **Contracts of Bailment and Carriage.** The kind and amount of risk that may be transferred is controlled to a certain extent by statutory law, particularly where a common carrier is involved. However, despite this the law governing the relative responsibilities of the parties is usually drafted in such a way as to allow considerable scope for the apportionment of these responsibilities by the terms of the contract. Usually the bailee and the carrier endeavour to transfer by contract all of the responsibility for financial loss back onto the owner or person purchasing the service.

(e) **Contracts of Sale, Supply and Service** as well as Purchase Agreements. There are many variations in these types of contract, and as a consequence many ways in which the cost of loss may be transferred, varying from hold harmless agreements to straight out transfer of ownership. In the former case only the cost of loss may be transferred, whilst with the latter both the cost of loss and ownership is transferred. Obviously this type of agreement will not work if the party seeking to transfer the cost of loss is not likely to ever have to meet that cost of loss.

(f) **Bonding** under which one party called 'the surety' agrees to guarantee that another party called 'the principal' will undertake some express obligation or task to a third party known as 'an obligee'. This type of agreement is often used with the larger supply contracts and construction projects as well as in certain circumstances where fees have to be paid on a regular basis to government or local government organisations, such as duty to Customs and wharf charges to Harbour Boards.

6.3.5   The element of transfer in these types of contract will take the form of an exclusion clause, a limitation clause, a disclaimer or indemnity clause which:

(a) transfers the responsibility or legal liability for a wrongful act to another person or organisation; or

(b) endeavours to make that other party bear the financial consequences of such act.

An exclusion clause in a contract removes or restricts the remedy or the liability arising out of a contractual obligation. It removes or restricts the liability of one of the parties to the contract.

A limitation clause in a contract seeks to set a limit on the amount of damages that are payable if a specified circumstance occurs.

A disclaimer clause is used by a property owner or occupier of premises to state he will not be responsible for any loss of property or injury of any other person.

Under an indemnity clause one party agrees to assume on behalf of the other party any financial cost of a specified event should it occur.

6.3.6   All of these types of risk control measures are subject to some problems of which the following are examples:

(a) the organisation or person to whom the risk or loss has been transferred may be a 'man of straw' and may not be able to pay for any loss. This can leave the transferor with a significant contingent liability exposure.

(b) the wording of the contract effecting the transfer may be:

   (i) limited to such an extent that effectively only a part of the risk or loss is effectively transferred.

   (ii) ambiguous or difficult to understand or its interpretation is uncertain until tested in a court of law. In these cases the courts will usually interpret against the drafter.

   (iii) such that public policy is contravened or that statutory or Common Law is substantially altered by the wording. In these cases the courts will usually apply a very narrow interpretation of the meaning of the wordings.

With all types of transfers there is no overall reduction in the risk that may be involved and no overall reduction in any loss that may eventuate. All that has occurred is that the responsibility for any loss may have been transferred to another party.

6.4 EMPLOYERS LIABILITY OR WORKERS COMPENSATION

6.4.1 Many countries have enacted legislation covering accidents at work and occupational disease. In most, insuring this type of risk is mandatory and readers should study the legislation that is applicable to the country in which they are working to ensure that all of the ramifications of the legislation are fully understood.

6.4.2 Despite insurance being a mandatory requirement there is much that can be done to control this type of risk. Amongst the measures that may be used are:

(a) good safety practices

(b) close supervision of work, processes and use of materials

(c) accident prevention surveys including Health and Safety Audits

(d) reporting of all incidents and claims coupled with a detailed investigation to ascertain the originating cause and to develop suitable prevention measures

(e) Health and Safety programmes

(f) back to work programmes and other rehabilitation measures

(g) managed care programmes

(h) training of employees in all aspects of their work and loss prevention.

6.5 RISK AND LOSS CONTROL FOR THE OTHER MORE SPECIALISED TYPES OF LIABILITY RISKS

6.5.1 Whilst there are a wide variety of specialised types of liability risk, such as the liability for:

(a) false arrest

(b) libel, slander, defamation etc.

(c) mental anguish

(d) misleading advertising

(e) infringement of industrial property rights, patents, copyright etc.

(f) infringement of human rights;

all may be controlled to some extent by a number of similar techniques

6.5.2 The exposure to claims involving these types of liability risk may be minimised by:

(a) being aware that such exposures can and do exist. Understanding of how the exposure may arise is also important in helping one formulate strategies to minimise the exposures.

(b) acting at all times with care and forethought. Using standard procedures, forms and wordings can go a long way to reducing the likelihood of claim.

(c) utilizing Total Quality Management or similar techniques in all aspects of each individual's work as well as the work of the business.

6.6 DIRECTORS AND OFFICERS RISK MANAGEMENT CHECK-LIST

As a Director ask yourself:

- do I understand what my company does?

- have I read all of the minutes of Board Meetings and do I agree that they are an accurate representation of what was said?

- do all members of the Board have the opportunity to speak their minds?

- am I as aware of the Company's current financial position as I could be?

- am I aware of any problems concerning the fundamental viability of any of the companies with which I am involved? If so, have I done my best to rectify the situation?

- have the accounts been filed with the appropriate statutory authority within the required period of time?

- have I met all the companys' professional advisers?

- am I satisfied with my fellow directors' performance?

- am I satisfied that I do not have any personal conflicts of interest?

- am I happy that I am serving the interest of shareholders at all times and not of myself?

- have I ensured there is a D & O policy in force plus all other relevant insurances?

- am I sure the company complies with all of the relevant legislation as far as possible?

- am I aware of any mergers, acquisitions, takeovers or other actual or contemplated restructurings and have I taken all reasonable steps to protect the position of those I owe a duty or care to?

- have I got adequate information to make an informed decision at Board meetings/management meetings?

- am I happy that all potential major problems are brought to the Board's attention without due delay?

- am I satisfied that all of the risks to which the company is exposed are being managed in a prudent way, which not only maximises the upside or profit but also minimises loss or the downside?

- am I satisfied that all of the risks to which the company is exposed are being managed in accordance with the overall plan that the Board has drawn up and do I understand all of the regular reports on the management of risk that management gives to the Board?

6.7   ENVIRONMENTAL IMPAIRMENT CHECK-LIST

Ask yourself:

- is the management of our organisation fully aware of the requirements and effects of any legislation and regulations covering the environment, hazardous materials and natural resources?

- do we monitor and provide input to proposed legislative changes related to environmental matters?

- does our organisation have a member of the senior management team who has been assigned the responsibility for all environmental matters?

- does our organisation have a written environmental policy?

- does our organisation have any quality control programmes in place with respect to processing?

- has our organisation implemented a programme of Compliance Auditing of all our existing processes and sites?

- does our organisation require that a Compliance Audit be carried out on any proposed acquisition (including land), mergers and divestments before any decision to proceed is made?

- are we aware of the uses to which the land on which our organisation is situated may have been put prior to our occupation of the site?

- does our organisation have any fully documented and regularly tested Contingency Plans for coping with emergencies involving the release of hazardous materials?

- do we have full records of all hazardous materials on the organisation's sites?

- do we keep up to date with new materials and processes and with disclosures about the newly discovered hazards of existing materials?

- are any of the materials in use at present able to be replaced by less noxious ones or can the processes be changed to use less of the noxious materials?

- are there any underground tanks on any of the sites used by our organisation? If so when were they last checked for corrosion leaks etc? Are they necessary?

- have asbestos or fibreglass been used in the construction or insulation of any of the buildings occupied by our organisation? If so is it currently in a safe condition?

- has our organisation implemented a programme of waste minimisation, energy and water conservation?

- With respect to waste produced by our organisation:

  - do we know how and where it is being disposed of?

  - are we aware of what happens to it at each stage of the process?

  - what steps are being taken to eliminate or reduce the amount produced?

  - what records do we keep with respect to the disposal of waste?

  - are all our disposal contractors suitably licenced?

- is our organisation proactive in taking steps to eliminate or reduce the use or production of pollutants?

- does our staff training cover environmental matters?

- do the employees understand enough about the hazards of the materials and processes used by our organisation?

- are the employees in our organisation fully trained in the handling, storage and transportation of all of the hazardous materials stored or used on our sites? Are they aware of the materials and their dangers? Are they aware of possible reactions between different materials if stored together?

- is sufficient suitable protective clothing and equipment available for the employees of our organisation to safely handle any of the hazardous materials or processes on our sites? Do we have any systems to ensure that these are being correctly used whenever such materials and processes are in use?

- are the employees in our organisation trained to handle any accidental release of any hazardous substance? Is sufficient equipment and materials necessary to handle such incidents available, in working order and regularly checked?

7

LOSS CONTROL – OTHER THAN FIRE AND LIABILITY

This nation was built on risk. Personal risk in tackling the wilderness, financial risk in business, risks in exploring the scientific unknown, enormous engineering risks, management risks. We shall continue to take risks of greater magnitude than in the past. But the consequences of failure are becoming less permissible. The political, social as well as economic and personal risks that now accompany our ventures can have enormous repercussions when failure occurs.

Growing risk factors require a more comprehensive approach to hazard management than in the past.

Jerome Lederer
Director of the Office of Manned Space Flight Safety for NASA

7.1 PERILS OTHER THAN FIRE

7.1.1 It is possible to take steps to prevent and minimise loss caused from virtually every one of the perils that may be insured and a lot of perils which cannot currently be insured. The methods used in controlling the fire losses depend by and large on the physical aspects of the organisation. For many of the perils other than fire, the physical aspects of the risk are also important in determining which of the methods should be used in controlling the risk.

7.1.2 **Extraneous Peril Loss Prevention** The aspects that must be considered in respect of Extraneous Perils and if possible improved, largely follow those considered for fire risks, though perhaps the situation of the property concerned has the most significant effect on the likely loss from many of the perils. In other words, if a reduction in risk is to be achieved much of the necessary action must be taken during the initial stages of deciding on where to site the property. The following are loss prevention measures for some of the major

149

Extraneous Perils that may be encountered.

7.2   THE PREVENTION OF DUST EXPLOSIONS

7.2.1   As with fire there are a number of key elements for an explosion to occur. If one of the following five elements is eliminated the explosion will be averted:

(a) fuel in the form of dust

(b) an ignition source

(c) oxygen (in normal air)

(d) dispersion of the dust

(e) confinement of the dust cloud

7.2.2   It is possible to take steps to prevent and minimise loss caused by the explosion of:

(a) **flammable or explosive gases and vapours by:**

(i) providing mechanical exhaust fans to ventilate the area of any build up of gases or vapours to a safe area outside the building

(ii) flame proofing all electrical equipment

(iii) eliminating all other possible ignition sources

(iv) using safe working practices and good housekeeping standards.

(b) **dusts** by:

(i) enclosure of plant, processes and equipment to prevent dust escaping and reaching ignition sources

(ii) dust extraction to a metal container outside the building so as to prevent the accumulation of explosive dust inside the building

(iii) removal or protection of ignition sources including the flame proofing of electrical equipment

(iv) working under inert atmosphere or under liquid. In many plants and processes where the dust is confined within an enclosure explosion may be prevented by the replacement of the normal atmosphere by an inert gas. In such a system oxygen is either excluded altogether or else is reduced below the level at which combustion will occur. This varies with the size and duration of igniting source, and the flammable material involved. It should however be noted that the inert gases used may also contain toxic compounds and extra care will be required in their use.

(v) the use of safe working practices and good housekeeping standards so as to reduce the amount of dust produced or allowed to accumulate

(vi) installing electromagnetic or metal detecting safety switches in the feed areas of grinders to detect all tramp iron or similar hard materials to prevent both sparks and damage to the machinery.

7.2.3   Prevention of the Accumulation of Dust

Layers of dust tend to have lower ignition temperatures than dust clouds. The difference can be very significant – over 200 degrees centigrade – in the case of many agricultural products and certain plastics. The ignition temperatures decrease, as layers become thicker. A layer 150 mm deep may ignite at a temperature 100 degrees centigrade lower than a layer 10 mm deep as shown in this table. When dusts are allowed to accumulate on surfaces that are apparently at a safe temperature they can begin to smoulder and an explosion may occur if the dust is subsequently dispersed or disturbed.

Difference in ignition temperature of clouds and layers of certain agricultural and plastic products		
Material	Ignition temp. of a cloud (degrees centigrade)	Ignition temp. of a 10 mm layer (degrees centigrade)
Cereal Grass	550	220
Flour (cake)	480	250
Milk Powder	490	200
Soya Flour	540	190
Yeast	520	260
Cellulose	480	270
Rayon	520	250
Alkyd resin	500	270

Dust dispersal into the atmosphere may be avoided by using properly designed plant and by good housekeeping. Where good housekeeping is ignored and dust is allowed to settle, if a primary dust explosion occurs it will dislodge this dormant dust, leading to a much more serious secondary explosion, often of great violence.

7.2.4   Ignition Sources

Work should be undertaken to eliminate the means of igniting any dust/air mixtures that may occur in buildings, mines, storage bins, elevators and so forth.

For example:

(a) **hot surfaces**

Electric and other lights should be shielded. Bearings should be kept clean and well lubricated so that heating does not occur. Hot pipes and flues likely to come into contact with dust/air mixtures should be well insulated. Grain elevators and similar material handling equipment should be kept clean so that friction does not arise between moving parts.

(b) **red-hot ash from tobacco**

Smoking should be totally prohibited in hazardous areas

(c) **naked flames**

Matches, fires and the like should be totally prohibited from the area. Sparks can be produced mechanically through the presence of stones or iron. Material to be ground should be screened and, if necessary, passed over magnetic separators. Where necessary non-sparking tools should be used.

(d) **sparks from electrical equipment such as switches, motors, fuse boxes and the breaking of electric light bulbs**

Dust tight or flame proof equipment should be used in the hazardous areas.

(e) **sparks from the discharge of static electricity that builds up on moving belts**

Static can be dissipated with the aid of radioactive material that ionizes the air, or by an increase in humidity. Electrostatic dust precipitators can also be used to collect airborne dust.

7.2.5   Methods of Limiting the Effects of Explosion

(a)   there are four main ways of limiting the effects of an explosion:

  (i) **correctly siting the plant** – so that an explosion in one item of plant will not damage others, or cause injury to people

  (ii) **protecting the plant** – by designs that withstand or isolate the explosions

  (iii) **relieving plant explosions** – by diverting the force of the blast harmlessly through vents, ducts or bursting panels

  (iv) **suppressing plant explosions** – by using the pressure from an explosion in its early stages to release a chemical that suppresses the explosion.

(b)   **siting of plant**

  (i) Open-air plant

       The simplest and probably the most effective method is to build the plant so that it is in the open air, or is open to the air. If necessary the equipment can be controlled from a separate control room. Items of plant should be adequately separated so that an explosion in one is unlikely to affect other items. Open-air construction and operation is especially useful when highly hazardous dusts such as aluminium, aluminium stearate and magnesium are being processed.

  (ii) Segregation

       It is not always practicable to place hazardous processes in the open air. A compromise approach is to situate the plant in a cubicle against an outside wall of a building. The cubicle should be separated from the rest of the building by walls of exceptional strength e.g. reinforced 350 mm brickwork and its outside wall should be of fragile material or left out completely. The roof can also be made of fragile material.

(c) **Protection of Plant**

(i) **strong construction**

Pressures of 700 kPa may be generated in an explosion. Plant for certain types of operation e.g. grinding and pneumatic conveying can be made to withstand and contain dust explosions of this order. But the effectiveness of this method of explosion control is limited since most plant cannot withstand pressures much greater than 20 kPa and in many cases it may be better use damage limiting or explosion venting construction. Equipment such as rotary valves can be made to withstand explosion pressures so as to isolate and protect other items of plant.

(ii) **separate dust extracting ducting**

Where dust extraction ducts are part of the plant design the ducts should not be arranged so that one duct is common to several items of plant. Each item of dust producing plant should have its own separate duct connecting it to the hopper outside the building.

Long lengths of ducting should be avoided and if a duct is over 30 m in length explosion relief should be provided. Vents should be placed adjacent to bends or branches in the ducting and at intervals as shown in *Figure 7.1*

Figure 7.1

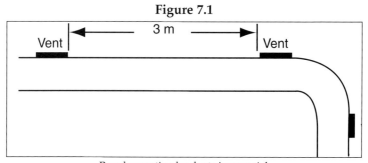

Regular venting by ducts is essential

The air velocity should be sufficient to prevent the settlement of dust in the ducting.

(c) **Vents**

Providing vents, which open when an explosion occurs, can materially reduce the disruptive effects of an explosion. They should be designed to open at a pressure well below that which would severely strain or distort the structure. The hot gases and other materials can then escape (see *Figure 7.2*).

Figure 7.2

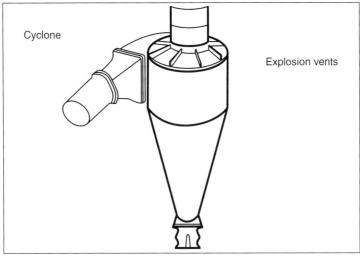

Cyclone

Explosion vents

A hot gases vent

The area of the vent should be related to the volume of the plant. For most carbonaceous dusts it is usual to allow 1 square metre for every 20 cubic metre of volume. For metal dusts larger vent ratios are required and 1 square metre for every 10 cubic metre of volume is recommended, for example, for plant handling aluminium and magnesium powders. Vents should be as close as practicable to the likely points of ignition. They should be placed so that they do not discharge burning material into workrooms or into places where a secondary explosion or injury to persons could result. Vents should preferably discharge into the open air; and according to the NFPA Standard, any auxiliary ducts should not be more than 3 m long. Other countries may have a different standard and reference should be made to the regulations or standards of the country in which the reader is working.

An inspection port in the auxiliary duct is desirable to permit observation of the vent closure. It should be noted, however, that with certain types of dusts the pressure rise following ignition is so rapid that the above systems will not operate in time to prevent damage to the enclosure. In order to obtain the maximum benefit from the explosion reliefs, correct placement of them is important.

7.2.6   Explosion Relief for Buildings

Where dust handling plant cannot be located out of doors, adequate explosion relief may be advisable for the buildings which contain the plant. This usually takes the form of specially designed, chained blow-out windows, wall panels and light structure roofs. (See *Figure 7.3*). The design should be such that flame and projected solids are not hazardous to any passer-by in the vicinity.

Figure 7.3

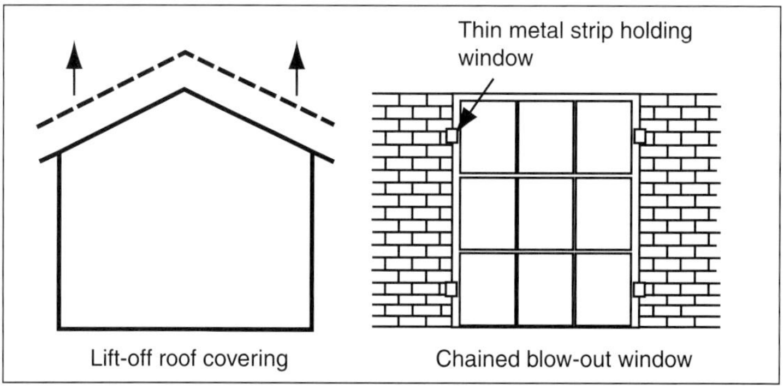

Thin metal strip holding window

Lift-off roof covering   Chained blow-out window

Specially designed buildings

7.2.7   Suppression of Plant Explosions

The very brief interval of time between first ignition and the attainment of peak pressure in an explosion can be utilised to suppress the explosion. (See *Figure 7.4*).

Figure 7.4

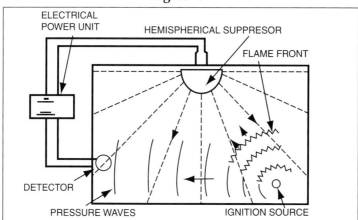

ELECTRICAL POWER UNIT

HEMISPHERICAL SUPPRESOR

FLAME FRONT

DETECTOR

PRESSURE WAVES   IGNITION SOURCE

The brief interval between ignition and peak pressure

A quick-acting pressure switch can be installed which will respond to the initial and comparatively slow increase in pressure. The switch releases a chemical to suppress the explosion. The effectiveness of the technique however is limited to volumes of a few thousand cubic feet.

One method is exploding a hemisphere of an explosion suppressant such as **BCF** into the protected area. (*See Figure 7.5*).

Figure 7.5

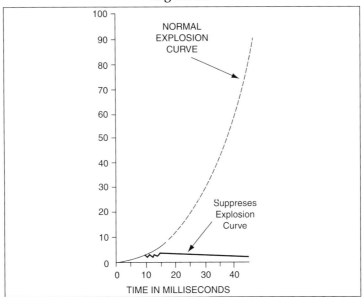

Exploding a hemisphere of an explosion suppressant into the protected area

Another method operates high speed discharge bottles of inert gas such as **carbon dioxide**. This technique can be extended to inert rapidly any plant connected to the one in which the explosion has occurred before the explosion can spread. Care has to be taken where such systems are installed because of the toxic nature of some of the suppressants. This form of protection can only be used where the containers can withstand an initial pressure rise of about 20 kPa.

A third method involves the use of **superheated water**, which is rapidly injected into the space using a quick action pressure switch. The water flashes to steam and quickly expands to fill the space inerting the incipient explosion.

7.3 FLOOD AND OTHER WATER PERILS

7.3.1   The following points should be taken into account:

(a) when considering whether or not to erect a new building on a new site or to lease into newly developed premises it may be prudent to have a full soil and site investigation carried out before the final decision is made. Known flood areas should be avoided if possible.

(b) where the building is adjacent to or near an open stream it is a good idea to keep a record of the usual high flow water level. If the stream becomes silted up or overgrown the water level will rise, therefore, the condition of the bed of the stream is important. Water courses should be regularly inspected and cleaned out when necessary.

(c) flood protection falls into three categories:

(i) **permanent protection** which are preventative measures that are always in place and are largely passive in nature such as:

- flood banks and similar protection

- bricking up of ground floor windows

- sealing off all openings to basement areas

- bunding of critical items of plant such as computers, switch gear, boilers etc

- providing flood tight doors for all ground floor entrances and exits

- installing back flow valves or non return valves on drains and other plumbing pipework.

(ii) **contingent protection** which are preventative measures that are able to be installed in a relatively short space of time, such as flood shields. These comprise permanently mounted brackets on the frames of ground floor openings onto which the shields may be bolted when a flood warning is given.

(iii) **emergency protection** which comprise measures that take some time to put into place such as:

158

- sandbagging ground floor openings

- removing stock and plant to areas outside the likely flood zone

- protecting plant with water and rust repellant or proofing compounds or materials

- ensuring that empty containers are either moved outside the likely flood zone or securely fixed so that they may not float away or become battering rams in the floodwaters.

(d) store goods at least 100 mm (4 inches) above the floor on pallets etc. This will allow water to flow around the floor and to run off without wetting the goods other than in a serious flood. This is effective in minimising water damage from plumbing leaks or fire fighting operations. In any event, from an ergonomic point of view, unless the goods are heavy they should be stored well off the floor (at least 18 inches).

(e) check the guttering and roof down pipes at least every six months to ensure that they are clear of obstruction and in good condition, more often if large trees grow nearby.

(f) maintain all plumbing in good working order and regularly inspect drains and valves and service those requiring it. If in a colder area ensure that the plumbing is well insulated to prevent freezing and consequent bursting.

(g) see that storm water drains around the building are not obstructed with leaves or other material. Ensure that there is adequate drainage from the site.

7.3.2 **Water Alarms**

There is at least one type of alarm that may be used to detect the presence of water. Such alarms may be used to warn that goods should be moved to higher ground or that special precautions should be taken to protect fixed equipment such as heavy electrical motors from possible inundation by water.

7.4   EARTHQUAKE

7.4.1   It is not possible to construct a building that is earthquake proof; at best, the building will only be earthquake-resistant. This being so, if there is ever an option to not move into any area that has a higher than average exposure to earthquake then it should be exercised. If an earthquake occurs in the area, the premises will suffer some damage even if it is constructed so as to be as earthquake-resistant as is possible.

7.4.2   The following should be noted:

(a) an earthquake-resistant building requires a degree of flexibility. Well-built wood frame buildings generally have high resistance to earthquake damage but are vulnerable to fire damage following earthquake. Steel frame structures generally are good with preference for bolting or riveting rather than welding. Reinforced concrete structures can be very good but are vulnerable to deficiencies in design and construction. Masonry structures have performed badly in earthquakes but improvements in specification make it possible to build structures of this material that have a good earthquake resistance.

(b) high-rise buildings need to be specially designed to resist the oscillating (shaking) forces that follow an earthquake. This type of building is particularly prone to damage caused by the building oscillating in resonance with the earthquake (40 seconds in San Francisco 1906, 3 minutes in Alaska 1964).

(c) the earthquake design building codes of many countries are gradually being strengthened with special attention being paid to:

(i) soil type and composition

(ii) location of building in relation to known fault lines

(iii) alignment of building in relation to fault line (beware of being parallel to a fault line)

(iv) foundations and especially the connection of the building to them

(v) building design with particular reference to being able to withstand the flexing and shaking motions; asymmetric buildings are particularly vulnerable

(vi) the standard of construction workmanship and materials used.

(d) other factors that should be taken into account are:

(i) **building use**

Some types of industry have equipment needs that make them very vulnerable to damage in an earthquake, such as paper machinery (very long lines), doors for aircraft hangers (usually very large), to mention just two. Services in buildings are also very vulnerable such as chemical flow lines and other utilities such as sprinkler lines (use flexible couplings). Any hazardous materials stored in and used in the building also add to the risk.

(ii) **fire following earthquake is a major hazard**

In the 1906 San Francisco earthquake a number of fires started which ultimately joined together to form a very large fire that lasted several days. Fire damage was estimated to have cost four times as much as earthquake damage. In an earthquake there are many sources of ignition. Water supplies may be disrupted and may fail totally and climatic conditions can add to that danger.

(iii) **tsunamis** are linked with earthquakes and are sea waves resulting from earthquake or volcanic activity. When such waves reach land they can be 60 feet in height and run up the beach area for several hundred feet causing severe damage and loss of life. Hawaii has been hit by many tsunamis, some coming from as far away as Chile and Alaska. The 1960 Chilean tsunami reached Japan with the loss of 180 lives (due to lack of warning). Tsunamis can travel at 500 Mph or more – in the deep ocean their effect is limited perhaps to a wave as little as two or three feet in height but they are very dangerous in port and shore areas.

(iv) **contents**

In an earthquake objects are likely to be shaken vigorously in any plane particularly if the building is relatively stable. The primary effects will be:

toppling – which may be prevented by:

- diagonally bracing racks either to each other or to the roof and floor

- providing special bracing for valuable objects

- storing heavier items on the lower storage shelves.

sliding – which may be prevented by:

- installing lips or restraining devices

- fastening to surface on which object resting with anchors and bracing

- storing hazardous chemicals in unbreakable containers

- securing mobile equipment by locking brakes and chocks

- installing seismic protection systems which will automatically shut down major equipment

- installing all interconnected equipment on the same foundation

- using vibration isolation mountings

- fitting liquid storage tanks with internal baffles to dampen wave action and providing sufficient binding to contain any spills

- not using magnetic catches on cupboard doors.

snapping – which mainly occurs to pipework and which may be prevented particularly where hazardous liquids are involved by:

- providing a clearance allowance around pipes which pass through walls and floors

- using sway bracing

- using flexible couplings and/or piping

- using welded connections rather than screw ones

- fitting automatic shut off valves.

The effects of an earthquake on the contents of a building may be magnified by the stability of the building structure itself. The greater the stability of the building the greater the likelihood that both serious injury will be caused to any occupants, and serious damage will be done to any contents which are not securely fastened down.

7.4.3   It is possible in many cases to improve the earthquake resisting capabilities of both buildings and equipment thereby reducing seismic risk. Measures could include:

(a) adding or strengthening shear walls

(b) strengthening support columns

(c) strengthening foundations or better still using seismic shock absorbers or isolators wherever appropriate

(d) closing over openings in walls such as doors and windows

(e) adding cords or collectors or cross bracing at appropriate positions in the structure.

7.4.4   Seismic Probe

There is a type of alarm that detects an oncoming earthquake split seconds before it actually occurs. Such an alarm can be linked to major items of heavy equipment so that the equipment is automatically shut down if an oncoming earthquake is detected. This can substantially minimise the damage caused by the earthquake to such equipment.

7.5   WEATHER LOSS CONTROL

7.5.1   The following are some of the precautions that may be taken:

(a) use heavy solid construction if the building is in an exposed location

(b) ensure that the building is well maintained at all times and that all drainage channels from the site are kept clear of any obstructions

(c) if possible avoid exposed locations such as coastal and riverside areas as well as the top of prominent hills

(d) if in an area that is prone to heavy snow or hail falls ensure that the roof and its supports are strong enough to bear the weight of the likely maximum accumulation of snow or hail.

7.6 CONSEQUENTIAL LOSS CONTROL

7.6.1 Here the aspects that should be considered, and if possible improved, are similar to those for fire risks, though there are a number of additional aspects that should be considered:

(a) are there alternative routes provided through the processes that eliminate likely bottlenecks in the process flow?

(b) are there alternative routes available into and out of the premises that enable any possible restrictions of access to be overcome?

(c) are there any other premises or facilities to which production may be switched if production cannot be continued at the original property?

(d) are there alternative sources of supply of raw materials, power, etc.?

(e) are there any alternative sources of essential plant and equipment and what is the shortest delivery time?

(f) is the organisation dependant on a few large customers or does it have a well spread customer base?

7.7 BURGLARY RISK CONTROL

7.7.1 Consideration should be given to a number of aspects, some of which if they are to be effective need to be considered and acted upon before the building is built, whilst others can be acted upon sometime later but before the burglary occurs.

It should be remembered that criminals:

(a) target the particular premises which they intend to attack and they will use considerable ingenuity to achieve their objectives

(b) rarely enter premises on a spur of the moment decision and they usually enter with some positive intent

(c) weigh the risk to themselves against the potential reward.

7.7.2   Thus, improving security and thereby reducing the risk of burglary or theft, involves the organisation in balancing the risk factors inherent in its operations against the potential losses and then giving consideration to a wide range of measures such as:

(a) **target hardening** – installation of a number of different types of physical barriers and detection devices

(b) **target removal** – move potential targets to another more secure site

(c) **reducing target value** – minimise value of potential targets

(d) **management of environment** – using the terrain, occupancy and traffic flows to eliminate or reduce opportunities to thieves and vandals.

In addition, consideration should be given to the location of the operation, the construction and layout of the premises and the occupation (ie. the types of goods) involved as well as possible protection, detection and deterrent devices.

7.7.3   **Location or situation** can only be acted upon prior to building, and the following should be taken into consideration when deciding where to build:

(a) the type of neighbourhood and the nature of the other businesses in the neighbourhood

(b) the level of lighting around the area at night

(c) the level of activity in the area during both daylight and night-time.

Some of the extra risk from the situation may be removed by the building being occupied by an occupation that is unattractive for thieves or by installing extra protection and other such preventative measures.

7.7.4 Construction

Most of the possible means of reducing the risk should be incorporated at the time of building, though some remedial work can be undertaken at a later date, such as providing additional protection for access points. The following should be considered:

(a) the construction materials used in the building. Do they offer resistance to the would-be thief?

(b) the layout of the building that offers possible areas of concealment, such as:

(i) yards and enclosed areas. Can the lighting be improved?

(ii) cellars. Are the locking devices adequate?

(iii) boundary walls and fences. Can glass or barbed wire be placed at the top of them to act as an additional deterrent?

(c) access points both internal and external:

(i) doors and windows. Are they heavy duty or sub-standard? Should bars be fitted to windows?

(ii) fall, down or drain pipes. Is a spiked umbrella fixed at a suitable height on each of them or are they rebated into the brickwork?

(d) security lighting. Is the level of lighting adequate to eliminate shadows in which intruders or vandals may hide whilst on the premises? Does the lighting illuminate both sides of the perimeter of the premises?

7.7.5 **Occupation** is perhaps the most important aspect as it determines to a large extent the attractiveness of the premises to the criminal because of the goods likely to be stored on the premises. It is difficult to see how the risks associated with a particular occupation may be eliminated, as they are a fundamental part of that occupation. However, the risks involved can and should be minimised.

In this the following should be considered:

(a) the type of goods stored and used in the premises. Are they easily transported and disposed? Can they be identified?

(b) is there ever a large accumulation of cash on the premises? Can this be avoided?

(c) how are the goods and cash stored?

7.7.6   Paying attention to the little things can often bring considerable benefits as far as deterring the would-be burglar from entering the premises, such as:

(a) ensuring that the site is able to be securely fenced after hours

(b) ensuring that all aspects of the exterior of the building are well lit at night, particularly doors and windows; planting of bushes and trees that will provide concealment to the criminal should be avoided

(c) not leaving ladders, wooden pallets or similar items lying around outside the building as these can be used to gain access to the roof or high level windows.

In addition to providing access these articles as well as any waste and unused packing material are often used to start fires that can cause major damage to the building.

(d) making sure that all of the doors and windows to your premises are securely locked so that the burglar has to use more time in trying to get into and out of the premises. Don't hide an entrance key outside the premises and ensure that all exit doors require a key to open them.

(e) not leaving attractive goods in the front window of the store without having substantial grilles or bars to prevent smash and grab

(f) not leaving attractive goods in unsecured areas inside premises during non working hours

(g) installing security lighting to highlight intruders both inside and outside the premises

(h) immobilising fork hoists, gantry cranes and any vehicles left inside the premises overnight

(i) not storing money in the till overnight. Always empty tills and leave them open at night.

7.7.7   Protection, detection and deterrent devices should be regarded as the last defence and they should only be used to supplement the other forms of protection outlined above. The objectives of this type of device is to:

(a) **deter** – make it hard for any thief to enter and get out of the premises

(b) **delay** – a thief wants to spend as little time as possible on the premises, as the longer that he has to spend the greater the chances of detection

(c) **detect** – a thief at every step whilst he is within the perimeter of the premises.

7.7.8   Most precautions do have an associated cost and this cost must be balanced against their likely effectiveness and the need for them. What is considered as being essential in the way of security and protection for a home appliance store or a computer centre is likely to be excessive for a wool store or an office building.

Protection must be looked at from the standpoint of overall security. It is useless to fit a good quality deadlock on one door if the rest are fitted with cheap locks or the building is built of corrugated iron or is all glass. Protection or security devices are essentially passive and include the following:

(a) **locks** There are many different types of locks but the one preferred for most normal uses is the mortice lock. Code (or combination) locks or time locks are usually fitted to safes or strong rooms.

(b) **safes and strongrooms** Whilst the better quality modern safes and strongrooms are resistant to explosives, drilling, oxy-acetylene and oxy-arc cutting, most of the older safes and strongrooms offer only a minimal resistance to the determined and well equipped thief

(c) **deterrents** are however both proactive and passive in action and include the following:

(i)   night watchman

(ii) guard dogs

(iii) security organisations

(iv) closed circuit TV

(v) psychological deterrents e.g. warning notices.

7.8 SECURITY DETECTION DEVICES OR INTRUDER ALARMS

7.8.1 Any detection device should be installed by a reputable company that specialises in alarm systems, and should be well maintained once it has been installed. To be effective the detection devices should be switched on when the premises are unoccupied, and this involves the human element.

Security alarms to detect entry or attempted entry are readily available. It is however, important to recognise that an alarm installation can only call for help and should, therefore, only be used as a back up for adequate physical protection measures.

7.8.2 The following points should be noted with regards to security alarms:

(a) security alarms may be fitted to cover:

(i) the perimeter i.e. doors, windows etc

(ii) the interior space

Whilst an alarm system covering both is likely to give the best results, either system on its own can be effective.

(b) the detection methods used in alarms do vary and a system which uses two different methods (e.g. sound and heat) to trigger the alarm is infinitely preferable to those systems which only use one method because there will be fewer false alarms.

(c) ff alarm sounding devices are incorporated into the system these must be mounted in a position which is inaccessible from the ground, and windows, the roof area or any shelving.

(d) there is little point in installing an alarm system with locally sounding alarms if there is likely to be no one nearby to hear it and call the police. In such cases it is better to have a monitored alarm that at least gets a response. This can be provided by a monitoring service company or by having the alarm activate an automatic telephone dialling facility that is connected to the manager's house and two or three other staff members as backup. The local sounding alarm could be silent for a period after activation to increase the chances of catching the burglar on the premises.

(e) security systems need to be continually re-evaluated and tested. As most modern alarm systems are quite sophisticated and require professional skills to service each alarm installation should have a service contract with the installer to ensure that it is thoroughly and regularly tested.

7.8.3   Every alarm system is made up of three circuits which are inter-related; if one section fails the whole system fails:

(a) the **detection circuit** – the alarm trigger

(b) the **control circuit** – the interpreter and decision maker

(c) the **warning circuit** – raises the alarm.

7.8.4   The detection circuit

(a) This may be either **Open** where the intruder causes the circuit to be completed and a current to flow or **Closed** where the intruder breaks the circuit thereby stopping the current. Once the detection circuit has been actuated it has to be manually reset.

(b) detection devices

(i) detection devices need careful siting. Multiples of a device or different devices in combination can be used according to circumstances.

(ii) wiring and devices should be electrically supervised to prevent tampering

(iii) use the devices as appropriate to provide the following forms of protection:

– Perimeter   e.g. outside wall or fence

– Volumetric   e.g. room

– Point   e.g. doorway or window

(c) detection mechanisms

There are many varieties, all of which have their particular uses.

(i) continuous wiring – a continuous wire around the perimeter of an area. It is actuated by the circuit being broken.

(ii) foil – instead of a wire, a narrow strip of foil is fitted usually on the inside of the windows

(iii) infra-red rays – an infra-red beam of light is transmitted to a receiver and the alarm is set off by the beam being interrupted

(iv) protective switch – which may be fitted to an entry point. The alarm is activated by the entry being opened and circuit being broken. There are the following types:

– mechanical contacts

– magnetic reed contacts

– mercury tilt.

(v) pressure pads – are usually made up to two sheets of metal separated by foam which when compressed allows a current flow and thereby sets off the alarm

(vi) personal attack switches – which are activated by the hand, knee or foot of a person such as a teller when faced with a threat or attack

(vii) knock-out rods – can be used to protect windows etc. They are used instead of continuous wiring and foil and consist of horizontal battens that carry the circuit between contacts from one side of the frame to the other. If a rod is removed the circuit is broken and the alarm activated

(viii) passive detection devices – are used in a closed circuit system and have no operational requirements until activated by an intruder.

Examples of this type of device are:

– mechanical vibro contacts

- electronic vibration detectors

- microphonic devices

- geophones

- passive infra-red heat detectors

(ix) active movement detectors – are devices which detect movement within the area of a continuously broadcast signal that they emit, such as ultrasonic movement, microwave or radar detectors

(x) pressure differential detectors – involve maintaining the air pressure within an area at a slightly different level to the adjacent areas and using a device to detect any pressure changes which is used to sound the alarm

(xi) proximity detectors – use the ability of a capacitor to store an electric charge. If the capacitor or anything metallic connected to it is touched by a person the charge leaks away and the alarm is triggered.

(d) installation

(i) the devices are more reliable if installed in parallel i.e. all must be activated before the alarm is sounded. Compared to the other method of installation i.e. in series, there are likely to be fewer false alarms

(ii) the devices may be installed so that they are set 24 hours a day which is perhaps the optimum, or may be turned on as and when required which creates the possibility of human error or forgetfulness negating the purpose of the alarm

(iii) the devices may be installed so that detection occurs:

- only when the intruder is within the protected area. This is sometimes referred to as **Trap Protection**

- before or as the intruder breaks in. This is referred to as **Perimeter Protection**.

7.8.5   The control circuit

In addition to using the alarm signals from the detection circuit to initiate a signal to the warning circuit it normally contains the means of setting and unsetting the system as well as testing it.

7.8.6   The warning circuit

This circuit is intended to alert those monitoring the system that an alarm has been activated, usually by audible signals such as bells and sirens, or visual signals such as flashing lights.

7.9   MONEY RISK CONTROL

7.9.1   Although the aspects considered above for Burglary Risk reduction must also be considered for static money, the major part of the risk associated with money is its movement from one location to another. To control this risk the following can assist:

(a) varying the method, route and timing of the movement of money on a random basis

(b) reducing the amount of money that has to be carried by adopting such actions as paying the staff by cheque or by using the bank money transfer services

(c) using protection devices such as:

(i) alarm bags

(ii) cash-carry waistcoats

(iii) specialist cash in transit services.

7.10   EMPLOYEE RISK CONTROL

7.10.1   The hazards are moral or morale and the control of the associated risks is extremely difficult. There are however a number of approaches to risk prevention that can be taken such as:

(a) carefully selecting the staff including fully vetting staff employed in sensitive areas such as foreign exchange dealing rooms, computer support staff and accounts staff

(b) implementing and enforcing strict procedures for handling financial transactions including transfers of money

(c) requiring two or more signatures before money is transferred or cheques are drawn

(d) enforcing a strict division of duties

(e) implementing a programme of regular financial audits

(d) maintaining good staff relations so as to eliminate the motivation to commit fraud or to embezzle.

7.11   COMPUTER RISK CONTROL

7.11.1   The risks arising out of the ownership and use of computers have become very significant in recent years. Organisations have become more heavily dependent on them, and the value of information that is stored on and processed by the computers of the organisation has grown significantly.

7.11.2   The risk reduction measures that should be taken therefore need to ensure that:

(a) the computer facility is available when required by the organisation

(b) misuse of computer time is minimised

(c) the information is not:

(i) corrupted

(ii) stolen or removed

(iii) destroyed either deliberately or accidentally.

7.11.3   Possible measures would include:

(a) careful selection of staff

(b) strict implementation of standards for:

(i) operating

(ii) programming

(iii) systems design.

(c) division of duties e.g. programmers not allowed to operate

(d) restricted and controlled access to the computer and its files

(e) integration of the clerical and computer systems

(f) control over the development and implementation of new systems and changes to existing systems in terms of both cost and time

(g) regular financial audits.

7.11.4   There are a number of ways in which the likely loss may be reduced such as:

(a) dividing up high value pieces of equipment into different fire compartments thereby reducing the likely maximum loss from any one incident

(b) installing facilities that will limit the spread of smoke from any fire so that the effects of the highly corrosive combustion products are contained within the compartment in which the incident occurs

(c) ban all temporary storage of combustibles such as paper, tapes and cables in computer rooms

(d) use fire resistive or non combustible construction and furnishings

(e) allow no doors in walls separating the computer room and the room containing uninterruptible power supply (UPS) equipment. When UPS batteries burn or overheat they give off an acid that can severely damage computer equipment

(f) install a smoke handling system

(g) staff the computer room 24 hours a day to ensure an adequate manual response to a fire

(h) where loss expectancies are unacceptably high, provide one of the following in the sub-floor:

(i)   cables that do not propagate flame; or

(ii) cables that are slow burning provided when smoke detectors are also present and an adequate manual response is available; or these are not available

(iii) CO_2 flooding systems, provided the sub-floor is an unoccupied enclosed space.

7.12   TERRORISM RISK CONTROL

7.12.1   Terrorism, being the unlawful use or threat of violence against persons, products or property to further political or social objectives, takes many different forms such as extortion, product tamper, kidnap and ransom, hijack and detention.

7.12.2   In order to exercise any control the organisation and its senior management need firstly to understand the threat and its likely objective. The organisation will then need to put the threat into the context of its own operations and its vulnerabilities. In this, factors such as symbolism (brand or name image), status, purpose and location of the organisation are all important.

7.12.3   Risk Control measures will vary from organisation to organisation and from country to country, but whatever is implemented essential elements will include all of the following:

(a) the involvement and commitment of the senior management of the organisation as well as the law enforcement agencies

(b) both physical and procedural safeguards. In the case of products, good quality control and security, together with good employee relations will go some way towards controlling the risks of product tamper. With the other forms of terrorism a major defence available to the organisation will be the use of a strong element of unpredictability together with both tight security and secrecy.

(c) The prior selection and training of specialist personnel to handle the negotiations, publicity liaison, legal, logistics, victim family support and financial matters. This, together with having a well formulated contingency plan, will go a long way to containing any crisis that may occur.

7.12.4   The control of the Terrorism risk has become highly specialised even though it involves the application of a considerable amount of common sense. A small number of specialist consultancy firms have developed in recent times who can assist the organisation in appraising the risks to which it is exposed as well as in determining the defence measures and a Crisis Management Plan for the organisation.

7.13   POLITICAL RISK CONTROL

7.13.1   With respect to the control of Political Risk, the organisation should seriously consider:

(a) concentrating proprietary research within the organisation in low risk countries such as the United Kingdom or in its home country

(b) making the local company dependant on the parent organisation for some essential materials or markets

(c) diversifying to the extent that local assets in any one country do not exceed say 5% of the parent organisation's total world wide assets

(d) divesting a proportion of the local company into local hands perhaps as a Joint Venture, as well as showing good faith and being a good citizen of the host nation

(e) conducting business as a local company as far as this is possible, e.g.:

 (i) by borrowing a significant proportion of funds required by the local company from local banks

 (ii) by purchasing as much of basic supplies for the local company as possible from local sources

 (iii) by leasing rather than owning

 (iv) by keeping the size of plant in high risk countries as small as possible.

(f) limiting acceptance of local currency to that necessary to meet local commitments

(g) avoiding local trademarks in preference to worldwide ones so as to secure market presence

(h) keeping the extent of the local company's value to its country of domicile in both political and economic terms fully documented

(i) developing a high level of export sales

(j) keeping a careful watch on the political, social and economic environment of the country

(k) carefully complying with all local regulations which affect all aspects of the local company's activities.

7.14 MOTOR LOSS CONTROL

7.14.1   Again, the majority of means are concerned with accident or loss prevention rather than risk reduction and largely commonsense. The following are some actions that may be taken and which may help reduce the losses involved with motor vehicles. Most are of a reasonably modest cost.

7.14.2   The Driver:

(a) all drivers should be carefully selected

(b) all drivers should have reasonable work schedules

(c) all drivers should attend a defensive or advanced driving course and should their performance start to slip, they should be sent on a refresher course

(d) drivers should have regular eyesight checks, including tests for possible night blindness

(e) every driver who has been involved in an accident should be counselled by his or her manager

(f) if the driver has consumed any alcohol he/she should be forbidden from driving. Either use a taxi or another competent sober driver.

(g) always lock the vehicle and close the windows if leaving the vehicle unattended

(h) seat belts should always be worn in both the front and rear seats of private vehicles

(i) if the vehicle fleet has a number of drivers, set up a competition based on remaining free of accidents.

7.14.3   The Vehicle

The vehicle should be adequate for the job that it has to do but it should not be overpowered:

(a) it should be adequately maintained so that it is always in a good road-worthy condition

(b) it should be fitted with an anti-theft device such as:

(i) an audible alarm

(ii) a cut-off in the electric circuit

(iii) steering lock

(iv) gear lever lock

(v) a non return valve in the hydraulic braking system

(vi) a cut-off in the fuel line.

(c) only purchase vehicles with bright readily visible colours; dark colours such as red, dark green and dark blue should be avoided. Scientific investigation has shown that brightly coloured vehicles that contrast with the surroundings are involved in fewer accidents.

(d) purchase vehicles with 'laminated' rather than 'toughened' windscreens

(e) fit 'high level' brake lights. These have been found to reduce rear-end collisions by approximately 50%.

(f) fit 'headlight' protectors if available

(g) fit a tow bar

(h) fit safe 'bull bars'

(i) fit the sides and rear outlines of all trucks and trailers with reflective tape

(j) fit all vans with convex mirrors on the driver's side

(k) etch all windows with registration number of the vehicle or some other form of identification

(l) purchase only vehicles whose controls and indicators have been optimally designed from an ergonomic point of view

(m) fit frontal impact sensors which will trigger the inflation of an air bag to protect the occupants of the front seats

(n) only purchase cars that have been fitted with additional side impact bars.

7.14.4 The Use

Would it be more cost justified to put the vehicle to a less hazardous use?

(a) do not overload the vehicle

(b) ensure that the vehicle is not driven at an excessive speed

(c) ensure safe stopping distances are maintained at all times

(d) don't dazzle other road users at night, dip headlights early on for oncoming traffic

(e) ensure that the vehicle is cleaned regularly paying particular attention to the windows if the vehicle is used at night.

7.15   RISK REDUCTION FOR OTHER TYPES OF ACCIDENT RISK

7.15.1   The assessment and the reduction of risk are closely connected and the possible means that may be used to reduce the risk of a particular class of risk can often be determined from the aspects covered by the survey of the risk, or from the questions asked so that the risk may be assessed.

7.16   MARINE HULL LOSS PREVENTION

7.16.1   The event of loss or damage in any organisation can have far reaching consequences. The loss or damage can cause problems in a land based location where there may be ready access to expert services to counteract and minimise the danger or adverse situation. Imagine then, the extra problems associated with water borne craft facing loss or damage, remote from shore and expert assistance, not only having to contend with the problem but often having to do so under very adverse conditions.

7.16.2   Clearly, some simple measures are available to minimise the potential for loss or to control situations once they arise to an extent that assistance can be obtained or the craft is placed in a position of relative safety. These relate to:

(a) hull of the Vessel

(b) engine room/machinery spaces/fuels

(c) navigational and other aids

(d) loss prevention/reduction equipment

(e) management. The best equipped craft is still likely to be put at risk if it and its facilities are not handled by competent staff and crew both onshore and offshore

7.17   CARGO LOSS PREVENTION

7.17.1   Investigations by the International Union of Marine Insurance has revealed that in excess of 75% of all cargo losses are preventable. Cargo will spend the majority of its time in the hands of third parties whilst it is transported from one place to another, and for cargo loss prevention to be effective the various parties involved must work together.

These parties are as follows:

the shipper

the consignee

the carrier

the port and/or terminal operator

the marine underwriter

In addition, loss prevention must be capable of working wherever the cargo is located, and whichever of the parties is handling it. There are however many pitfalls and using a marine surveyor to supervise both the loading and discharge of cargo may help avoid most if not all of them.

7.17.2   Another factor to be taken into consideration is that the whole transport system is built on documentation, with receipts being given at each point in transit, where the cargo is handed over by one party to another. It is therefore, vitally necessary that when the cargo is handed over, that the receipt is noted if the cargo is found to be damaged or pilfered at that time. If this is not done, it is then impossible to pinpoint where the loss has occurred. Besides not being able to hold the responsible party liable, it also does not assist in being able to take active loss prevention measures.

8

FIRE LOSS CONTROL – LOCATION AND CONSTRUCTION

8.1. INTRODUCTION

8.1.1   The methods of preventing and minimising loss from fire are related by and large to the physical aspects of the organisation:

(a) the **building** in which the organisation is situated.

Whilst the major hazards associated with buildings arise out of its occupation there are a number of areas of hazard arising out of the building itself that can assist or in rare cases start a fire. These are the hazards which are associated with:

(i) the **location** and **exposure** of the building

(ii) its **size**

(iii) the **construction** of the building

(iv) the **design** of the building

(v) the methods used to provide **heat, light** and **power** in the building;

(b) the **occupation** of the organisation which provides an indication of the materials, processes and plant used by the organisation. Occupation usually provides the major causes of loss.

(c) the **management and employees of the organisation**.

8.1.2   Fire losses like all other types of loss may be reduced by:

(a) **reducing the level of risk** involved thereby making losses more unlikely

(b) implementing measures that **prevent losses from occurring**

(c) **detecting and limiting the extent of any loss** that may occur

8.1.3   In addition the measures which may be implemented can be further classified into those that are:

(a) **passive** such as fire resisting construction, fire doors or use of less hazardous processes which are implemented before the loss and which assist in containing the loss

(b) **proactive** such as sprinklers or alarms which are installed before the loss and which at the time of the loss become active in reducing the possible extent of the loss.

8.2   THE BUILDING

8.2.1   Location and Exposure

(a)   the position of buildings or stocks of materials in relation to each other can have material effect upon both the risk of fire outbreak and the possibility of fire spread. Despite the enforcement of strict building regulations by many countries in relation to new properties and, so far as is possible or practicable, to existing buildings, most cities and towns have areas of old closely sited buildings, often several stories in height, of inferior construction compared to modern standards. In many cases these buildings are currently occupied for purposes that were not envisaged at the time they were built and are not only a fire hazard in themselves but endanger the adjoining properties.

Even though constructed of non combustible material such as brick, the amount of internal timberwork, such as in the floors, stairs and roof members, is often extensive. A fire commencing in one such building can readily spread to an adjoining building as a result of:

(i)   the radiated heat; or

(ii) unprotected opposing windows; or

(iii) the upsurge of heat from the burning building that can carry with it sparks and flaming debris, which may fall on an adjoining roof.

Height, window area, occupation and distance from neighbouring buildings are all involved in the risk of fire spread. The presence of sprinkler protection or external drencher protection can materially reduce the exposure hazard in such instances.

(b)   where buildings are built close together fire-fighting is often impaired. Access to the fire may be made so difficult that the activities of fire fighters are hampered. The prime aim of the fire brigade is always to get trapped occupants to safety and this creates special problems where there is limited space to deploy ladders and similar appliances. In addition, a fire in a suburban housing area can remain undetected for a considerable period particularly if it happens during the night, and there may therefore be undue delay before the attendance of the fire brigade.

(c)   if the property is situated in an isolated area, for example, a country farm or a moorland farm, there is clearly no exposure hazard – except perhaps to the extent that the buildings on the property may be undesirably close to each other. However the possibility of a fire burning undetected for a considerable time coupled with a poor water pressure or supply and the distance from the nearest fire brigade are obvious factors in the assessment of the size of the risk. The risk associated with country properties therefore depends partly upon the water supplies available and partly on the speed with which the fire brigade could attend.

Also in the country areas forest, grass or scrub fires are an ever present possibility, particularly in times of drought. The assessment of the risk is difficult but the periodic cutting and removal of long grass, bracken or other scrub vegetation, which is liable to grow to a hazardous degree close to buildings, should be a high priority. In dry conditions such vegetation may provide ready fuel for fires that are difficult to extinguish. Fires may be caused by cigarettes or matches thrown down carelessly or by deliberate acts or irresponsible or malicious persons, or by picnickers, campers, or hunters. The focussing of the sun's rays through a broken bottle is another possible cause.

(d)   as a general rule it is not the single or "unit" fire that is the principal factor in total fire losses, but rather the fire that passes from its place of origin to other sections of the building or to other buildings. This is what is called the exposure hazard. Most architects and owners neglect exposure hazards. Very often a building of good construction is turned into a poor fire risk by being situated next to a poor fire risk.

(e)   the positioning of new buildings therefore should take into account the possibility of a fire spreading from a neighbouring building or site and appropriate action taken to minimise the likely effects. If at all possible the building or buildings on the site should be positioned so as to:

(i) minimise the possibility of a fire spreading from a neighbouring building or site by use of one or more of the following:

- adequate spatial separation of buildings; this is the most effective safeguard

- avoidance of easily ignitable construction materials

- installation of outside sprinklers or drenchers

- barrier walls (self supporting) between buildings

- elimination or adequate protection of openings to reduce spread e.g. fire doors and shutters, wired glass

- elimination of waste between the buildings.

- any outdoor waste bins should be covered and

- placed well away from the buildings

- elimination of vegetation growth close to the buildings

- elimination of yard storage of combustible materials. If this is not possible then the materials should be subdivided into separate stacks with not less than 15 metres between each stack

(ii) provide adequate access for fire-fighting to all parts of the site and the buildings on it

(iii) be close to a good fire-fighting water supply (e.g. the town main).

(f)   in addition, the following should be taken into account when selecting the site on which to build:

(i) the surrounding environment e.g. urban or rural

(ii) the distance from the nearest fire brigade and its type.

(g)   it is also possible to increase the resistance of a building to fire by:

(i) coating the surface of the building with a material such as intumescent paint. When a flame heats these paints, they soften, then decompose, then froth, then char. This charring provides an effective insulation and hinders burning. These paints have never been widely adopted since the resultant froth and char had difficulty in adhering to the material, on which it was painted, thus reducing the effective barrier. In addition surface coatings tend not to be durable and are susceptible to mechanical damage that reduces their effectiveness in a fire.

(ii) impregnate surfaces with fire resistant materials

(iii) surface coatings such as salt, water glass, white wash, gunite (sand and cement).

All of the above provide a physical barrier.

8.2.2   Fire Risk in Relation to Size

The amount of the potential loss by fire in a building depends not only on the size of the building but also on the value of its contents. In assessing the risk, however, the larger building will always present the greater hazard because:

(a) a building of such size contains a larger number of factors that may initiate a fire

(b) the spread of a fire once initiated will be assisted by the greater quantity of goods or merchandise that the building may contain and which therefore may contribute to the propagation of the fire.

The fire risk is consequently directly associated with size. To say that hazard increases with the size of the building is generally valid. Both the total height of the building and the size of the separate fire compartments within the building have a significant impact on its hazard.

8.2.3   Height

Probably the greatest single factor from a structural point of view affecting the extinguishment of a fire in any building is the height of the burning structure. Height causes the following problems:

(a) it is extremely difficult to prevent fire spreading upwards and outwards as the direction of the natural draught caused by a fire is upwards

(b) in working its way upwards, the fire becomes larger and the heat more intense as it devours flammable and combustible material in its path until the fire reaches the maximum intensity

(c) as the fire increases in temperature, more water is required to extinguish it and the pressure and flow of water becomes increasingly vital

(d) there are often considerable problems in ensuring that a sufficiently large water stream is supplied to the higher floors of a tall building. This problem is recognised in many countries by having regulations that set the maximum height for a building that does not have an automatic sprinkler system. For example, a very high water pressure is needed to get water on to the roof of a burning building that is over 40 m high

(e) assuming that the water supply is adequate, it is often impossible for the firemen to obtain a position that is high enough for them to be able to direct a stream of water down onto the structure in the desired direction. Furthermore unless they can find a safe position from which to fight the fire, firemen are at a distinct disadvantage in trying to control a fire high up in a tall building.

(f) there is a danger to firemen attempting to enter a burning building because of the likelihood of the floors, walls or roof collapsing upon them. In such cases the efforts of firemen to get to the seat of the fire may be seriously restricted.

(g) extinguishing an extensive fire on the higher floors of a tall building involves the use of a large quantity of water. Most of this water finds its way down to the lower floors causing much damage so that often the water damage exceeds the fire damage. The problem may be overcome by grading the floors so that the water either flows down the lift well or else flows through specially made scuppers in the exterior walls of the building and down the drain pipes provided for that purpose.

(h) the actions and usefulness of the fireman are often severely curtailed by the surroundings of a tall building

(i) the following points are important in taller buildings:

(i) the provision of adequate escape routes from all floors for the occupants of the building

(ii) the provision of adequate access to all floors of the building for the fire fighters

(iii) the provision of adequate supplies of water, particularly on the upper floors, together with sufficient drainage on each floor to minimise the water damage on the lower floors if a fire should occur.

(iv) ideally each floor should become a single compartment or series of compartments by using fire resistant floors and walls both internal and external in the construction of the building. This will help prevent the spread of fire from one floor to another.

(v) provision should be made for the firemen to get above the building if possible so that they may direct water down onto a fire on the top floor of the building.

N.B.　The above weaknesses apply equally to the storage of contents or stock within a building as they do to the structure itself. Consequently the possibility of fire in a storage building may be low, but the probability of serious loss may be high.

8.2.4　Cubic Capacity

(a)　it is recognised that there is a limit to the size of a building in which a fire is capable of being controlled and extinguished in the early stages by even the most efficient fire-fighting service with the best apparatus and water supplies available. The maximum floor area that is generally allowed without sprinklers being installed is 1000 square metres. However, to obtain a true measure of the risk of any section or compartment of a building which constitutes a separate fire risk it is necessary to take into account the height to which the goods are stored in the area, thereby converting the measure into one of cubic capacity. As a measure of hazard, cubic capacity is used by insurers for various warehouse risks and other buildings designed for high density storage such as wool stores, cool stores, furniture depositories and bonded stores. In the case of single storied buildings, however, the floor area may be taken as the measure of the degree of risk.

(b)   experience has proved that usually the easiest type of fire to extinguish is the one in a low one storey building in which there are no highly combustible contents. Accessibility is good and water pressures are at their best. In most cases such buildings are rarely completely destroyed.

(c)   there has been a trend in recent years towards building very large single storied warehouses and factories with very little compartmentation within them as this makes for easier operations particularly when modern flow line techniques, mass production and automation are involved. However a large building is likely to become a roaring furnace in a very short time and to defeat all efforts of the firemen to extinguish it before extensive damage has been done.

> It follows naturally from this example that it is better to have risks spread rather than concentrated.

(d)   cubic capacity provides a good way of assessing the fire risk in a warehouse or store but it relates primarily to the propagation risk or the potential extent and spread of the fire. It does not take into account the degree of activity within the building that gives rise to fire outbreak hazards. Accordingly for certain occupations a good indication of the size or extent of the risk is the number of personnel employed or the number of machines engaged in production.

8.2.5   Compartmentalization

(a)   all buildings should be subdivided into a number of fire resistant compartments by the use of:

(i) party walls

(ii) fire resistant floors

(iii) fire breaks;

so that any fire that may start may be contained within the compartment in which it starts.

(b)   for single storied buildings the use of:

(i) curtain boards and roof curtains

(ii) roof vents;

can also be effective in limiting the spread of fire within a compartment.

(c)   in order to restrict the spread of fire, a building should be sub-divided into as many sections as possible by walls and floors of adequate fire resistance as shown in *Figure 8.1.*

Figure 8.1

Sub-divided walls and floors of adequate fire resistant materials restrict the spread of fire

Whilst building regulations in many countries specify maximum compartment sizes and minimum fire resistance gradings, as requirements for personal safety, consideration should be given to smaller compartments and higher degrees of fire resistance in order to protect the buildings themselves and their contents from the effects of fire. Fire resistance should be sufficient to withstand a complete burn out of the contents of the individual compartment. Thus a fire is contained within its compartment of origin. One set of regulations requires that the vertical sub-division of buildings should be such that each sub division not exceed 7000 m3 or in the case of storage areas 280 m3. Reference should be made to the local regulations of the country in which the reader is working to establish the actual limits that apply.

8.3   HAZARDS OF CONSTRUCTION

8.3.1   Since different materials employed in building behave in different ways in a fire, consideration must be given to the way in which the degree of fire resistance of elements of structure constructed of such materials may be measured. The following are the building materials most commonly found:

(a) **traditional materials**

    (i) brick and concrete

    (ii) slates

    (iii) stone and reproduction stone/slates

    (iv) clay tiles.

All are non-combustible. Some are heavy and could therefore contribute to early collapse in a fire. Often a timber frame is required to carry the building load in which case building paper or bitumous felt is sometimes used as lining, both of which are combustible.

(b) **materials requiring support**

    (i) Mastic, Asphalt; combustible but burns only with difficulty

    (ii) Aluminium, Lead and Stainless Steel; Non-combustible but conduct heat and will distort if heated

    (iii) Glass; sheet glass shatters on exposure to heat unless it is reinforced by wire cast within the glass. However, radiated heat will pass through wired glass as it only prevents the passage of smoke and flames.

    (iv) Aluminium Sheeting; Normally non-combustible but has caught fire and burned in a few exceptional fires. However, due to its low melting point it may expose any combustible material at an early stage of fire.

    (v) Asbestos or Cement Sheeting; Non-combustible. Shatters readily in fires, which can be an advantage in many cases.

    (vi) Plastic; All plastics are combustible but fire risk varieswidely depending on particular plastic. Usually melt at very low temperatures. Thermoplastic sheeting can be used for venting purposes.

N.B.:   The supporting slabs and structural framing for these materials may be combustible.

(c) **self supporting materials**

    (i) Timber; Combustible if heated over 200 degrees

centigrade. However large timber beams have a considerable capacity to resist destruction by fire.

(ii) Steel and Iron; Non-combustible but it has two characteristics, which are very important under fire conditions.

Fire temperatures rapidly climb to a point where steel loses much of its strength and reaches its yield point, that is, it can no longer carry the load for which it was designed. This failure occurs when the steel has been heated to approximately 538 degrees centigrade. Generally speaking, most unprotected structural steel subjected to the standard fire test will fail by the 30 minute mark.

This means that a steel beam under fire conditions becomes physically longer and this exerts pressure at the ends of the beam on to other structural members. The result is the failure of the columns with consequent collapse of the structure that they support.

(iii) Concrete; Non-combustible but the fire resistance of this material depends on the free water content and the type of aggregate used. When heated to 100 degrees centigrade any free moisture is converted to steam and, if the moisture is excessive the pressure developed can be sufficient to break up the surface and even dislodge large pieces from the main body (spalling).

Concrete loses strength at 600 degrees centigrade, but although this temperature is reached under fire conditions, concrete absorbs heat quite slowly and a concrete member should not fail until this temperature is reached throughout the member and not just on the surface.

(iv) Single Brick Walls; Better than wood or iron but not equal to a double brick wall. Usually tied at intervals to a wooden frame by wire embedded in the mortar. If the frame is burnt from the inside the bricks have no support and may collapse. Fires coming from the outside usually do not encounter very stiff resistance.

(v) Double Brick and Reinforced Concrete Walls; The minimum or standard requirement is a 225 mm brick wall or 150 mm reinforced concrete wall. Either of these walls is assumed to give adequate separation from buildings of the same construction or between buildings or groups of buildings of "wood". To be effective the wall must be as high as and extend as far as the building from which it is proposed that it be separated, and it must have no openings of any kind unless such openings are protected by approved double fire-resisting doors.

8.3.2   Construction

(a)   insurers are normally concerned with the whole structure and its degree of exposure to loss. Buildings are therefore graded broadly in terms of the resistance to fire of their construction. This can vary from those with a very high resistance to those that have very little resistance to the effects of fire. The terminology used varies from country to country and reference should be made to ascertain the correct terminology for the particular country in which the reader is situated.

For example in the United Kingdom a building with a very high resistance to fire (2 hours or more) is referred to as being of Standard I, II or III construction depending on the length of time of resistance, or as being of Fire Resisting Construction (F.R.C.). By contrast in New Zealand the term Massive Construction is used. Many buildings are not built of materials that will resist fire for as long as this so for a building that is constructed of materials that will resist a fire for 2 hours or more the term Construction Grade 1 is used. However if the structure will resist a fire for at least an half-hour the term Construction Grade 2 is used in the United Kingdom. In New Zealand for example the terms used for buildings with a lower fire resistance relate to the predominant material used in the fabric of the building; for example brick, mixed, or wood.

(b)   **F.R.C. or Massive type of Construction**

    (i)   for a building to be considered as being of this type of construction all of the walls, roofs and supporting columns must be constructed entirely of load bearing brick, mass concrete, reinforced concrete, or concrete block

    (ii) a fireproof building does not exist, the name "fire-resisting" building being closer to reality as far as structures composed of non-combustible materials such as brick, steel, terra cotta or concrete are concerned, but a building can be erected that will resist fire if five cardinal features are included in its construction i.e. :

- protection of iron or steel work

- protection of floor openings

- protection of exterior openings

- avoidance of wood trim, finish and wood transoms

- thin glass skylights over enclosed shafts.

(iii) a so-called fireproof building bears about the same relation to its contents that a furnace or stove does to the materials put into it to burn. As a rule the fire-resisting building will prevent the spread of fire to other buildings, just as a fire will not spread from one stove to another placed near it. However the contents of a fire-resisting building will be consumed once the fire is well under way just as thoroughly as the coal and wood in the stove. Further, the heat will be retained in the fire-resisting building and human beings, if they fail to get out quickly, will be killed. This is particularly true of a building filled with merchandise, or other types of combustible material, such as partitions, office records, etc. If large quantities of combustible materials are stored on the lower floors of a tall building and they each catch fire, the upper floors will quickly become untenable because the stairs and elevators act as chimney shafts, carrying up the heat to the upper floors.

(iv) a building constructed entirely of fire and heat-resisting materials is fire-resisting as long as it contains no combustibles. However the contents of such a building are frequently many times more liable to destruction than the same material in an ordinary type building. Many losses have demonstrated this, with contents completely burned out.

(c)   **Other types of construction**

(i) brick construction

Such buildings will have all external walls including gable ends constructed entirely of load-bearing brick, poured

195

concrete, reinforced concrete or concrete block. Roofs and floors may be of inferior (i.e. less fire resisting) construction without affecting the overall level of risk providing the materials used are incombustible.

(ii) wood construction

This type of building is constructed with a wooden frame and wood, iron or other inferior cladding.

(iii) mixed construction

With the wide variety of building materials that are available today a wide range of different combination of materials may be used in a building all of which result in a building of a lower fire resistance. Examples of such types are:

- brick and steel

- all steel

- brick and wood

- brick veneer;

(d)   **Linings**

It is usual for the inner surfaces of walls of a building to be lined. Also linings in ceilings are usually affixed below the joists of the upper floors or at the level of the eaves under the roof. Plaster linings are most common, whilst lath and plaster is often found in the older buildings and fibrous plaster in those of more recent construction. However, wallboard made of gypsum, which is incombustible is now used extensively.

Fibrous plaster lining is preferred because of its better fire resisting qualities. Lath and plaster is quite effective but in a fire the plaster is inclined to spall exposing the wooded laths. Such a fire can be extremely difficult to extinguish.

Wallboard linings, unless made of gypsum, are combustible and will materially assist the spread of the fire. Combustible linings such as these have been a feature of several large fires in recent years.

(e)   **Internal partitioning**

Whilst internal partitioning is not intended to have a major effect in preventing the spread of fire it should not assist in the spread.

Partitions of wood or other combustible material add fuel to the fire and help to spread it to other contents. The only really effective means of division is by walls which extend up to the ceiling lining and which are made of a material that will stand up to the effects of being exposed to fire for a reasonable period of time.

Where rapid attendance of the Fire Brigade can be ensured, such as where a fire alarm system is installed, a building with even light weight partitions is preferable to an undivided building. This is because the partitions may slightly slow the fire growth as well as slowing down the spread of smoke to a limited extent, and they provide the brigade with a point at which to hold the fire. However, many of the modern materials used in internal partitioning produce large quantities of toxic smoke when involved in a fire.

8.3.3 Fire Rating

The fire rating of a material or structure is the term expressed in time for which that material or structure will resist a laboratory controlled fire. The fire rating allotted to a particular material is the time it takes until one of the following conditions occur:

(a) **Collapse**

For all elements of structure it is required that the elements shall not collapse during the fire test and during the hose stream test if this is required

(b) **Passage of flame**

For all elements of structure whose function is to separate spaces and to resist the passage of fire from one space to another it is required that cracks, fissures or other orifices through which flame can pass shall not develop even during the hose stream test if required

(c) **Failure of Insulation**

For all elements of structure it is required that the average temperature of the unexposed surfaces shall not increase by more than 139 degrees centigrade above the initial temperature. This requirement may be waived for elements such as doors, shutters and glazing against which combustible materials would not normally be placed.

The standard gradings allotted following the test are half an hour, one hour, one and a half hours, two hours, three hours, four hours and six hours.

8.3.4   The various elements within a building can contribute to or help control an outbreak of fire. These are the roof, the walls and the floors.

(a)   **roof**

(i) **fire within the building threatening the roof from beneath.** In a single storey building the roof is immediately vulnerable to the rising heat from a fire. The roof structure may be weakened and collapse. Combustible material in the roof may be quickly ignited and fire may spread laterally throughout the building. Burning material may fall from the roof to ignite contents on the floor ahead of the fire, and radiation between the fire on the floor and in the roof may intensify the effects. If the roof is penetrated, combustible material in the covering (such as wooden shingles or asphalt based tiles) may be ignited and spread fire on the outer surface. Burning brands may break away and alight on, and ignite neighbouring roofs.

In multi storey buildings and many single storey buildings a ceiling provides a protection to the roof from the fire below. Once fire penetrates that ceiling, or if a fire breaks out in the roof space, many of the effects described above may occur. As in many buildings the roof space extends over the whole building without a break, there is no barrier to the spread of fire at roof level.

(ii) **fire in a neighbouring or adjoining building threatening the roof from above.** A roof is also vulnerable to the radiant heat from a fire in a neighbouring building, either through the ignition of a combustible upper surface or the penetration by heat of the surface to ignite combustible material within the roof. A neighbouring building on fire may also shed brands that may alight on the roof to start a fire. This situation is likely to be aggravated if the roof has already been subjected to radiant heat from the burning neighbouring building.

(iii) **a roof may be subject to three potential risks:**

- its ignition from a fire within the building and the subsequent possibility of its spreading fire throughout the building.

- a fire within the building heating the supporting structure thereby causing complex stresses that may bring about its collapse. This collapse, in turn, can cause extensive damage to the contents and inhibit the ability of fire fighters to control or extinguish the fire, as well as destroying fixed fire fighting systems within the roof structure such as automatic sprinklers. The collapse or partial collapse of the roof may expose external surfaces to an internal fire; thus causing external as well as internal spread.

- its ignition by a fire in a neighbouring building that could thus spread to the building.

(b) **walls**

Modern Load Bearing Walls – for large buildings are usually constructed with piers, girders (or beams) and panels, particulars of which follow:

(i) **piers** – are vertical columns and carry the load of the floor girders and offer a means of tying the building together. They may be:

- solid brickwork of sufficient thickness at bottom to allow of an average reduction of 57 mm at each floor level and be not less than 35 mm at seating of the roof girders

- rolled steel "I" beams (R.S.J) which should be encased in brick not less than 115 mm thick, or reinforced concrete not less than 75 mm thick, with standard connections such as cleats, spice plates and stools, bolted or riveted to the "I" beam at each floor level to carry girders

- reinforced concrete columns.

(ii) **girders** – are the horizontal supporting members. Usually rolled steel joists (R.S.J) or reinforced concrete, or heavy hardwood

(iii) **panels** – carry no load beyond their own weight, and are also known as "curtain walls" or "filling". They should be properly bonded or keyed to the piers by reinforcements. They should also be built of one of the following materials:

- reinforced concrete which is not less than 150 mm thick, and which was poured at the same time as the reinforced concrete piers are poured

- solid brickwork which is not less than 230 mm thick or cavity type of two brick walls, each not less than 115 mm thick, set in concrete mortar, forming a cavity not more than 200 mm wide, with galvanised iron truss in staggered formation at vertical intervals of not exceeding three courses and horizontal distances of not exceeding 600 mm

- terracotta hollow blocks which are not less than 150 mm thick set in cement mortar and rendered on both sides with cements (not allowed by some authorities for external walls)

- aerated concrete of approved type which is not less than 150 mm thick (not allowed by some authorities for external walls).

(iv) **fire walls**

Fire walls are used to provide a fire-rated separation of two attached buildings or separate fire compartments. The required Fire Resisting Rating (F.R.R.) is four hours, which is inflexible. Sometimes the term party wall is used for a wall separating two buildings on a common site. This wall has the same function as a fire wall.

The fire wall plays a vital role in preventing critical temperatures being transmitted and maintaining structural integrity during the process of the most severe fire. When a fire wall separates premises constructed of combustible materials, or the separate buildings have combustible roofs, the wall should extend above roof level to form a parapet.

To be of any practical value, dividing brick walls must be at least 225 mm thickness and should pass through the roof and form a parapet of at least 300 mm above. In earthquake prone areas such parapet however should not exceed 150 mm. Openings in such dividing walls should be protected by double fire-resisting doors. Any combustible roof linings should be cut away for not less than 300 mm on each side of the wall.

(c) **floors**

A fire resisting floor must be non-combustible and also resist the transfer of heat. The usual materials employed are concrete or reinforced concrete and these materials are usually implied when the term "fire resisting floor" is used. Any columns, piers or girdles supporting a fire resisting floor should have a similar fire rating to the floor itself. This applies in particular to any structural steelwork that supports a floor. The resistance of a timber floor to fire from below can be considerably increased by the addition of a properly fixed non-combustible ceiling such as fibrous plaster or plasterboard. Such protection will not, of course, affect the resistance of the floor if the fire starts on its upper surface. An open joisted timber floor offers little resistance, especially if the boards are only butt jointed and not tongue and grooved. Surfacing a floor with wood or other similar material does not usually reduce its fire resisting qualities but it is preferable for such materials to be laid directly on to the floor without intervening air space. If such an air space were to be left it could lead to a rapid spread of fire if it gained hold in the space. However, this is not considered as serious a risk as a ceiling with air space below a floor.

9

FIRE LOSS CONTROL – DESIGN

9.1   THE HAZARDS OF DESIGN

9.1.1   Many design features of the building are important because they may assist a fire to spread or they may slow down or prevent it from spreading. Such features all need careful assessment and comprise:

> (a) floor openings such as staircases, hoists, lifts
>
> (b) wall openings such as doorways, windows, loading docks, ducting for services
>
> (c) atriums, light wells and light areas
>
> (d) cavities and voids.

9.1.2   It should also be noted that many of these features often play a part in losses from other causes such as injury (e.g. unfenced floor openings or loading docks), burglary (e.g. unsecured wall openings), and climatic excesses (e.g. flood damage through doorways with an inadequate sill).

9.2   FLOOR OPENINGS

9.2.1   The main cause of fire spreading so rapidly in tall buildings is the number of floor openings. These floor openings may be either hoists, well holes, trap doors, staircases or lift wells, the two most common being lift wells and staircases. A fire starting near a lift, staircase or other opening will immediately be drawn up and into such an opening and on up the building, thus enabling the fire to spread from floor to floor. This occurs because the fire creates large quantities of hot air and gases, which quickly rise and seek to escape through any vertical openings. Cold air rushing in to take the place of the warm air causes a draught and supplies additional oxygen to sustain and increase the fire and carry it higher and at a faster rate. By this means, floor after floor catches fire and soon the building becomes a blazing mass.

9.2.2   The measures that may be taken to control loss include:

(a) all lift wells, hoists, dumb waiters, service lifts and staircases should be totally enclosed in brick and/or concrete of approved thickness according to the height of the building and the class of contents. The opening on to each floor should then be protected by means of an approved fire-resisting door. An automatic door with a fusible link is the most efficient and suitable type of door, but nevertheless a manually operated fire door can provide protection. It should be possible to close all the doors leading in to the floor openings and so restrict the fire to the floor on which it occurs. Under ordinary circumstances if the building is of fire-resisting construction and is split into compartments a fire in one compartment may burn itself out and not damage or affect the remainder of the building. Such a compartment is termed a **Fire Resisting Compartment.**

(b) if the building has wooden floors then the closing of the doors will only act as a temporary measure in restricting the fire. The closing of all openings by fire doors would give employees time to leave the building and time to bring first-aid appliances (if any) into action. It would also assist the fire brigade to the extent that the fire would tend to be limited to one part of the building and not on every floor when they arrive at the scene of the fire.

(c) the use of space underneath wooden staircases should be discouraged. If unavoidable, then the walls and undersides of the stairs should be plastered with some type of non-combustible material.

9.3   WALL OPENINGS

9.3.1   Both internal and external walls are pierced by many different types of openings that serve a variety of different purposes such as allowing access or to allow in light or to enable the building services to be distributed around the building. Most of these openings are unavoidable but all have the effect of lowering the fire resistance of the walls.

Modern buildings usually have a large number of window openings so that a considerable percentage of the wall area is actually glass. Glass does not present an obstruction to the passage of radiated heat and so large areas of glass may increase the likelihood of any combustible contents in the building being ignited by a fire in an adjoining building. This exposure may be reduced to some extent by the use of external drenchers.

9.3.2   Measures that may be taken to control loss include:

(a) ideally a fire wall should have as few openings as is possible. However, if such openings are protected by double automatic-closing fire resisting doors of an approved type or fire damper, shutter or window, a wall would still be regarded as perfect separation.

Such doors must be installed on each of the doorway openings so that the two doors are separated by an air space equal to the full thickness of the wall. Fire doors installed on openings in the walls are designed only to resist the passage of fire and are not expected to offer much resistance to the passage of smoke.

Under most building regulations however a single fire door, which has a minimum rating of two hours, may be accepted as perfect separation for the protection of an opening in a fire wall. In general, as stated above, a fire door is preferred on each face of the opening.

(b) **types of door**

For many years the only type of fire door available to serve this purpose was the automatically closing tin clad fire door that was made up of several layers of timber. This core material was covered with interlocking zincaneal plates, hence the term tin clad. These doors are manufactured to conform with the specification issued by the appropriate authority in each country. Doors of this type have been subjected to the standard fire test in many countries and have always passed that test. In addition, even those that have not been tested in this way have been found to perform satisfactorily under actual fire conditions. Other types of automatic fire doors are now available and these are sometimes referred to as "composite doors". These doors have a core of inert material, such as calcium silicate usually overlaid with a type of asbestos board and a surface finish of timber veneer or metal.

(c) **one or two doors?**

The minimum fire rating required for a fire resisting door is two hours, but some doors have achieved ratings of three, four and five hours. As the rating normally required for a fire wall is four hours it might seem, at first glance, that any opening in a fire wall could therefore be satisfactorily protected by a single fire door with a rating of four hours. It is generally the practice for two doors to be installed, one on each face of the wall, each with minimum rating of two hours. If one door alone is relied upon then if for some reason the automatic closing mechanism fails to work, or the closing of the door is obstructed, perhaps by stock, the opening will be unprotected and fire will pass through from one side to the other. There are many reasons why a fire door might be non-operational at the time of the fire and therefore, if there is a door on each face of the wall and one door fails to operate the other is there as backup.

(d) **automatic closing doors**

The majority of these fire doors are not hinged but operate on a sliding track. Normally, the automatic closing mechanism consists of a system of wires connected through pulleys to weights and the system incorporates a temperature sensitive mechanism. This temperature sensitive mechanism might be either a fusible link that is merely two pieces of metal held together by a type of soft solder with a low melting point, (usually 71 degrees centigrade) or a Quartzoid bulb which acts as a link between two metal sections. In the case of the fusible link the soft solder melts at the designed temperature allowing the two metal sections to part. With the Quartzoid bulb, which is filled with liquid that expands and bursts the bulb at the designed temperature, again allowing the two metal sections to part. In either case the parting of the two metal sections brings the closing mechanism into operation. In the case of a fire door with a horizontal track a wire cable connects the temperature sensitive element to a set of weights. When the two sections of the element part, at the fusing temperature, the wire suspending the weights is released and the weights then exert force on the door which pulls the door along the track into the closed position. For a door with an inclined track (which was the common method for installing the tin clad doors) the temperature sensitive element is again connected by wire cable to weights. However in this case the weights exert a force on the door during normal day-to-day operations and counterbalance the door so that it can remain in any position on the track without sliding down the incline. When the temperature reaches the level at which the solder melts or the bulb bursts the two metal sections part, and the weights which hold the door back are released, the door then slides down the inclined track into its closed position as shown in *Figure 9.1*.

Figure 9.1

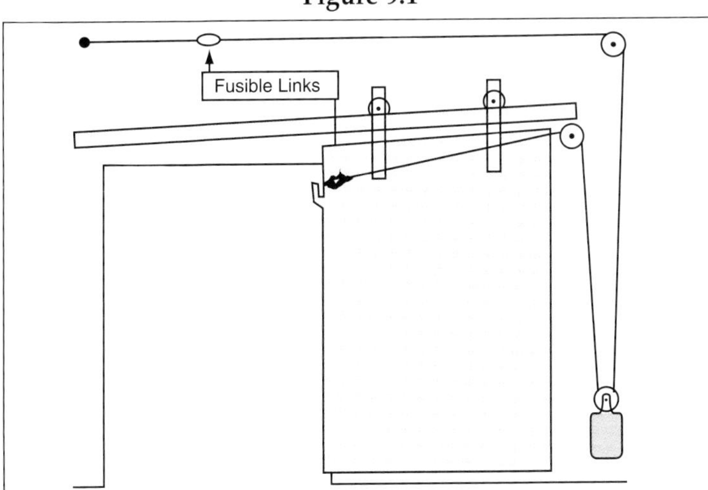

An Automatic Fire Door

An important feature of these automatic fire doors is that they will remain open in any position along the length of the track during normal operation and, therefore, there is no need for people to chock them open in order to take goods through the opening. Chocking would of course prevent the door from closing automatically in the event of fire. The five common reasons for the failure of the various types of self-closing doors are:

(i) damaged track

(ii) snagged cable or chain

(iii) inadequate spring tension

(iv) blocked opening

(v) the working parts have not been lubricated properly.

It is therefore essential that properly trained personnel regularly service all doors of this type.

(e) **self closing doors**

These close immediately upon release and which are spring, pneumatically or hydraulically operated and are not normally acceptable for openings in fire walls. This is because when people wish to take goods through the opening or if there is constant pedestrian traffic, there is a strong temptation to put a chock under the door and hold it in the open position, thus negating the protection.

(f) **Fire Dampers or Shutters**

Openings in fire walls which are smaller than normal doorway openings, such as conveyor openings, may be protected by fire doors of a reduced size or, if the openings are of very restricted size (normally not over 0.37 square metres), fire dampers may be used. Fire dampers are made of a single thickness of a mild steel and may be in the form of a single plate or made up of a number of blades with the appearance of a louvre. These reduced size fire doors and dampers are normally held in the open position by a temperature sensing element (of the same type as described for fire doors) and when the element fuses the doors would be normally arranged to close by gravity.

(g) Fire Windows

These windows are usually installed only for the protection of exposures in external walls. The total area of windows in any one external wall need to be carefully monitored and cognisance should be taken of the exposure to flames and heat from neighbouring properties. The opening to be protected should not exceed 5.2 square metres for any one window as tests have shown this to be the maximum size opening that may be protected in this way under normal circumstances. The fire window is constructed of wired glass with metal frames and moveable sashes that are connected to a temperature-sensitive element arranged so that the window will close automatically in the event of a fire.

9.4 ATRIUMS, LIGHT WELLS AND LIGHT AREAS

9.4.1 Atriums are large vertical spaces within a building, onto which a number of different floors look and are a feature of the entrances of many modern buildings. Atriums are a special form of light well which usually have a skylight which allows light into various floors that look out onto the light well. Light areas are similar to light wells except that they are usually found between different buildings, thus giving light to each, and that there is no skylight in their use, the bottom of the area being the ground. Usually such areas are accessible to employees and other occupants.

Figure 9.2

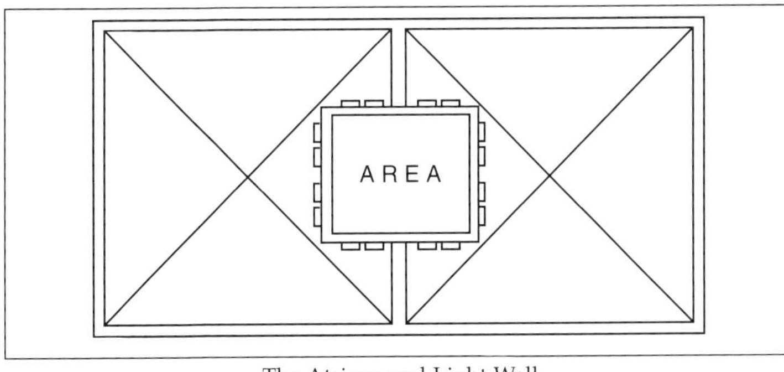

AREA

The Atrium and Light Well

If different tenants and various trades occupy the various buildings that abut onto a light well, the risk of a fire starting in one of the tenancies and spreading across the area is very real. Even if the individual buildings are of fire resisting construction with each floor ostensibly forming an independent compartment, this feature of fire-resisting construction may be of little practical benefit so long as there is the risk of fire being transmitted from building to building.

9.4.2   Measures that may be taken to control loss include:

(a) all vertical openings should be covered at roof level by light glass or shutters held closed by a fusible link. Should a fire get into the vertical opening, the glass would break or the shutters would open forming a kind of chimney. By this means hot gases, heat and smoke, which would otherwise collect on the upper floors are released into the air, thus possibly preventing a fire spreading onto these floors.

(b) windows looking onto these types of area should be fitted with approved wire glass windows in metal frames, or with approved shutters, or with approved wire gauze in a metal frame, or with drenchers fixed over each window. Any doorways onto the area should be protected by approved fire doors.

(c) minimal combustible material present within the atrium itself.

9.4.3   With some atriums:

(a) provision is made for the air pressure within the atrium itself to be increased to a level that is sufficient to hold the smoke within the tenancy in which it is being generated

(b) if extremely tall, the smoke in the atrium will tend to cool quickly and will, as a consequence, stratify. When this is likely to occur it is necessary to introduce additional energy (such as fans) in order to help the smoke to disperse.

9.5   CAVITIES AND VOIDS

9.5.1   Cavities and voids are present in some form in virtually every building. Usually they are concealed from view; in many cases they are functional and are created intentionally, but sometimes they are only incidental to the construction. Cavities commonly occur as part of the external envelope:

(a) in a cavity wall, which may consist of two leaves or of hollow block construction

(b) between the constructional wall of the building and an external cladding

(c) between the external wall and an internal lining, or as part of the internal divisions of the building

(d) between floors and ceilings where the separation is caused by beams, joists or even hollow tile

(e) between a structural ceiling and false or suspended ceilings

(f) roof voids in their various forms – the space between a flat or a pitched roof and its outer skin (a common feature in industrial buildings), the 'loft' space between the ceiling of the top storey and the tiled or sheeted roof above it, the space between vertical walls and the sloping roof of attic or mansard type construction, and in numerous other circumstances.

Any of these spaces may be filled (or partially filled) with insulating materials that may or may not be combustible.

9.5.2   There are three reasons for concern about the fire hazards of cavities and voids:

(a) they are generally concealed spaces of which the occupants are often unaware, and a fire starting in them, or breaking into them from outside, can develop to large proportions before being noticed

(b) they form channels, either individually or in a group, if they interconnect with other cavities along which fire, smoke and water used in fire-fighting, spread unnoticed and rapidly, often over a considerable distance, to other parts of the building. They often act as a chimney in a fire.

(c) access to these spaces for effective fire fighting is difficult.

9.5.3   The following are general principles for good construction involving cavities or voids:

(a) one cavity or space should not communicate with another, and the separation between them should be fire-resisting

(b) the size of any cavity or space should be limited by the insertion (if necessary) of fire-resisting barriers. (Example: the space between a false ceiling and the structural ceiling could extend over the whole floor area, which in a large building could be a very large area. Fire-resisting barriers in the form of walls should be used to divide such a space into smaller areas).

(c) no cavity or void should cross the boundary between fire compartments – a fire-resistance barrier should be used to separate them at this point.

(d) the storage and use of combustible material and the installation of plant inside a cavity or void should be avoided as far as possible but where essential, fire-resisting barriers should be incorporated to limit any possible fire spread. The choice and use of thermal insulating materials should be carefully considered in this respect.

9.6   RISING DUCTS AND OTHER SERVICE DUCTS

9.6.1   Rising ducts are common in all high rise buildings and service ducts are common in all modern buildings. All are a special form of cavity or void being used to route the various services such as power, water and air conditioning to the various areas within the building. As a consequence, all will allow the easy passage of fire and smoke around the building.

9.6.2   The basic precautions to consider are:

(a) service, ducts and/or other enclosures together with any insulation should as far as possible be made of non-combustible materials

(b) services should be routed and protected so that they do not readily assist the passage of fire, heat and smoke from one part of a building to another

(c) all service ducts should be filled with automatic closing dampers or should be sealed at each floor level and at each wall with a fire resistant compound so that they do not facilitate the spread of fire between compartments

(d) air conditioning systems should be designed so that there is no direct communication between fire-resisting compartments of the building. This can be achieved by using a separate air conditioning system for each compartment. If there is a central plant room and air is distributed throughout the building by a system of ducts, then main air shafts should be of fire-resisting construction.

(e) the fire dangers from the consequences of electrical faults can be greatly reduced by careful consideration to other services run in the same duct or in close proximity:

- electrical services should not be installed in air ducts

- piped services, e.g. for gas and water, should not be in close proximity to electrical services unless these services are electrically bonded to the earth of the electrical installation

- combustible insulation, e.g. foam plastic and cork of other services should not be allowed in the same duct or close to electrical services.

(f) pipes that have a temperature that exceeds 100 degrees centigrade should be separated from wood and other combustible parts of the building by an air space of at least 50 mm. Pipes hotter than 50 degrees centigrade should in addition be lagged with non-combustible materials.

(g) waste disposal chutes and associated hoppers should be completely enclosed by fire-resisting construction. Openings into such chutes should be fitted with self-closing fire-resisting flaps.

(h) rising ducts should be sealed at each floor level with a fire resisting sealing compound.

9.7 SMOKE AND HEAT VENTING

9.7.1 Control of Fire and Smoke Within a Building

(a)   the initiation and growth of a fire can be regarded as a cycle of processes which require sufficient heat to cause a fuel to give off flammable vapours which ignite, consume oxygen and release more heat. Some of this heat then becomes the initial heat for adjacent fuel and the cycle is repeated.

(b)   heat may be transmitted by direct contact or conduction, by convection or by radiation. Some 75 per cent of the heat from most fires is convected and the hot products of combustion, including smoke may have a temperature of 800-1200 degrees Centigrade. This will heat any materials near the fire to such an extent that if they are combustible they may in turn be ignited and so add fuel to the fire.

(c)   the products of combustion from a fire consist of fumes and visible smoke. Smoke consists of small carbonaceous particles and droplets of materials such as tar. It can cause panic by obscuring vision and by affecting eyes, nose and throat. It can also cause severe damage to building decor and contents. Carbon, which is present in most combustible materials, can form carbon dioxide and carbon monoxide. If other chemical elements are present various other dangerous gases can be produced. As a consequence victims in a fire usually die from asphyxiation or poisoning due to these fumes.

(d)   there are a number of precautions that can be taken:

   (i) selection of building materials that do not produce excessive visible smoke or especially toxic fumes when burning or heated by a fire

   (ii) fire venting of single storey buildings. The rapid accumulation of heat and smoke may be checked in the early stages of a fire by means of automatic ventilators. These ventilators are used in association with non-combustible screens within the roof space. Automatic lantern lights in theatres are an early example of roof venting

   (iii) venting of basements Special venting arrangements for basements are usually necessary and pavement lights, normally for fire brigade use, are commonly provided. Provisions should also be made for fresh air entry.

   (iv) measures to protect stairs and corridors include:

   • siting of stairs at the periphery of a building so that windows can be used for venting

- permanent mechanical ventilation of stairs not located against an outside wall

- pressurisation of stairwell

- ventilated lobby approach to stairwells, with smoke-stop doors in corridors.

(e)   it must be realised that five minutes from its discovery a fire could have spread throughout the building:

(i) **initiation**

Lighted match in wastepaper basket: combustible materials in vicinity ignited

Figure 9.3

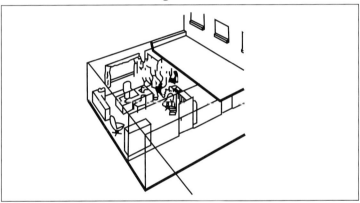

Initiation

(ii) **enlargement**

Someone tries to enter, panics, leaves door open: flames and smoke billow into corridor

Figure 9.4

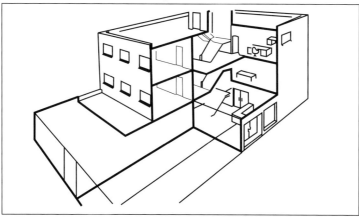

Enlargement

(iii) flue effect

Hot gases and smoke reach stairwell and rise to top floor, igniting combustible materials in their path

Figure 9.5

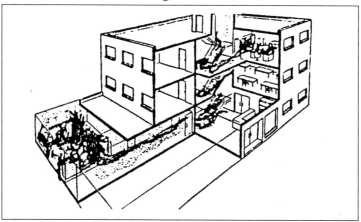

Flue Effect

(iv) failure of roof

The fire in the first office has burnt through the roof and the fire is now also affecting all upper offices from the outside.

Figure 9.6

Failure of Roof

9.7.2   Smoke and hot gases can become confined within the building during a fire and these will interfere with access and visibility for escape as well as fire and rescue. They will also assist in maintaining high temperatures and fire spread within the building and, if the hot unburned products of combustion are allowed to accumulate, they will ignite explosively when a supply of oxygen is suddenly made available. This is known as the smoke explosion. It is therefore generally beneficial to incorporate curtain boards or vents in the building so as to facilitate the exhausting of smoke and heat and to limit the horizontal spread of fire and smoke.

9.7.3   Curtain Boards as Aids to Venting

In large area buildings, unless vented areas are subdivided by means of walls or partitions, curtain boards should be regarded as being essential. They also may be used to good effect around special hazard areas such as metal heat treatment plants. They delay and limit the horizontal spread of heat and smoke by providing ponding area that ideally should be less than 185 cubic metres in size. See *Figures 9.7, 9.8 and 9.9* for various examples of curtain boards and their effects.

Figure 9.7

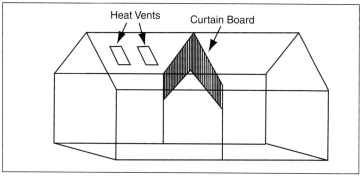

Figure 9.8

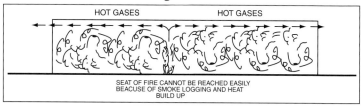

Figure 9.9

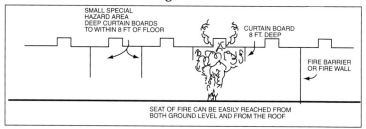

9.7.4   Roof Vents

Heat venting consists of either automatic opening purpose built vents, or burn-out panels which allow the heat above the seat of the fire to escape. Some Standards such as NFPA suggest that at least 2% of the roof area should be heat venting in high hazardous areas such as warehousing and that 1% be allowed for less hazardous occupancies. Venting of roofs can be done in the following ways:

(a) **monitors**

Roof monitors with louvres or thin glass windows in the sides may provide the needed venting if properly spaced and subdivided, but glass may be slow to break as the performance of glass in a fire is unpredictable

(b) **continuous gravity vents**

This type of vent is a continuous narrow slot opening with a weather hood above. If provided with shutters, they should be fitted with automatic opening devices in event of fire.

(c) **unit type vents**

These are relatively small and the local regulations will usually specify a maximum allowable size, such as 16 to 100 square feet in area. Some consist of a metal frame and metal housing with hinged dampers. Others are transparent or translucent plastic domes that open on release of spring loaded lifting levers. See *Figures 9.10 and 9.11.*

Figure 9.10

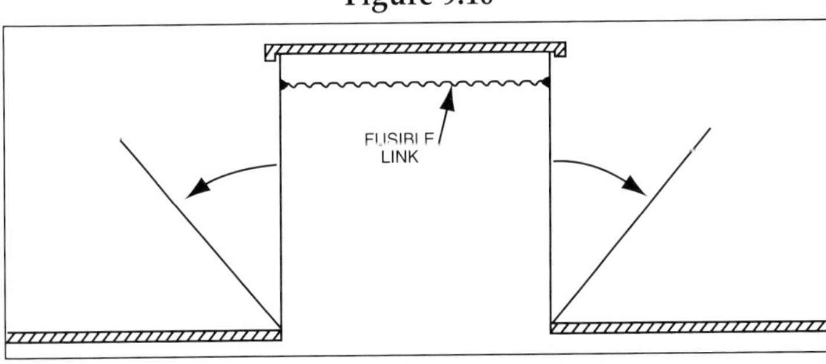

Vertical Shutters held in place by Fusible Link. When Fusible Link gives Shutters Open under own weight.

Figure 9.11

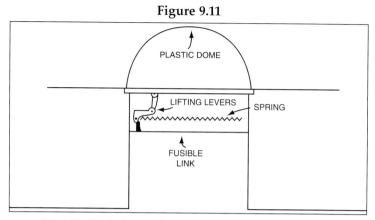

When Fusible Link gives Spring Forces the Plastic Dome to Lift

(d) sawtooth roof skylights

This type of skylight is only useful for venting if the glass used is of normal strength, (not wired) or if an automatic opening mechanism is provided which operates in the event of fire. Protection against falling glass should be provided for the fire fighters.

(e) external wall windows

Ordinary glass in the windows on the upper floors of a building may break in the event of a fire and would provide some limited degree of venting. However, glass further down the building, especially if below the lower edge of any curtain boards, is of much less value for venting purposes.

(f) automatic release

Where the automatic operation of venting facilities is provided, operation should be actuated by fusible links or interlocked with the operation of a sprinkler system or other automatic protection equipment covering the same area.

9.7.5   Venting Effects

(a)   whilst venting does appear to improve combustion during the early part of the fire and it cannot fight the fire, it appears to offer a number of significant advantages.

(i) it allows the fire brigade more time to respond to the alarm

(ii) it is very successful in restricting a fire, by keeping temperatures down, thereby limiting the risk of flash-over or explosion. Under certain conditions it may facilitate the fire burning itself out without any spread.

(iii) it assists fire fighting by:

- ensuring cleaner and more complete combustion which reduces the amount of smoke produced

- evacuating the smoke and toxic gases produced, thereby enabling firemen to locate the source of the fire more quickly

- keeping the fire temperature down, thereby enabling the firemen to get closer to the source of the fire

- keeping the fire smaller, thereby reducing the amount of water or other type of extinguishing material needed to put it out

- improving the effectiveness of any fixed fighting system such as sprinklers because of its quicker activation.

(b)   the effectiveness of venting can be further increased by providing a means of manually activating venting. This will provide the fire brigade with a further means of controlling the fire and its effects by opening vents remote from the fire to:

(i) clear smoke and toxic gas accumulations

(ii) admit air so that the spread of fire is limited.

9.8   HIGHLY PROTECTED RISKS

9.8.1   Whilst design plays an important part in creating a Highly Protected Risk it is not the only factor that must be taken into account. These are major industrial properties that meet rigidly enforced standards with respect to:

(a) construction

(b) protection against the risks of the building and its occupancy.

9.8.2   For an industrial property to be considered as a Highly Protected Risk it must have:

(a) a management that is committed to protecting the property from loss and that takes an active interest in loss prevention

(b) regular inspection services to prevent or minimise loss

(c) proper housekeeping

(d) single occupier of the site

(e) a sufficiently large floor area and value to generate the level of premium necessary to pay for the inspection services

(f) a sound construction and design so that the relative importance of such external factors as location exposures and public protection are reduced. The property must also be maintained in good repair and must be adequately subdivided internally by standard fire walls

(g) sufficient fire protection equipment to provide adequate protection for the type of occupancy, construction and exposure conditions likely to be experienced in the building

(h) satisfactory watchman or alarm service and the tenancy limited to one business

(i) an adequate public or private fire protection system that has sufficient hydrants and a satisfactory water supply.

9.8.3   Such properties warrant a special lower rating than the average property but they are subject to the following:

(a) regular inspections, usually several times a year, with a report detailing any necessary improvements submitted following each visit

(b) an undertaking by the industry itself to design, build and maintain plants in which adequate steps are taken to reduce ordinary losses and to guard against catastrophic ones

(c) if a larger exposure, continual and intensive study aimed at:

(i) maintaining the level of risk at the lowest possible level

(ii) Improving the standards of loss prevention.

(d) a larger excess, thus providing an incentive for the management to avoid and reduce loss

(e) rate adjustments that are based on the statistical data of exposure and loss analysis for the particular industry concerned.

Ideally all the necessary measures to create the Highly Protected Risk should be allowed for in the design stage so that they may be incorporated in the construction of the premises. Failure to do this invariably means either the expenditure of very large sums of money later to correct the faults, or the premises do not gain the advantages of being classified as a Highly Protected Risk. The measures should cover prevention and minimisation of loss from all types of risk associated with the building and its occupancy.

9.8.4   There is obviously a very high initial cost involved in incorporating all the necessary measures but this is usually more than offset by the savings in:

(a) insurance costs which tend to rise over a number of years. This saving can be quite large.

(b) avoiding the cost of:

(i)   damage to property and loss of earning capacity

(ii) loss of customers and/or market share

(iii) loss of confidence of shareholders

(iv) loss of goodwill

(v) loss of life (customers, employees and the public)

(vi) loss of profitability of patents, trademarks, etc., following a loss;

which, even if the risk is fully insured, would not be anywhere near fully covered. In many studies it has been found that for every unit of currency able to be recovered from insurance in respect of a loss, at least three are not so covered.

10

FIRE LOSS CONTROL – BUILDING SERVICES

10.1   BUILDING SERVICES

10.1.1   Building services may:

(a) **cause** fires

(b) **feed** fires

(c) **spread** fires, toxic gases, smoke and extinguishing water.

10.1.2   Precautions

Precautions must be taken in the design and installation of services supplying, using or conveying:

Hot or Cold Water	Refrigeration
Steam	Compressed Air, Oxygen
Electricity	and other Gases
Gas	Fuel Oil
Telecommunications	Waste
Air	Exhaust Fumes

Special precautions are necessary for major items of plant and for service tunnels, ceiling voids and other spaces containing large quantities of services.

10.1.3   Fires in building services may result amongst other causes from:

(a) faulty electrical cables and fittings

(b) combustible materials in contact with hot pipes or other hot surfaces

(c) leaks from piped services containing flammable gas or liquid

(d) rubbish in waste disposal chutes being ignited by, for example, a lighted match.

10.2   ELECTRIC CURRENT

10.2.1   An electric current is electricity flowing in conductors from a point of higher potential to a point of lower potential in a closed circuit.

10.2.2   Conductors, Resistances and Insulators

Examples of good conductors are silver, copper, gold, aluminium and of good insulators are slate, ebony, glass, porcelain, rubber, mica, P.V.C (Poly-vinyl Chloride) and (rather importantly) air. In between these are the not so good conductors that often do duty as "resistances" e.g. carbon, tungsten, nichrome alloy. It is, however, only a question of degree, because even the best conductors offer some resistance and the best insulators will permit some flow of current even though it might be minute. If the driving force of the current is increased to such an extent that a current flows through an insulator, the insulation is said to have "broken down".

10.3   THE EFFECTS OF AN ELECTRIC CURRENT

10.3.1   Heating Effect of Electric Current

Whenever a current flows it has a heating effect. This in fact is made use of in heating, lighting and cooking, e.g. electric light is produced by a fine wire of high resistance which is brought to white heat by the flow of current. The heat developed is proportional to the resistance of the conductor and the square of the current, i.e. doubling the current gives four times (2 squared or 2 x 2) the heat.

The current flowing through wiring increases as devices that consume current are switched on and if the heating effect is not controlled, enormous increases of heating could result from the increases in current. Normally, this does not occur because the installed wiring is of sufficient thickness that when the wiring is fully loaded, with full current load flowing, the heating of the wire itself is negligible. Wiring that is too thin to carry full current load may, however, become hot enough to be hazardous. Thus the thickness of the wiring is analogous to the need for a water pipe to have an internal diameter that is large enough to carry the required flow of water without excessive loss of pressure through friction.

10.3.2 Chemical Effect of Electric Current

Some liquids are affected chemically by the passage of a current. If a current is conducted into and out of the liquid by means of immersed metal plates, the substance of these plates may also be acted upon, metal being removed from one plate, and deposited upon the other. This is the basis of electroplating.

10.3.3 Magnetic Effect of Electric Current

Some metals, principally iron, can be made to develop, either temporarily or permanently, the properties of a magnet. This effect is used to good effect not only in electric motors but also in alternators or magnetos and a wide range of electronic apparatus. As with the other effects described above the magnetic effect (or electromagnetic induction) can be used to produce an electric current. For example if one end of a bar magnet is thrust into a solenoid (a coil of wire wound uniformly on a cylindrical former) a flow of current is generated momentarily in the coil. When the magnet is withdrawn there is another flow but in the opposite direction. Whenever lines of magnetic force cut across a conductor an electric current is induced in that conductor, the current generated being proportional to the rate at which the lines of magnetic force are cut. This principle is used in the dynamos that are used to produce electricity in power stations.

10.4 STATIC ELECTRICITY AND LIGHTNING

10.4.1 In addition to electrical current there is also static electricity in which electrical charges may be built up within or upon a body, (piece of equipment or machinery) which does occur in the course of many industrial processes. A considerable potential difference can be built up between two bodies subject to such charging and when the potential difference reaches the point of electrical "breakdown" of the intervening air gap, a spark discharge could occur. Such a spark could have sufficient energy to cause a fire or explosion if, for example, it occurred in a flammable atmosphere.

10.4.2 The repeated contact and separation of two different types of material produce a static charge. When two objects are in contact, electrons can move from one to another. Subsequent separation of the objects prevents the re-establishment of electrical neutrality and thus results in the accumulation of a negative charge on one object and of an equal and opposite charge upon the other. If the material concerned happens to be electrically conducting and is earthed, the charge will flow away rapidly after separation. On the other hand, if the material is a non-conductor, the charge cannot leak away and remains on the surface. Static electrical effects are caused by the accumulation of these charged particles upon, or within, a body.

Like charges repel and unlike charges attract each other. Charges accumulating on a body can induce a charge upon an adjacent object and charge accumulation by this process of induction is of major importance in problems relating to static electricity.

10.4.3 Examples of circumstances in which static electricity is produced are:

(a) processes involving driving belts running over pulleys or rollers, conveyor belts and rollers

(b) processes in which sheet material passes over rolls, such as newsprint, plastics and rubber

(c) the use of rubber tyred vehicles

(d) the accumulation of charges on personnel due to movement

(e) any process involving the production of a dust cloud

(f) the passage of liquids (particularly hydro carbon liquids) through pipes and discharge into tanks. The transfer of petrol or other spirits to storage tanks or wagons and from the garage pump to a motor vehicle requires special precautions.

10.4.4 Static electricity can be prevented from building up by conducting it away as fast as it is generated. The methods of preventing sparks from static electricity are as follows:

(a) effective earthing of the surfaces on which the charge collects – this may take the form of trailing wires or chains or combs with pointed teeth which are positioned to sweep the surfaces of the moving material. Machinery, containers and piping should be properly bonded and grounded.

(b) use of humidifiers so that the whole surface of everything becomes covered with a film of moisture which provides a "leakage path" for any charge

(c) use of high voltage to neutralise the electrostatic field – limited use only because the high voltage itself introduces a possible fire risk

(d) use of radioactive materials to ionise the air and again provide a "leakage path" for any charge

(e) personnel may need to wear special conductive footwear in areas that include metal flooring.

10.4.5   Lightning is a form of static electricity that is built up and discharged from a particular type of cloud. Under suitable conditions a charge builds up within the cloud until the potential difference between the top and bottom of the cloud is sufficient to cause a discharge to another cloud or to earth. The potential difference may be insufficient until the cloud passes over a particularly high building that in effect reduces the size of the air gap to be traversed. This is the reason why high buildings are liable to be struck and damaged by lightning unless fitted with an adequate lightning conductor.

10.4.6   Lightning Protection

The basic purpose of any lightning protection system is to direct the lightning current to earth. Protection against direct strikes is provided by the use of:

(a) **ground** or **static** wires installed above the overhead power transmission lines

(b) in the case of tall buildings and outdoor electrical equipment grounded masts or rods that extend above the building or equipment down to the ground.

Surge protection is very important for all major electrical equipment (transformers, motors and generators). This is provided by a system of appropriate interconnected and well-grounded arresters and surge capacitors.

10.5 HOW ELECTRICITY CAUSES FIRES

10.5.1 Insulation Failure

(a)   whenever wiring is used to provide a path for the flow of electrical current it is (with certain exceptions) covered with a sheath of rubber or plastic. This sheath is the **insulation**. These materials are bad conductors of electricity, and when current is flowing it does so through the copper core, because the high conductivity of the copper offers the easiest path, and the surrounding insulation the most difficult path. If the insulation should be weak or perished, wet or damaged mechanically, the resistance to the flow of current offered by the insulation would be low, and the voltage would probably succeed in forcing some current through the defective insulation. There would be a leakage because the insulation fault may provide an easier path for the current than the legitimate one through the cable and the comparatively high resistance, say, in a lamp. If the current flows directly from one conductor to the other, via a parallel path with minimal current passing through the consumer's appliances, there is said to be a SHORT CIRCUIT. If the current in the parallel path is sufficiently high it will trigger the cable's protection device (blow the fuse). When the insulation fault allows current to flow to earth it is known as an "earth fault". It should be noted however that every electrical cable suffers from some insulation leakage that in the case of a top quality cable is extremely small.

(b)   short circuit currents can be very great because the resistance of the circuit without the resistance of any intervening appliances may be very low. Arcing will often result in such situations and this may lead to fire.

(c)   the flame retardant finish of conductors and self-extinguishing properties of insulating materials now in use on most wires and cables does not mean that they will not burn. Single wires with self-extinguishing insulation may not support combustion when well separated, but piled together in a cable tray or junction box in large numbers, they can become involved in a self-spreading fire. In a normal commercial environment there are other factors that will aid combustion, such as the presence of other combustibles, oily deposits, dust, air currents and higher operating temperatures due to load or environmental conditions. Cable trays are therefore often the site of fires and these can remain undiscovered for some considerable time.

10.5.2   Fuses

(a)   the purpose of a fuse is akin to that of a safety valve in a steam boiler, which releases steam if the boiler reaches or exceeds a predetermined pressure that is considered to be undesirably high. A fuse is usually a short length of special wire, such as tinned copper, forming part of the circuit. In the ordinary way the current taken by heaters, lamps and motors flows through a pair of fuses, just as if they were part of the feeding cables. When, however, an excessive short-circuit or overload current flows, the fuses heat up and melt. This breaks the circuit, the whole installation becomes dead, and no more current will flow.

(b)   a fuse is designed to prevent the overload but does not always do so. A fuse wire has to reach a certain temperature (through the heating effect of the short-circuit current flowing through it) before it will melt, so there is a time lag between the occurrence of the insulation fault and leakage and the blowing of the fuse. In this time the magnitude of the short-circuit current at the point of leakage may be sufficient to heat up neighbouring flammable material such as rubber, wood lining, skirting or flooring to ignition point and set it alight. This is precisely what a "fire of electrical origin" means. The build up of heat in such circumstances may even melt a neighbouring gas pipe and set fire to the gas.

(c)   in addition, it is well known that when a fuse blows, instead of this being regarded as a danger signal that indicates over-loading or leakage, people sometimes deal with the problem by inserting a heavier fuse instead of investigating and rectifying the fault. The workman who claims – with an air of triumph – that he has "cured" the trouble by inserting a hairpin or paper fastener in lieu of fuse wire, has merely created a very similar situation to that which would arise if he had suspended an additional weight on the safety valve of a boiler. In both instances a far greater overload may occur before the safety system (the fuse or safety valve) will operate.

10.5.3   Arcing

(a)   if two conductors between which there is a potential difference are brought into contact, the circuit will be completed and current will flow. If they are then separated quickly, and held wide apart, the circuit will be broken and current will cease to flow. If, however, after the wires are brought into contact they are separated slowly for only a short distance, it may be found that the circuit will not be broken but that current will surge across the small intervening air space and will form a white hot arc.

(b)   the temperature of such an arc is very high and is quite capable of causing fire. Arcing may occur in a roof space, under a floor, in wood casing or where the wires pass through cupboards, racks or compartments stacked with flammable material. Apart from the possibility of the arc igniting surrounding material, it is almost certain that it will ignite the wire's own insulation. Furthermore if a number of wires are bunched in one conduit or casing, the insulation of all the wires may be involved and thereby further short circuits may be caused.

10.5.4   Dangers of Multi-Adaptors

(a)   one of the most outstanding causes of a fire particularly, in private dwellings, is the use of multi-point adaptors that are necessitated by the unfortunate practice of providing too few power points in each room.

(b)   many domestic fires are caused through the inadvertent switching on of the wrong appliance through the misuse of multiple adaptors. For example multiple adaptors are often used to connect appliances that need to be permanently switched on such as an electric clock with appliances that need only be switched on from time to time such as a radio or electric heater.

10.5.5   Overloading

(a)   all wiring must contain a conductor of sufficient thickness to carry all the current that can flow through the apparatus connected to it. If it is too thin, the heating effect of the current will gradually cook and weaken the insulation, which will ultimately break down and permit a leak, which may cause a fire. A potential fire danger is created when the original wiring installation is extended as business expands and more electrical equipment and appliances are introduced.

(b)   a second cause of overloading arises when additional circuits are connected to a distribution board without a corresponding increase being made in the size of the wires that supply the latter. As the heating effect varies in proportion to the square of the current, it will be apparent that even comparatively small overloads may cause an appreciable increase in temperature. Whereas the effects of heavy overloads are easily realised, those of small overloads are not always fully appreciated. The continuation of a small degree of overheating will tend to carbonise the insulation and make it brittle, leading ultimately to its breakdown. At the same time the prolonged heating of combustible materials in proximity to the electric circuit may in course of time cause those materials to ignite.

10.5.6 Earth Faults

(a)   if there is a leakage of current through an insulation fault, and if the current should then flow through to an adjacent metal work it would become alive. The metal might then become so hot as to become incandescent or even melt and so cause a fire by igniting adjacent combustible material. An earthing lead should prevent this, for as soon as the leaking current flows through the metal work it should find a very easy path to earth. This would immediately help to increase the flow of current to the level needed to melt the fuse wire. This isolates the installation from the supply and prevents any local heating that might cause a fire.

(b)   earthing systems, however, are not always perfect and failures do occur. A common cause of fire is the persistent earth fault that remains uncleared because the impedance of the earth-fault-current-path is too high to pass sufficient current to operate the circuit breaker or blow the fuses. The rapidity with which the fuses blow is dependant on the current value and it is possible for a fuse to take minutes, or even hours to reach its melting point, during which time destructive arcing can continue at the fault or point of breakdown.

10.5.7 Unsafe Location of Heating

(a)   with electric heating appliances such as fire and radiators, soldering irons, electric irons and all industrial equipment including furnaces and the like, the fire risk may be divided into two distinct types.

These are those that:

(i) arise from electrical faults

(ii) are due to the generation of heat.

Special types of heaters, such as panel heaters are merely heating elements suitably encased in fire-resisting framework and let into walls or partitions so that they are inconspicuous and eliminate loose wiring. In situations such as public buildings, restaurants, places of entertainment, department stores and the like, they prevent the possibility of persons setting fire to their clothing through standing too close to unprotected elements. Accordingly, they are designed so that they heat a fairly large area at a low temperature. Obviously it is necessary for the heating unit to be protected suitably when in the vicinity of woodwork or other flammable material.

(b)   **bulbs near flammable goods**

The tremendous heat that is produced by gas-filled bulbs in unventilated situations such as in shop windows, necessitates care in ensuring that flammable material is prevented from touching the surface of the bulb. For the same reason, paper decorations should not be allowed to come into contact with the bulb surface. The heat may also be responsible for the rapid deterioration of the insulation of the wiring in the lampholder, and this should be examined regularly. Note however, florescent lights which operate at a comparatively low temperature do not produce as much heat, although the ends of the tubes near to the electrodes may become hot enough to char fabric such as curtaining that may be in contact with tubes.

Goods should not be stacked in storage areas to such a height that cartons are situated near to light fittings.

10.5.8   Control of the Exposure to the Risks Arising out of Electricity

The great variety of electrical equipment, applications and environmental conditions make it impossible to provide a detailed discussion of specific safeguards. There are, however, several general rules that should be kept in mind:

> (i)   equipment should be of the appropriate design to meet the particular operating demands and environmental conditions
>
> (ii) installation should be in accordance with electrical codes and manufacturers' literature
>
> (iii) equipment should be subject to regular maintenance, which should be recorded
>
> (iv) equipment should be kept clean, dry and cool, with tight connections and, where needed, provided with adequate lubrication

(v) visual inspections should be conducted regularly during operating and shutdown periods

(vi) the various electrical tests, as detailed in data sheets for specific equipment, should be carried out on the basis laid down in the data sheets.

The only way to forestall fires from short circuiting is the regular testing of the resistance of the insulation. If the insulation stands up to the insulation test, then there is no immediate leakage or local heating hazards which may initiate a fire.

10.6   HEATING AND LIGHTING

10.6.1   All methods of heating and lighting, with the exception of electricity, involve the hazards associated with naked flame and lighting up.

A naked flame may be a luminous flame such as a candle or a simple lamp burning kerosene at a wick, or a non-luminous flame that produces light by heating a mantle to incandescence. In either case the main hazard is the ability of a naked flame to set fire to flammable material in contact with or close to the flame. This applies particularly to flammable vapours because the property of diffusion possessed by gases means contact can be made with the flame even when the source of the gas is not close to the flame.

The naked flame also produces heat that is capable of setting flammable material, which is not in direct contact with the flame, on fire by conduction and by radiation.

10.6.2   Because the effect is almost immediate, everyone realises what the direct application of intense heat does to flammable material. We all know that we can light a taper or piece of paper by holding it for a short time in the flame of a gas burner and we would not do the same with say, a handkerchief, unless we wanted to destroy it. The effect of heat conveyed by conduction is generally delayed, maybe hours and even years while drying out and pyrophoric breakdown occurs, so the danger to flammable material is often overlooked and it may not be realised that the danger exists.

10.6.3   We normally enclose the source of heat with material that will not burn but often overlook that such material may be a good heat conductor and place it too close to something that will burn.

Iron is a common material for such containers, because it is non-flammable, is easy to fabricate into the shapes we require, relatively cheap and readily available and it is not fragile. It is, however, a good conductor of heat so an iron "container" must be suitably heat insulated from combustible material. Material for such insulation must be a bad conductor of heat and, of course, non-combustible. Brick is a common example of good insulator or bad conductor. Air is another.

Even the best insulator will conduct some heat and were it not for the fact that the surface not directly exposed to the heat source is constantly losing heat to its surroundings (usually the air), that surface would in time reach the same temperature as the heat source.

10.6.4   Temperature of the "surface not directly exposed to the source of heat" is always the key factor for fire prevention and it should always be kept below the ignition temperature of adjacent combustible material. Nothing will burn until its temperature reaches its "ignition temperature".

10.6.5   The convection currents developed when air is heated are important in assisting "loss of heat to its surroundings" because it means a constant supply of cool air as the "surroundings". This presupposes a free movement of air in the surroundings and it helps to explain why heat insulation fails sometimes when the air is not allowed to move freely and on very hot days when there is no supply of cool air. The thicker the insulation the slower the passage of heat, so, for any given source of heat, the thickness of insulation required is governed by the probable rate of loss of heat by the unexposed surface and the temperature of that surface that is considered safe in the conditions applying. A higher temperature would be more acceptable in a foundry than in an oil store. It will be realised also that the higher the temperature of the source of heat, the thickness of the insulation must be increased to keep the "unexposed surface" temperature at the safe level.

10.6.6   The effect of heat transmitted by radiation is also delayed and so, is often forgotten. The man standing with his back to the gas fire is sometimes astounded if the backs of his trousers start to burn, as is the housewife who finds that garments left to dry in front of the fire have been burnt.

10.7   ELECTRIC SPACE HEATING APPARATUS

10.7.1   Electric heaters of various types need special consideration in relation to fire hazards, not because they are more liable to electrical faults than other equipment, but because they are designed to be heat sources and they are often carelessly placed or inadequately guarded. Clearly, portable radiant heaters such as open-bar heaters or reflector heaters should not be located near combustible material. If the heaters are of a fixed type, combustible material should not be stacked or placed in their vicinity so that accidental dislodging or the collapse of a stack of material brings it into the proximity of a heater element. Particular care is required in storage areas.

10.7.2   Convector heaters and thermal storage heaters should be so placed that there is an adequate circulation of air around and through the casings, otherwise serious overheating may occur. In particular, these types of heater must not be covered or have equipment or materials placed on or near them.

Other types of heater operating at black heat, such as tubular heaters or wall panel heaters, should also have free circulation of air around them and it is highly desirable that they be fitted with indicator lamps to show that they are in operation.

10.8   CENTRAL HEATING

10.8.1   The essential feature of any central heating system is the one source of heat in a building – the stove, furnace, burner – where the heating fuel is burnt. From that single source heat is conveyed to all parts of the building to where it is required by any of the following means:

(a) low pressure hot water pipes

(b) high pressure hot water pipes

(c) steam pipes

(d) hot air ducts.

10.8.2   In all these systems the source of the heat should be installed in such a way that it is not a fire hazard in the building that is being heated. It should be in a separate compartment of fire resisting construction, but in small buildings this may be too much to expect and it is sufficient if:

(a) the heating unit is suitably insulated from combustible material in the building structure

(b) no combustible goods or waste is permitted in its vicinity

(c) the fuel supply is suitably housed.

10.8.3   Low Pressure Hot Water

The system is open to the atmosphere at some point so it operates at atmospheric pressure plus any pressure due to the "head of water" in the system.

The heating unit, in this case a "boiler", is installed at the lowest part of the building and the water circulates on a normal convection principle that hot water, being lighter than cold water, rises. As the water is heated it rises up the flow pipe, passes through the radiators (room heaters), losing heat in the process, and returns to the boiler by a return pipe. A cold water tank supplied from the mains via a ball valve replaces any water lost through evaporation. Being open to the air, and having a constant supply of water, the temperature of the circulating water cannot get above boiling point (100 degrees centigrade) unless there is an appreciable pressure due to "head of water". Temperatures are usually well below the 150 degrees centigrade which is regarded as the maximum for a low pressure system and so, with these systems the hazards are primarily those of the boiler compartment and the fuel storage.

10.8.4   High Pressure Hot Water

Pressure due to "head of water" builds up at a rate of 10 kilopascals (kPa) for every metre of head. The pressure from "head of water" raises the boiling point temperature of water as follows:

kPa	Temperature Degrees Centigrade
100	120
200	134
300	145
400	153
600	164
800	174

A twelve-storey building with each storey 3 metres in height, cold water tank in a room above the top floor and boiler in the basement, would have a "head of water" of 36 metres and generate a pressure of 36 x 10 = 360 kPa. So the water in the system would be close to 150 degrees centigrade before boiling.

If the temperature of the water in a system is no more than 150 degrees centigrade the system is considered to be a "low pressure" system. Anything over that is considered to be a high pressure system and temperatures over 150 degrees centigrade can be expected in the pipes and radiators. The significance of this is that fluffy deposits common in textile works, upholsterers and similar risks may have an ignition temperature as low as 125 degrees centigrade, and wood exposed constantly to a temperature of 150 degrees centigrade or more becomes very easy to ignite.

10.8.5   Steam Pipes

Steam heating systems are similar in all respects to a hot water system except that the boiler is designed to boil water continuously. (In the hot water systems the water should never boil).

The operating temperature of the steam boiler is higher than the hot water boiler so it should be housed in a fireproof compartment or in a separate building. In general, pipe and radiator temperature will also be higher, but this depends on the pressure at which the system is designed to operate.

The temperature of most steam pipes is quite sufficient to cause pyrophoric action on woodwork, which can lead to a reduction of the ignition temperature – and even achieves ignition – so insulation must always be interposed between steam pipes and combustibles.

10.8.6   Hot Air Ducts

The source of heat is used to heat the air and the heated air is carried through ducts to wherever it is required. Individual regulators control the flow of warm air in each room. These systems may rely for distribution on the fact that hot air rises, but large installations must use a fan. In all hot air systems there is the danger of the ducts becoming very hot and it is important that they be kept clear of woodwork and other combustible material. Ducts should, therefore, be constructed of metal and should be fitted with dampers that close automatically in the event of a fire occurring.

10.9   FIXED ROOM HEATERS

10.9.1   **Fireplaces** – for the burning of solid fuel – (wood, coal, coke, briquettes).

The hazards of the open fireplace are:

(a) the ignition of joists or other woodwork close to the fireplace being inadequately protected from the heat

(b) the burning fuel or embers falling onto carpets and wood floors in front of the fireplace

(c) the chimney fire, and the possibility of its spread to the rest of the building through cracks in the brickwork or chimney liner – perhaps due to deterioration over a period of time, earth movement or earthquake.

10.9.2   **Gas Fires** – these consist of burners heating clay or asbestos "candles" to a red heat. They should be installed on a properly constructed hearth or on a suitable non-combustible base if the floor is of wood. Properly constructed, the only hazards are those of the open flame lighting up and the flammable gas.

10.10   PORTABLE LIGHTING AND HEATING

10.10.1 Portable non-electric lighting and heating appliances can be placed carelessly in the vicinity of flammable material, or where they can fall or be knocked over easily in much the same way as electric heaters.

10.10.2 Portable Room Heaters – these are often kerosene stoves and are divided into those burning oil at a wick and those using a vaporising system. Hazards are similar to those of portable oil lamps – (see below).

10.10.3 Oil Lamps and heaters present the further hazard that they require filling from time to time with flammable liquid, and many fires have been caused by people trying to refill a lamp while it is still alight. The filling risk is especially hazardous when the liquid is petrol because it is highly volatile, and the diffusion of the vapour makes it possible for a match struck several metres away to ignite the vapour or even set off an explosion.

In mineral oil pressure lamps the oil must be vaporised before entering the burner. This is done by creating an air pressure in the fuel reservoir by means of a hand pump and this forces oil through the vaporising tube that is heated by the burner itself. It is, however, necessary to heat the vaporising tube in the first place to start up the lamp, and if this is not done properly, warm oil instead of vapour comes out when the tap is opened. This may cause an unpleasant or dangerous flare-up.

10.10.4 Portable Gas Heaters and Lamps – these have all the same hazards that have been outlined above, plus the hazards of instability and the ability to be placed too close to flammable materials.

10.10.5 The risk control measures that should be followed with the various forms of portable lighting and heating appliances include not only complete and regular maintenance and cleaning, but also full training of those people who will use the appliances to ensure that they fully understand:

    (a) how to operate the appliance, particularly its filling and lighting operation

    (b) the importance of correctly placing the appliance so that the likelihood of it being tipped over or setting fire to adjacent material is minimised.

All such appliances should be fitted with a safety device that stops the flow of fuel if the appliance is tipped over.

11

LOSS CONTROL – INDUSTRIAL MATERIALS

11.1 OCCUPATIONAL HAZARD

11.1.1   It is the occupation of a building that provides the majority of hazards to be found in or around the building, particularly with respect to fire and injuries to people. These hazards are associated with either the materials used or stored in the building or the machinery and processes used in the building.

11.1.2   Every human activity creates some human hazard and therefore risk, although in many cases this may be relatively small. When a person occupies a house or unit for his or her own occupation a host of items, which constitute fire and explosion hazards or an exposure to harmful or injurious substances are brought into the property. Supplies of power are introduced in the form of gas and electricity with which to operate the heating and cooking appliances, and all the other electrical paraphernalia of the modern dwelling. Highly flammable and often toxic solvents, adhesives, paints, cleaners and the like, are frequently used and stored in the dwelling. The car stored in the garage may contain 30 or more litres of petrol close to the workshop where an electric drill, polisher and paint sprayer, etc., may be used. Yet a dwelling house is considered a relatively non-hazardous fire risk, because the householder has a personal interest in ensuring that his property is not misused, damaged or destroyed. The dwelling and its contents commonly are one of the largest investments that a person is ever likely to make and he or she is naturally concerned for its continued preservation. This is evidenced by the care that most people take to minimise the fire inception hazards and their possible consequences.

11.1.3   In industry, such considerations apply only to a lesser degree except at ownership or management level, and there are much greater hazards resulting from the purposes for which the premises are used, the processes involved and the materials employed. There are risks common to both dwelling house and the factory, which are referred to as 'general' fire or health hazards. Examples include the careless siting of a space heater in proximity to combustible materials, the thoughtless disposal of a lighted cigarette, the accidental spilling of a flammable liquid near a source of ignition or the inadvertent fitting of a fuse with the wrong rating. In the factory however the predominant risks arise from the nature of the work carried out, the materials used and the employees.

11.1.4   It is essential that a building be designed and constructed in a manner that is relevant to the type of fire which might occur within it, and this is naturally dependent upon the purpose for which the building is to be used and the materials it contains. It is necessary to know the relative hazards of different occupancies so that the appropriate measures may be taken to reduce the risk involved and to limit any losses that may eventuate. In order to determine the best type of sprinkler system to install, it is often the practice to classify occupancies in many countries, for example in New Zealand occupancies are classified into one of the following:

(a) extra light hazard

(b) ordinary hazard (subdivided into groups of increasing hazard)

(c) extra high hazard.

Sprinkler systems are considered in more detail in Chapter 13

11.1.5   In addition there are the hazards resulting from the storing of large quantities of certain materials which would result in an occupancy being considered as presenting what is termed an **'abnormal fire risk load'**. It is not merely the flammability of such materials, which is taken into account. Different materials may have the same calorific value per unit weight or volume but can present considerable differences in the overall fire risk, examples of such differences being:

(a) ease of ignition and rate of burning

(b) hindrance of fire fighting, or encouragement of the burning of other materials

(c) a risk of frequent outbreaks of fire due to a process involving the application of heat to a combustible substance

(d) the geometry of the stored materials, whether they are able to be closely stacked with few air spaces in the stacks or whether there is plenty of air spaces because of the shape of the stored material.

11.1.6   Therefore the presence or use of significant quantities of any of the following may create an occupancy with an 'abnormal fire risk load':

(a) explosives

(b) compressed, 'permanent' liquefied and dissolved gases

(c) substances which become dangerous by interaction with:

(i)   water, or

(ii) air.

Substances falling under (i) also become extremely dangerous by interaction with moisture in the air and to that extent can be included in (ii).

(d) all substances with flash point below 48 degrees centigrade

(e) corrosive substances

(f) poisonous substances including those that are carcinogenic, narcotic, toxic and irritants

(g) miscellaneous, such as:

(i)   oxidising agents

(ii) substances liable to spontaneous combustion

(iii) readily combustible solids

(iv) radioactive materials.

11.1.7   Three categories of substances which are likely to create special hazards of fire in buildings are:

(a) substances likely to spread fire by flowing from one part of the building to another, e.g. all oils, fats and waxes, rubber, bitumen, pitch etc.

(b) flammable gases which may escape from a safe enclosure within the building and come into contact with an ignition source, e.g. butane, propane, chlorine dioxide etc.

(c) substances in such form as to be readily ignitable, e.g. wood shavings, paper, pieces of fabric, cotton, rags, fibre, down, flock, kapok and similar materials, flour, coal dusts, metal dusts and other combustible dusts and powders.

It must be remembered that many new processes and materials are being introduced each year and that the hazards associated with these innovations may not be immediately recognised.

11.1.8 Whilst occupational hazard is primarily dependent upon the activities carried on within a building and the nature of the materials employed, it is also affected by the method of storing such materials. This is because the method of storage may:

(a) make fire fighting more difficult

(b) reduce the efficiency of fire fighting appliances

(c) encourage the spread of fire.

Poor methods of stacking and overstocking can lead to gangways and even stairways being obstructed so that access to the seat of a fire may be difficult or virtually impossible. Bulk storage in high stacks can delay the operation of automatic sprinklers and impair the designed distribution of water when they eventually operate. The operation of fire alarm detectors can be prevented or delayed by the close proximity of badly stacked stock that deflects the rising heat.

11.1.9 Certain trades and occupations are classified as **'extra high hazard'** and so require special sprinkler protection, but the classification **'extra high hazard'** is also applied to what are termed **'High Piled Storage Risks'**. These risks are subdivided into categories in ascending order of hazard and reference should be made to the appropriate regulations to ascertain into which category a particular trade or occupation will fall.

Reference should also be made to the same source in order to determine the height above which a particular type of stock is deemed to be **High Piled**.

11.2 HAZARDOUS MATERIALS

11.2.1 Materials

Each of the materials used in the processes of the business should be stored in the quantity and the way best suited to the nature and hazards of the material. Some will not require any special precautions to be taken whilst others will require very careful handling of storage and disposal. It is essential that the hazards of storage and handling of every type of material used by the business should be known not only to the management but also to all of its employees. The physical and chemical properties of each material provide an indication of its risk with regards to:

(a) fire

(a) explosion

(b) toxicity etc.

(c) emission of toxic gas, vapour or dust.

In addition to these properties which are important with respect to the fire risk are the physical and chemical properties of materials that present risk because they are dangerous to the health of anyone exposed to them without the appropriate protective clothing and equipment. This particular data for each of the materials used in the business should be freely available to all employees and to the fire brigade. Many countries have regulations covering the handling storage and movement of hazardous materials and reference to the local regulations will assist in understanding the hazards involved.

Many substances, by virtue of their chemical and physical attributes, are classed as being hazardous. To reduce the hazard in their storage and use the conditions under which these occur need to be considered from the view point of the likelihood of the goods in question causing a fire or increasing its intensity or size.

In assessing the fire hazards of a particular substance, three main factors should be taken into account:

(a) the risk of goods originating a fire

(b) the risk of them spreading a fire already started

(c) their susceptibility to damage.

11.2.2   Originating Risk

(a)   **result of contact**

Spontaneous combustion may result if substances that should be kept separate are allowed to combine and set up chemical action.

For example combustion may be initiated by such as:

(i) Nitric acid (strong i.e. about 40 deg. Beaume) saturating hay

(ii) Potassium permanganate combining with glycerine and sulphuric acid

(iii) Sodium peroxide in contact with moist organic matter

(iv) Oils – some vegetable and animal oils, particularly linseed oil and turpentine, if allowed to soak into cotton waste, hemp, sawdust, lampblack, may initiate combustion

(v) Hydrogen peroxide and other strong oxidizers may ignite if brought into contact with organic or carbon based matter.

(b)   **effect of moisture**

Combustion may be induced by storage of some materials in a damp place, or in one exposed to risk of flooding.

For example:

(i) Quick lime generates intense heat when slaked with water

(ii) Calcium carbide produces acetylene gas when in contact with water

(iii) Potassium peroxide and sodium peroxide liberate oxygen while being dissolved in water

(iv) Bronze powders, powdered magnesium, powdered aluminium, powdered zinc, metallic potassium and metallic sodium all liberate hydrogen when exposed to moisture. The chemical reaction develops considerable heat and combustion is liable to result.

(c)   **proximity to heat or light**

Combustion may be induced by storage of a flammable substance close to a source of heat or light. However it is far more likely to occur if the substance is handled in dangerous proximity to artificial light or heat.

Those substances which give off flammable vapour at low temperatures need to be stored in such a position that the risk of such vapour coming into contact with a flame or source of heat is entirely absent or reduced to reasonable proportions.

Naptha, ether, carbon di-sulphide, acetone, methyl alcohol, petrol and similar volatile liquids are obvious examples of this type of substance. Where handling of the liquid is done by way of drawing off, or filling cans etc., the need for care is greater. Varnish containing volatile solvent, is especially liable to give off flammable vapours when drawing off, mixing, or using. Vapours that are heavier than air may travel quite a long way to some point where ignition takes place. The flame flashes back to the vapour source, and the whole source is set alight often in an explosive manner.

(d)   **precautions disregarded**

Combustion may be initiated by some bad feature of the construction of the building or by disregard of reasonable precautions.

Precautions are commonly disregarded, often because the chemical attributes of substances being stored and handled are not fully appreciated. For example, a stone/concrete floor is incombustible, but in some circumstances it is not as safe as a wooden floor. A workman wearing iron-tipped or heavy nailed boots may strike a spark on a stone floor. If flammable vapour is present, naptha or benzene fumes, or if chlorate has fallen on the floor and become mixed with dust, sawdust etc., a spark may be sufficient to cause ignition, possibly an explosion. Overshoes should be worn under such conditions, particularly where a dry-cleaning process uses naptha.

11.2.3   Fire Extension

(a)   **oxygen carriers**

A fire burns up strongly when a blower or draught-shield is placed over the fireplace, or when bellows are used, because the draught of air is increased. This has the effect of supplying oxygen at a greater rate and so intensifying combustion. The result is the same if the oxygen is supplied in any other way. The term **'oxygen carriers'** refers to those chemical compounds which contain a large proportion of available oxygen, that is held within the compound at ordinary temperatures, but which is released when subjected to heat. In many cases the release takes place at comparatively low temperatures. The liberated oxygen greatly intensifies the conflagration. The following are some of the more important oxygen carriers:

Chlorates	eg: Potassium Chlorate
Nitrates	eg: Crude Nitrate
	Potassium Nitrate
	Chile Saltpetre
Others	eg: Lead Dioxide; Peroxide,
	Red Lead, Chromic Acid.

(b)   **substances that develop exceptional heat**

As a fire progresses the heat developed by burning substances raises the temperature until the ignition point of the general contents is reached or passed. This rise in temperature is influenced to some extent by the calorific value of substances involved, and this can affect the intensity of the fire. Examples of the comparative calorific values are:

Dry Wood	1	
Alcohol	1½ to 2	Increasing
Coal	2	calorific
Charcoal	2¼	value
Butter	2¼ to 2½	
Ether	2½	
Petroleum	2¾	
Mineral Oils	2¼ to 3	
LPG	2½	

(c)   **highly flammable materials**

A fire will be greatly intensified if highly flammable substances are present. A combination of this type of substance with oxygen carriers will create a very intense fire.

The physical condition of the substance does affect the flammability of material, e.g. a given weight of wood in the form of a heavy beam compared to a mass of wood-wool. The wood-wool is very much more flammable than the beam. Those substances that have a low ignition point are specially flammable, and the following involve great risk of intensification of a fire:

Guncotton	Ethyl Alcohol
Celluloid	Methylated Spirits
Alcohols	Acetone
LPG	Petrol
Naptha	Ether

and substances which use highly flammable spirits as a solvent.

(d)   **flammability**

Not all mixtures of a flammable gas or vapour with air will burn, and the speed of burning varies with the relative amounts of fuel and air. If the fastest burning mixture is diluted either with air or fuel, a slower burning mixture results. Ultimately, mixtures containing only a small proportion of fuel or of air are reached, which will only just burn. These concentrations are known as the lower and upper flammability limits respectively. The range of mixtures of gas and air at normal atmospheric temperatures and pressures are shown in *Figure 11.1*. The explosive limits for these gases would fall within the ranges shown.

Figure 11.1

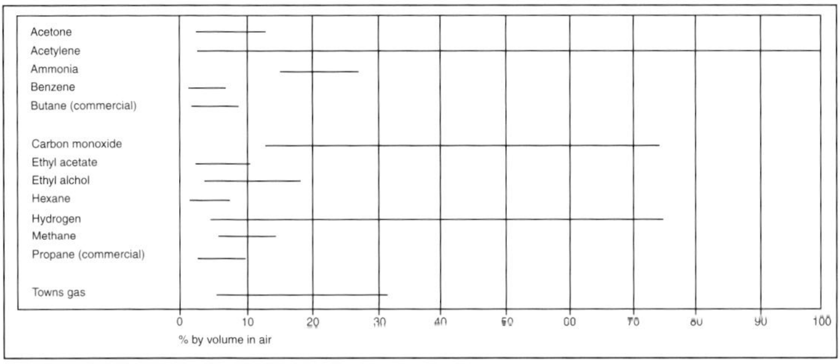

Atmospheric Temperatures and Pressures

Most vapours and gases, with the exception of ammonia and carbon monoxide, have a lower flammability limit where the mixture involves less than 6 per cent of the fuel. They therefore readily form flammable mixtures when only small quantities are released in air.

(e)   **flammable liquids and liquid fuel**

Flammable liquids are widely used in industry today in a variety of processes and for a number of different purposes. The danger associated with this type of substance arises from their ability to form a flammable or even an explosive mixture with air or oxygen. Containers being damaged or overturned and their flammable contents escaping may spread the fire zone. The storage of flammable spirits, alcohol, acetone, benzene, petrol, naptha, tar, varnishes, turps and oils in general present an exposure to this risk. If a fire has broken out, and as a result of the fire, tanks are damaged and a large volume of oil or spirit escapes and becomes ignited, the fire zone will be extended very rapidly to wherever the liquid may flow, possibly down from one floor to another. Flammable vapours are always associated with flammable liquid because, when a liquid appears to be burning, it is in fact the vapour that is doing so. Wherever flammable liquids are used or stored precautions must be taken on the assumption that vapours will be present. Storage in sealed metal drums to prevent vaporisation is usually desirable. Many flammable gases and vapours are toxic and health regulations usually do not permit concentrations that approach the lower danger limits. Removal of any possible source of ignition is another necessary precaution.

(f)   **liquid fuel**

This is a mineral oil with a flash point of at least 65 degrees centigrade, although sometimes it may have a flash point as high as 121 degrees centigrade. The temperature at which vapour is given off sufficiently freely to maintain combustion is usually about 27 degrees above the flash point. It is burnt in the furnace in the form of a fine spray mixed with air; being 'atomised'. The oil is warmed before it is injected, usually electrically. Hazards may arise through accumulations of vapour in the furnace or flue following accidental extinguishment of the burner or through lighting up with closed dampers. The vapour may be ignited by, or an explosion caused by a hot surface in the combustion chamber or by an attempt to re-light the furnace by hand. This should never be done without first allowing time for the combustion chamber and flue to become clear of vapour, or cleaning them by injecting steam or air. Oil-fired furnaces are sometimes lit by hand, but oil-fired hot water boilers for central heating are usually thermostatically controlled and fitted with automatic electrical ignition. A control that automatically shuts off the fuel supply as soon as the flame is extinguished is a partial safeguard against explosion. The chief hazards lie in the storage of the oil. (See 11.3)

(g)   **flammable solids of low melting point**

A similar hazard exists in the case of flammable solids that melt readily and form a liquid. The risk with tallow, butter, greases and wax is comparable to that of oils. Sulphur and resin are similarly liable to form a molten stream that spreads the fire zone in its passage. In the case of liquids and fusible solids that are flammable, the storage conditions should provide against this particular risk of the fire zone being extended by burning liquid flowing from point to point, or from floor to floor.

11.2.4 Susceptibility to Damage

If plant, material or other goods are easily damaged by smoke or water, a heavy loss may result from even a small fire in a building in which they are stored, e.g. tobacco, meat, fish etc. In addition, some forms of plant may also be easily damaged by smoke even in small quantities e.g. computers, electronic circuitry.

11.3 THE STORAGE OF MATERIALS

11.3.1 Storage of the many types of materials that may be found in today's commercial and industrial premises is an extremely important part of the organisation's operations. Not only from the point of view of ensuring that sufficient quantities are available for production to continue but also that loss is prevented or minimised. Good housekeeping is an essential part of ensuring that the storage of materials is properly controlled. It is also essential that full information about the up to date state of all of the different types of materials stored on each site is made available to the employees.

(a) **flammable materials**

Flammable materials should be stored under carefully controlled conditions which will vary in detail from material to material but should generally be stored in places which:

(i) are cool enough to prevent accidental ignition in the event that flammable vapours mix with air

(ii) have adequate ventilation, so that normal leakage of vapours from containers will be diluted enough to prevent a spark from igniting them

(iii) are located well away from areas of fire hazards

(iv) are kept well apart from powerful oxidising agents, materials susceptible to spontaneous heating or materials which react with air or moisture to generate heat

(v) have ample fire fighting equipment readily available

(vi) have the storage area posted with 'no smoking' signs

(vii) do not have filament heaters or other sources of ignition anywhere near the storage area

(viii)   have all electrical equipment grounded. This equipment should be periodically inspected

(ix) should be equipped with automatic smoke or fire detection equipment

(x) enable the quantity of flammable liquids in the process area to be limited to that required for the process. This should be stored in a metal container with a secure lid whilst not in use

(xi) are bunded so that any liquid that may escape from its container is prevented from escaping from the immediate area.

See 11.4 for specific details on storing fuels.

(b)   **oxidising agents**

These substances should be stored:

(i) away from liquids that have a low flash point

(ii) in a fire resisting cool and ventilated storage area

(iii) away from all types of fuel.

(c)   **water sensitive substances**

Substances which react with water, steam or water solutions to produce heat or flammable gases or explosions must be stored in well ventilated, cool, dry areas. Because many of these materials are also flammable, it is essential that no automatic sprinkler be used in a storage area. The building must be waterproof, located on high ground and separated from other storage. Particular attention must be paid to:

(i) light gases collecting in pockets under the roof

(ii) the introduction of sources of ignition

(iii) periodic inspection

(iv) providing automatic detection and alarm of dangerous concentrations of flammable gases.

(d)   **acid and fume sensitive materials**

These substances react with acid and acid fumes to produce heat, hydrogen, flammable gases and explosions, therefore it follows that:

(i) acids should not be stored close to these materials

(ii) the area should be kept cool, well ventilated and periodically inspected

(iii) sources of ignition should be kept away; construction of the storage area should be as for the storage of hydrogen

(iv) because acid and fumes can attack structural alloys producing hydrogen, acid might best be stored in ventilated wood sheds

(v) if metal is used in the construction of the store it should be painted or otherwise rendered immune to attack by acid

(vi) possible hydrogen pockets should be eliminated

(vii) if electric lighting is required in the storage area it should be of an approved type complying with the appropriate national standards.

(e)   **compressed gases**

Cylinders of compressed gases should be stored upright and chained or otherwise securely attached to some substantial support. The storage area should be kept cool and well ventilated out of the direct rays of the sun and away from hot pipes and surfaces. The building should be fire resisting and there should be some means (such as a sprinkler or drencher system) of keeping the cylinders cool in case of fire. Care must be taken to prevent damage to cylinders in handling, particularly the valves that must not only be operated carefully but also kept in good condition.

(f)   **toxic substances including those that are carcinogenic, narcotic, irritant, or harmful to human beings**

Materials that are toxic should be stored in a cool well ventilated place, well away from areas of fire hazard. Incompatible materials should be isolated from each other. In addition handling procedures should be strictly adhered to and protective clothing worn whenever the materials are being handled.

(g)   **corrosive material**

Corrosive Materials can often breach their container and get into the atmosphere of the area in which they are being stored. Some are volatile, others react violently with moisture whilst others are toxic:

(i) such materials should be kept cool

(ii) there should be sufficient ventilation to prevent accumulation of fumes, there also should be regular inspection of the containers and of the general area

(iii) containers of corrosive materials should be carefully handled, kept closed and labelled

(iv) all exposed metal in the vicinity of such storage should be coated with a suitable protective surface and should be regularly checked for weakening by corrosion

(v) corrosive materials should be isolated from materials (such as cyanides, sulphides etc.) reaction with which can produce highly toxic fumes.

If a leaking container is discovered put on protective clothing, block or rope off all contaminated areas and post with DANGER signs and report the following information:

(i) what is leaking?

(ii) where the leaking container is now located?

(iii) whether anything or anybody has been contaminated by the spilled material?

Be sure that a responsible person properly guards the affected area until necessary instructions are received.

Before you open a container, or handle a toxic or corrosive material in any way, you should put on complete protective clothing. To open drums, set the drum with the bung end under a ventilating hood.

(h)   **spontaneous ignition**

Good housekeeping is the key safeguard against spontaneous ignition of stored materials. Avoid the build-up of rags and other debris contaminated with vegetable and animal oils. Ducts, ovens and spray booths should be cleaned out regularly to avoid the build-up of deposits. Certain products that have undergone a heated drying process should be spread out to allow sufficient cooling off before being stored in tight, solid piles.

(i)   **radioactive substances**

Radioactive substances must be handled with care at all times and they must be stored in a manner that is appropriate to their level of radioactivity . Usually such substances need to be stored separately from other substances and from each other in a cool dry area that can be secured. As with other substances that can be injurious to health it is essential that the fire brigade and other emergency services are made aware of their location on a site so that the necessary protective measures will be taken in the event of an emergency.

11.3.2 the dangerous goods store

Where there is any quantity of dangerous goods it is desirable, and in many cases necessary by Law, to have a Dangerous Goods Store. Dangerous Goods Stores should be located as far away as possible from other buildings and plant in order to reduce the effects of any fire and/or explosion. Dangerous Goods Stores usually are built with a light roof and strong or heavy walls. This allows any explosion to vent out through the roof, thus keeping any consequent damage to a minimum. In addition, if the store is used to store liquids the building should be bunded so that any spilt liquid is contained in the immediate area from which it may then be recovered. Where separation by distance is impractical the next best location is in a compartment against an outside wall. The separating wall(s) should be sufficiently strong to withstand an explosion, whilst one side of the compartment can be of light construction so that any explosion or escape of chemicals may vent directly to the outside.

11.4   FUEL STORAGE

11.4.1   In order to keep the fire hazard of fuels to a minimum it is clearly desirable to have only small quantities of fuel in the immediate vicinity of anything burning, such as a stove or furnace. For economical operation, however, many organisations purchase fuel in large quantities and have it delivered and stored as near as possible to where it is to be used. It is, therefore, necessary to reach a reasonable compromise.

11.4.2   Solid Fuels

Black coal, brown coal briquettes and wood are the solid fuels in common use. All may under certain conditions spontaneously combust. Although they are usually used in their solid form they may be ground into powder for use in certain kinds of modern boiler. In this form there is a risk of explosion as well as of spontaneous combustion. Coal, particularly black coal in large stacks, is prone to over-heating and spontaneous combustion and it is recommended that:

(a) it be stored on clean, firm ground away from sources of heat such as the boiler-house wall

(b) the quantity in any stack should be under 200 tonnes

(c) the height of the stack should not exceed two to three metres

(d) ventilation should be adequate or completely suppressed.

With briquettes the worst fire hazard is the flammable dust produced that needs no more than a spark to ignite it. Wood is not subject to overheating but should be kept clear of any source of heat.

11.4.3 Liquid Fuels

(a)   although these have a high flash point and do not give off flammable vapour at ordinary temperatures, liquid fuels will give off vapour freely during a fire, when the presence of burning oil renders extinguishment difficult and intensifies and spreads the fire. It is normal for several thousands of litres (several tonnes) of fuel to be stored even in a medium-sized installation. If it is stored outside the buildings, it may flow in during a fire or escape from a fractured pipe, unless adequate precautions are taken. The bulk supply of oil should be stored outside the building, above ground, and a catchpit or bund of greater capacity than the tank should be provided. It should be stored in accordance with the appropriate Dangerous Goods Regulations.

If the storage tank must be inside a building, it should be in a fireproof chamber with a fireproof door and a high sill to the doorway to form a catchpit. The capacity of the catchpit should be greater than that of the tank, so that it will retain all the oil that may escape from the tank. The tank chamber should be against an outer wall and should be located at the lowest possible level in the building. A vent pipe to the open air should be fitted to the top of each tank.

Feeding the oil from the tank to the burner by gravity feed is hazardous since, in the event of leakage, oil may flow unchecked into the grate and spread a fire. The feed pipe from the tank should preferably be from the top of the tank and should be fitted with an anti-siphon valve, oil being drawn from the tank by a pump. With such an arrangement, the surplus oil in the pipe will flow back into the storage tank when the pump ceases to operate. A fire valve should be fitted to cut off the flow of oil at least two metres from the burner. The sensitive element of such a valve should be mounted above the oil inlet to the combustion chamber.

(b)   LPG (Liquified Petroleum Gas) is being used in industry for heating and providing energy for certain types of processes, such as cutting steel where it is used with oxygen. It is supplied either by tanker refilling a fixed tank or as cylinders of gas which are filled by firms specialising in their supply and delivery to the premises, the empty cylinders then being removed. There is a risk of explosion of the tank and the cylinders and a danger of boiling liquid evaporating vapour explosion (BLEVE) or a vapour cloud explosion (VCE) occurring which can be very destructive. The gas is a butane mixture and is usually stored in liquid form in small cylinders at a pressure of about 150 kPa. On release of the pressure the liquid changes to a gas and enters the supply pipe of the apparatus in this form.

In its pure state, butane has no smell and chemicals are added to give it a distinctive smell for the purpose of detecting leaks. The gas is very penetrating and metal tubing is preferable. Butane is a petroleum gas and the hazards are similar to those of other petroleum gases used in industry, such as propane. An additional property possessed by both butane and LPG is that they are both heavier than air and can accumulate in hollows should there be a leak. Cylinders should be stored in the open, or at least with low level ventilation if stored in a building. Both gases are extremely flammable.

There is an increasing demand for LPG as a fuel for motor vehicles and for bottled gas as a fuel for use in caravans, small boats and camping. LPG has been the cause of many fires and explosions when used in this particular way which have resulted from the build up of gas from undetected leaks.

(c)   CNG (Compressed Natural Gas) is another fuel like LPG that is used as a fuel for industrial premises and motor vehicles and as fuel for both heating and lighting in the home, caravans and boats. It is lighter than air and therefore rises quickly when it escapes, but like LPG it is extremely inflammable and can cause an explosion.

11.4.4   Gaseous Fuels

Reticulated gas is not normally a problem for the consumer because it can be piped to where it is used. It is, however, flammable and will in certain situations form highly explosive mixtures with air. If such a mixture is ignited a considerable amount of damage will occur. For 'bottled' gas such as those mentioned above and acetylene when supplied in cylinders the following should be noted:

(a) storage areas should, wherever possible be well clear of buildings

(b) a protective covering should be provided for the storage area

(c) adequate ventilation should be provided

(d) storage areas should be kept free from all combustible materials. No other materials should be stored in the cylinder enclosures.

(e) cylinders should always stand upright and be secured

(f) for security and ventilation purposes a wire mesh fence should surround the storage area

(g) notices prohibiting smoking and naked lights as well as notices describing the colour code for cylinder contents should be prominently displayed.

If a detached storage area is not available and the storage area forms part of a building used for another purpose, the following should apply:

(a) position the store against an outside wall

(b) segregate the store from the rest of the building by walls having a fire resistance of at least two hours and which are strong enough to withstand any explosion

(c) the external wall should preferably be of light construction to vent explosions outwards

(d) doors should only be provided in external walls

(e) ventilate the area at both high and low levels. If satisfactory natural ventilation cannot be provided, then mechanical ventilation should be installed.

11.4.5   It will be realised that escaping flammable gas or liquid may supply additional fuel to a fire and that escaping air from a compressed air system, air delivered by an air conditioning system which continues to operate, or oxygen from a fractured oxygen line, may assist and accelerate combustion; therefore, it is suggested that:

(a) pipes, fittings and jointing materials for flammable liquid, flammable gas and compressed air should not be made from materials such as plastics and aluminium which are easily melted or damaged by fire

(b) fuel supplies should not be routed through hazardous areas such as boiler rooms and the pipe runs should be as short as possible

(c) valves in fuel lines should be conveniently sited so that supplies can be cut off in emergencies. Valves should generally be provided in the following positions:

(i) at the bulk supply point

(ii) at the point of entry into each building

(iii) at the beginning of each branch line from a main supply line

(iv) near each item of plant supplied by the service;

(d) automatic fire valves are normally recommended for oil fired furnaces and other oil burning equipment.

11.5   THE STORAGE, MOVEMENT AND USE OF MATERIALS

11.5.1   Many countries have now enacted legislation or regulations covering the use and storage of hazardous substances. Reference should therefore be made to the legislation and any associated regulations that apply in the country in which the reader is working in order to discover the complete picture as it applies in that country. In most instances full and adequate records are required to be maintained by any organisation that manufactures, stores or uses a wide variety of substances. These records would normally include such details as:

(a) the generally recognised identification of the substance

(b) its composition

(c) the hazards associated with the substance

(d) its physical and chemical properties

(e) its stability and reactivity

(f) conditions necessary for its safe storage and handling

(g) any precautions that need to be taken when handling or using the substance

(h) essential fire fighting measures

(i) the handling of accidental releases or spills and the safe disposal of such

(j) first aid measures

(k) ecological information

(l) precautions to be taken when moving the substance

(m) correct labelling

(n) its location on the site

(o) quantity on site.

11.5.2   The hazards of dangerous substances are increased when they are removed from where they are produced or stored because the safeguards that are in place in both of those situations may not be effective whilst the substances are being moved or used.

11.5.3   Today most countries have legislation or regulations in place that prescribe the manner in which dangerous substances may be transported e.g. moved by road, rail or sea. Here again the reader should refer to the regulations that apply in the countries through which the substance is being transported.

In most instances specific duties are placed on not only the owner of the dangerous substance but also on the operators and drivers of any vehicle and on the owner and captain of any vessel used to carry the substance. These usually include the regular testing and examination of not only the tanks being used but also the vehicle or vessel itself. It makes common sense for the driver of the road vehicle and the captain of the vessel that is carrying a dangerous substance to be fully informed as to the identity and nature of the substance that is being carried. In addition information on the action to be taken in the event of an emergency should also be provided. Furthermore it is usual for the legislation or regulations to lay down specific rules for the labelling and packaging of such materials as well as the labelling of any conveyance in which they are being transported.

11.5.4 Where dangerous substances are being used in a process the chances of an accident occurring are greatly increased and it is therefore essential that:

(a) as far as is possible the employees are kept away from having any direct contact with the substances

(b) all employees are properly trained in:

(i) using the equipment used in the process

(ii) handling any emergencies involving the substance

(iii) recognising possible problems;

(c) all necessary protective equipment and clothing is supplied, is maintained in a good condition and is used

(d) all employees are kept informed about the dangerous substances that are present in the workplace and on the site.

12

LOSS CONTROL – INDUSTRIAL PROCESSES

12.1 INTRODUCTION

12.1.1 The majority of industrial processes involve the use of energy. Energy can take a number of different forms such as heat, pressure and involve various types of motive power such as steam and electricity. As was seen earlier, energy plays a major part in many losses particularly those that involve injury or are the result of fire or explosion. It follows therefore that most of the risk reduction and loss control measures are concerned with ensuring that energy is controlled and is kept within the designed parameters of the system in which it is being used.

12.1.2 Chemical Reaction Control

A basic safeguard in chemical processing is knowledge and understanding of the hazard characteristics of the chemicals being handled. Equipment should be properly designed to contain and confine chemicals. Adequate instrumentation and operating controls should be provided so that the typical process variables of temperature, pressure, flow and liquid level can be monitored. Safety controls to prevent or minimise sudden changes in these variables should be fitted and used. Operator training is still vital despite widespread automation. Familiarise operators with normal conditions as well as with what should be done if abnormal conditions develop. Finally, maintenance of equipment including the process equipment itself, as well as the operating and safety controls, is important.

12.2 SOURCES OF MOTIVE POWER

12.2.1 Whilst electricity, and to a lesser extent gas, diesel and petrol are used to power industrial machinery, considerable use is still made of steam. Steam is usually generated in a boiler at a pressure that is greater than normal atmospheric pressure. As a consequence, the boiler together with any associated steam receivers and containers, may not only start a fire but also may explode.

12.2.2   A pressure vessel is a closed vessel that operates at a pressure that is greater than normal atmospheric pressure. Steam boilers, steam receivers and steam containers are classed as pressure vessels as are air receivers that involve the use of compressed air. Because the failure of such vessels can lead to serious injury and extensive damage, pressure vessels are subject to extensive statutory regulations in most countries covering such matters as testing, operating and maintenance.

12.2.3   Many countries have enacted legislation or regulations governing the use, testing and maintenance of all types of pressure vessel, boiler etc and reference should be made to these in order to ascertain the requirements that apply in a particular country.

12.2.4   Boilers

(a)   **vertical boilers**

These basically comprise a metal cylinder containing water surrounding the combustion chamber with the hearth at the base and a vertical flue through which heat and flames pass up into a chimney.

These are used for driving small engines or for heating tanks or presses. They are not set in brickwork and so must be lagged to prevent loss of heat. However note that there may be a health problem associated asbestos that may have been used in the lagging of older boilers. Water tubes may be arranged across the flue so as to increase the rate of heat transfer.

(b)   **horizontal boilers**

These are generally larger than vertical boilers and are often set in brickwork, leaving only the top to be lagged. The firing place is at one end and heat and flames pass through a horizontal flue or flues to a brick chimney. The flues or fire tubes are surrounded by water or, as in the water tube boiler, the water is contained in a series of steel tubes that pass over and through the combustion chamber. The water for feeding the boiler is sometimes pre-heated by leading it through pipes situated between the boiler and the chimney. This device is known as an Economiser.

(c)   **boiler fittings**

The fire hazards of boilers and boiler-houses arise from combustible material being situated too near such an intense heat source as the boiler, its firing place or its flue. Examples of such combustible material include timbers in the boiler-house roof or nearby buildings, fuel or waste materials, or goods brought in to dry. There is also the hazard of explosion of the boiler. This may occur if the steam should accumulate at such a high pressure that the shell of the boiler, or some other part, bursts. There should be an arrangement that permits the excess pressure of steam to be relieved automatically by fitting one or more safety valves through which steam can blow off by overcoming the opposition of the valve loading to prevent this from occurring. All steam boilers, receivers and containers are subject to corrosion that can not only lead to boiler failure but also explosion. In addition, steam boilers can overheat and explode as a result of the water level in the boiler falling below a safe level. Regular inspection and testing by a qualified engineer is, therefore, essential.

(d)   **location and precautions**

(i)   The boiler should be sited in a separate building, which is preferably of fire resistant construction. The next best arrangement is a fireproof compartment within the building, against an external wall, with a doorway to the open only. If an opening in to the building is unavoidable, it should be protected by a fire door. Sometimes in old buildings the boiler is in a timber-partitioned compartment, a very hazardous arrangement, or situated in the factory without partitioning of any kind. In such circumstances any small outbreak of fire may quickly involve the whole building whereas, if the boiler is in a fire resistant compartment, little damage might result from such an outbreak.

(ii)   Steam boilers as well as steam receivers and containers and other types of pressure vessels are subject to statutory regulations in most countries which normally provide for not only regular inspection and testing, but also that they:

- are fitted with a pressure gauge, suitable safety valves and appropriate stop valves

- show both its maximum and safe working pressure

- be fitted with a blow down valve and a high water alarm; in the case of a steam boiler which, if it is not externally fired, should also be fitted with a fusible plug or a low water alarm.

A lack of testing and maintenance of controls and alarms,

inadequate operating methods and a failure to regularly test and check pressure vessels will lead to eventual failure and possibly an explosion.

12.2.5   Internal Combustion Engines

(a)   Internal combustion (i.e. petrol and diesel) engines should be sited in a separate compartment constructed of incombustible material and having a door fitted to every opening. Sand should be provided to soak up oil drips, or a drip tray should be provided and any adjacent woodwork should be lined with sheet metal to prevent splashing with oil. The engine should stand on a concrete floor or base. Exhaust pipes, which may become very hot, should be positioned well clear of all woodwork and should vent into the open air. On no account should an exhaust pipe vent into a chimney because this may allow the accumulation of unburnt gases that will lead to an explosion. Oily rags or wipes should be placed in metal bins and removed and burnt each day. Dirt and rubbish should not be allowed to accumulate around an engine.

(b)   **petrol engines**

An explosive mixture of gaseous fuel and air is drawn into the cylinder and a spark ignites the charge. A very rapid increase in pressure occurs because of the heat energy liberated by the combustion, and this gives motion to the piston. With petrol engines, the low flash point of the fuel makes it essential that the compartment in which the engine is situated should be well ventilated and that no naked lights should be allowed in the vicinity of the compartment. No fuel, apart from that in the tank, should be kept in the building, and the fuel tank should not be filled when the engine is running. The main supplies of fuel should be stored in a properly constructed underground tank outside, or in cans in a locked metal bin in the open. The arrangement whereby the fuel is fed by gravity from a tank above the engine is a poor one because if a pipe should break the contents may escape onto the floor. If such an arrangement is unavoidable the tank should be placed so that the heat or vibration from the engine will not affect it. In addition a stopcock should be fitted near the tank on the feed pipe which should itself be made of metal. A more preferable arrangement is for the fuel tank to be situated as low as possible with the fuel being fed to the carburettor by a pump. In any case, the fuel tank should be as small as practical so as to limit the amount of fuel that it can contain.

(c)   **diesel engines**

This is an oil fuelled engine. The oil (which is far less flammable than petrol) is injected into the air in the cylinders which has been raised to a temperature high enough to ignite and burn the fuel without the assistance of a sparking apparatus. Many of the precautions outlined above for petrol engines, however, still apply to diesel powered engines.

12.2.6   Electric Power

(a)   In most situations electricity is considered to be the safest form of power from the standpoint of fire hazard. The main advantage is that by using one motor to each machine or small group of machines, the hazards of power transmission are reduced.

(b)   **generators or dynamos**

Current is usually taken from the public supply, but may be generated on the premises. In a generator, mechanical energy is converted into electrical energy. An electric motor converts electrical energy into mechanical energy. The hazards of generators themselves are similar to those of the motors. A greater hazard with generators is the engine used to drive the generator. Usually a steam or internal combustion engine is used and the appropriate precautions should be taken.

Generating plant should be sited in a separate compartment away from combustible materials and flammable dusts or vapours. The main switchboard should be in a dry, well ventilated situation, away from combustible material, and no rubbish should be allowed to accumulate in the vicinity. Small generating plants, often driven by petrol/diesel engines, are frequently used to provide electric lighting as well as power to remote locations. They are often installed in unsuitable situations, and hazards may arise from lack of skilled attention.

(c)   **special precautions in hazardous situations**

Electrical machinery needs to be designed for the area in which it is to be used e.g. motors may need to be flameproof or damp-proof. Accordingly, danger sometimes arises when firms take over premises that were designed for purposes other than those for which they are now being used. Under normal circumstances little difficulty would be experienced in substituting the correct equipment for the special circumstances. However, in abnormal times it frequently happens that firms cannot obtain delivery of such equipment for many months, and in the interim the existing equipment, which may be unsuitable, may continue to be used. Thus, even though an installation may have been erected in complete conformity with the regulations, fire risk will often be increased by a subsequent failure to modify the arrangements when new hazardous processes are introduced.

12.3   ELECTRIC PROCESS HEATERS

12.3.1   Electrical immersion heaters are employed in some industries to heat flammable liquids such as oil or bitumen. In order to deal with large quantities of liquid, several heaters may be required at different levels in the tank and there is a danger that an explosion may occur if the liquid level falls below that of the uppermost heater. The exposed heater may ignite the flammable vapour/air mixture in its immediate vicinity.

12.3.2   In many industrial processes combustible materials are carried on conveyors exposed to infra-red heating units, and it is necessary to provide electrical interlocking between the conveyor drive and the heaters, so that the latter are switched off automatically if the conveyor should stop for any reason. The heaters themselves should be mounted so that little or no residue from the process can be deposited upon them.

12.4   FRICTION

12.4.1   When a body moves over another body, its motion is opposed by a resistance along the surface of contact of the two bodies. This resisting force is called friction. In other words, friction is the opposition to motion between the surfaces of two bodies. One of the by-products of friction is heat. The higher the speed of a particular machine the greater the friction and therefore the heat generated, but in comparing different types of machine the size of the surface over which the rubbing occurs, and the type of work being done, must also be considered. For example although a sewing machine works at a very high speed the work is very light and the friction negligible compared with a disintegrator, which may work at a slower speed but has far greater stresses imposed on it.

12.4.2   With any group of machines, shafting and gearing, and indeed all of the mechanical plant in a factory, frictional losses will occur. It is the engineer's concern to reduce these losses to a minimum, and so keep efficiency as high as possible, with the least possible waste of power. The power expended in overcoming friction is converted to heat. Through wear or lack of lubrication, especially if this should occur at one particular spot, the heat produced from the power expended in overcoming excessive friction might become very intense. If such heat is not dissipated it may raise the temperature of adjacent material, such as wood, to its ignition point and so cause a fire. An overheated bearing would cause such local excess heating, and this is a common cause of fire. (Bearings are the supports of moving parts). In addition, the parts involved may fracture or break leading to considerable damage and spoilage.

12.4.3 A disintegrator is a high-speed grinding machine, usually driven by direct coupling with an electric motor. The material to be ground is fed into the top of a drum, which is stationary; it is reduced by a grinding or pulverising by force of percussion, and the powdered product falls out of the bottom of the drum. If a very hard foreign body is accidentally introduced into the disintegrator, such as a nail or other piece of 'tramp iron', considerable damage may be caused. The revolving parts will try to grind this foreign material, together with the normal material, but in doing so an excessive quantity of power has to be used because of the abnormal hardness of the foreign material. The hardness of the foreign material causes excessive friction and thus, together with all the additional power, which is used by the machine in trying to grind the hard body, is transformed into heat. This heat may be sufficient with or without sparking, to cause an explosion and perhaps also a fire if the material being ground is flammable, such as corn, plastic, aluminium or cork. Even when working normally disintegrators and grinders give off heat because of the work being done against friction.

12.4.4 Friction should be controlled in the case of:

(a)   **processes that involve friction**

The key to preventing friction is adequate lubrication and maintenance. Be sure to use the proper lubricant at an adequate frequency. Check alignment of machinery components. Operators can minimise the possibility of misalignment problems by being aware of unusual sounds or other signs of faulty operation.

(b)   **processes that produce mechanical sparks**

Where processes involve quantities of combustible dusts, powders, vapours and gases, the equipment should be designed and maintained to avoid the spark-generating impact of steel parts. In-process materials should be inspected or otherwise screened, such as by magnetic separators, to remove metallic debris before they enter the process. Hand tools made of wood, plastic or special alloy metal tools should be used for very highly hazardous operations.

12.5   HEAT TREATMENT

12.5.1   In quantity production extensive use is made of continuous processes for dipping and drying materials on a conveyor system. This is very hazardous as the dip tank and oven hazards tend to be in close proximity to each other. Mechanical ventilation is a necessary safeguard as well as automatic extinguishing devices to protect the dip tank. Competent operators are needed to ensure that the equipment is operated at its proper temperature levels and to monitor temperature indicators (gauges and recording charts). Temperature controls, whether manual or automatic, must be reliable and high temperature alarms and interlocks that will shut down the equipment if necessary should be provided. Plating operations should be filled with high limit and low-liquid-level interlocks to shut off the immersion heaters if the plating solution evaporates.

12.5.2   Salt Baths

Heat treatment baths contain either molten nitrates or cyanides at temperatures from 150 degrees centigrade to 550 degrees centigrade. The salts are non-combustible but leaking, overflowing or splashed hot salts can ignite combustible materials. Nitrates are strong oxidising agents and in the molten state they will react violently and ignite combustible material producing toxic nitrous fumes. For example, ordinary clothing may catch fire when contaminated with molten nitrate. Cyanides, which are also sometimes used, are extremely toxic. They may be decomposed by acids to form hydrogen cyanide, which is a very poisonous gas. Even a few drops of water, oil, and other liquids cause violent scattering of the molten salts that are so hot that they can cause severe burns.

12.5.3   Installation

Salt and quenching baths should be installed on the ground storey of a building in a section that should be separated from other sections by fire-resisting walls and floors. A typical salt and quenching bath installation is shown in *Figure 12.1.*

Figure 12.1

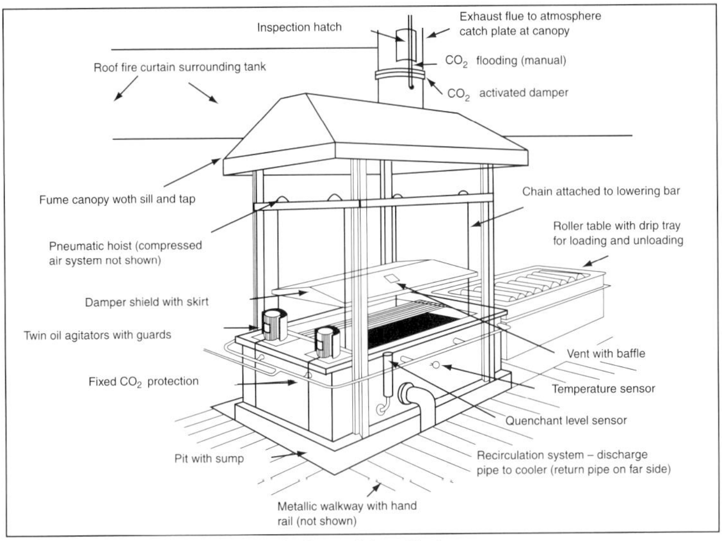

A Quenching Bath

Good ventilation should be provided and maintained. The baths should be placed so that there is no likelihood of water entering them from leaking pipes or dripping condensation. There should be no combustible material in this vicinity. For example, wood should not be used for duckboards, platforms and floors. Each bath should be sited in a catchpit capable of containing all of the liquid in the bath, plus 10 percent. The catchpit should be fitted with a noncombustible cover that is both hinged and counterbalanced or is capable of being slid into position. Quenching tanks should be at lower levels than the salt baths and, unless they are sufficiently far away from the baths, should be protected against the accidental flow of molten salts by curbing and drainage. A roof curtain or deep curtain board to prevent smoke and heat from mushrooming throughout the plant should surround each bath.

12.5.4   Storage of Salts

The salts should be stored in a dry area with a separate

storeroom set aside for each type of salt. The containers should be clearly labelled and any cyanide salts should be kept in sealed metal containers.

12.5.5   Special Atmosphere Furnaces

These are used to improve the quality of metals by exposing them to protective gases, many of which are combustible, during the heat treatment process. In most cases the gas is used to prevent oxidation of the metal during heat, but gas may be used for such things as preventing the removal or addition of carbon. Explosion risks occur when the plant is being started up as, during this process the air is being replaced by flammable gas, and when the plant is being shut down when the gases are being replaced with air. The furnace itself should be fitted with explosion flaps and have a pilot flame (to burn off surplus gas) together with a flame failure alarm. Facilities should be provided to purge the furnace with inert gas when starting and stopping the plant. The gas generator room or storage area for gas cylinders should be in a detached building as far away from the main plant as possible. Adequate ventilation must be provided and the roof and one wall should be constructed of light materials to allow an explosion to vent. All electrical installations must be explosion-proof.

12.5.6   Hardening Processes Using Oil

Quenching systems vary widely in size and arrangement, according to the type of workload, rate of production and various other technical factors. In addition to the tank itself, equipment will normally consist of agitators, filters, pumps to circulate the oil, heating and cooling systems etc. Quenching tanks and associated plant should only be located on the ground floor of the building and they should be segregated from surrounding areas by fire walls with a minimum fire resistance of 2 hours. The quench tanks should be placed so that the risk of fire spreading to adjacent equipment such as electric motors, cables and instruments is reduced to the minimum. Overheating must be prevented and an automatic alarm system should be incorporated which will give a warning when the oil temperature is about 20 degrees centigrade below its flash point.

12.6   DRYING

12.6.1   Many processes of manufacture necessitate the drying of articles produced or of materials used, and many different methods of drying are employed, all of which have the same intention – that of evaporating any excess moisture from the materials or articles. Most methods use a flow of air, the hotter the air the greater its absorbent powers, but when saturation point of the flow of air is reached a fresh supply of air is required to continue drying.

12.6.2 Drying without the aid of outside factors and relying upon normal elements of sunlight and air circulation is quite satisfactory for certain materials e.g. timber stacked in open air. If artificial means of drying are used it is customary to have a special drying compartment e.g. kiln.

The degree of hazard involved depends on:

(a) the combustibility of the articles or materials being dried

(b) the construction of the drying compartment

(c) the heating process used.

12.6.3 The drying compartment should be an entirely separate section of any factory and it should be built of materials that withstand the effects of prolonged exposure to fire. Wood or fibreboard must never be used in ovens, even those that are steam heated. All timber and other combustible material used in the construction of floors, racks etc. of the drying compartment will be dried out by the drying process and will become easy to ignite. Woodwork near to the drying compartment may be similarly affected. To guard against this hazard all heated pipes passing into or from the drying compartment should be installed so that they have plenty of clearance from all combustible materials.

12.6.4 The heating of drying rooms is carried out in many ways. The least hazardous method being by low pressure hot water in which the piping is fitted into the compartment and low pressure steam systems in which steam coils are placed outside the compartment and air is blown over the coils into the compartment by fans. This latter system requires fans to circulate the air in order to remove the saturated air. As these fans need to operate at high speed, the likelihood of over-heated bearings is always present.

Where higher temperatures are required in the drying compartment, high pressure hot water or steam pipes, gas or oil-fired burners or electrical resistance heaters may be used. It is hazardous to have sources of heat such as these in the drying compartment and the higher the temperature, the greater the hazard. Any materials in the compartment should be kept well clear of the source of heat.

12.6.5   Drying Ovens

Drying ovens are extensively used and these again should be installed in an isolated position in the building. For economic operation, and to prevent loss of heat and for reasons of safety, they should be built of insulating material. Brick ovens are used for very high temperatures but they have the disadvantage that considerable heat is required to raise the temperature of the oven to its operating level. Drying ovens are required to dry, set and bake on to any article a variety of coatings such as paint, lacquer or varnish. Drying ovens are also used to bake insulating compounds and varnish, etc. on to armatures and coils. The use of high temperatures in ovens treating goods coated with flammable material gives rise to serious hazard. Ventilation is, therefore, necessary to supply fresh air for any burners and to remove the products of combustion and any flammable vapours. Drying ovens may be direct-heated, semi-indirect-heated and indirect-heated and they are classified according to the method of heating and not the fuel used. Coal or coke, oil, gas, steam and electricity are all used in each of the methods.

Coal-fired or oil-fired ovens should have the combustion chamber cut off from the baking chamber, and the fuel should be stored sufficiently far away from the oven so that radiated heat will not cause fires.

Gas should not be used in direct firing of the oven, indirect firing of the oven is preferred so that any drips from materials in the oven cannot fall on the superheated surfaces in the oven. The gas flame and pilot light should be placed well away from the dip-tank and other sources of dangerous vapour. The leakage of gas into the oven chamber may cause a serious explosion.

Electrically heated ovens are extensively used because of their ease of operation and cleanliness, though where the heat requirements are large and constant the expense may become an important factor. Electric resistance heating units may be a constant source of danger as they are exposed to flammable vapours. Loose or broken contacts may cause high temperature arcs to occur. Heating units should be located so that they will not be dripped upon. Whatever the method of heating is used, adequate ventilation and explosion vents should always be provided to cope with the danger from flammable vapours in the oven.

The intensity of any explosion is in proportion to the size of the oven.

12.7   OTHER PROCESSES INVOLVING HEAT

12.7.1   Processes Involving Molten Materials

The refractory linings of furnaces used for molten materials should be inspected regularly by visual means as well as by infrared instrumentation (thermography). Combustible construction materials and the storage of combustible materials near molten material processes should be avoided. Position electric cables, cooling water lines, hydraulic oil lines, machinery and control panels so as to avoid exposure to spills. The accumulation of water should be avoided wherever molten metal is being poured. Any water or moisture in ore and scrap metal should be removed before it is charged into a melting furnace. Cooling water lines should include accessible valves to allow the water flow to be stopped in the event of a line rupturing or leaking.

12.7.2   Processes Involving the use of Open Flames

Portable open-flame equipment should be avoided if at all practical, as this type of equipment is more prone to cause fires than other types of heating processes. Alternative procedures should be considered for equipment such as the blow-torches used to thaw out frozen water lines, bunsen burners in laboratories, blow-torches used to heat roofing materials. If the use of such equipment is unavoidable close supervision is essential. Fuel burners should be properly designed, installed, operated and maintained. Combustion controls, combustion safeguards and various interlocks are needed to ensure that an adequate supply of combustion air is available, that unburned fuel vapours and products of combustion do not accumulate and that pilot flames are on. Operators should be properly trained in lighting, relighting and shutdown procedures for such equipment. Adequate safety (exhaust) ventilation should be provided at processes where flammable vapours are given off.

12.7.3   Exposure to Hot Surfaces

The basic safeguard is to avoid the contact of a combustible material with any hot surfaces. Besides having adequate clearance, the circulation of air and insulation are important in most cases. Piping that contains flammable liquid should be well maintained with clearly marked shut-off valves and remote control switches to shut down any pumps installed. On large fixed equipment automatic temperature controls and high temperature alarms help prevent overheating.

12.7.4 Combustion Spark Safeguards

Lift trucks powered by gasoline or diesel engines should not be used where flammable vapours, flammable gases or air-borne combustible dusts are normally found. Spark arresters should be fitted to stacks and chimneys from which sparks and embers are frequently emitted. Incinerators and solid-fuel-fired equipment should be well designed and maintained to prevent the escape of combustion sparks and embers.

12.8 PAINT SPRAYING

12.8.1 Paint

Paint may be applied by brush, by hand, by dipping in a bath of paint or by spraying. Paint in general is a mixture of various substances which may include pigments, plasticisers, drying oils, solvents, thinners, nitro cellulose, natural or artificial resins. Many of the pigments used are powerful oxidising agents and may become involved in a fire of extreme severity. Others are of inorganic materials and do not present fire hazards. Plasticisers may be castor oil or similar high boiling esters with high flash points. Their purpose is to keep the paint finish flexible. Solvents are those liquids that dissolve the nitro-cellulose. Thinners are liquids that can be added to the solution forming the base of the paint without degrading it. Both thinners and solvents are flammable liquids with low flash points and are very hazardous. One obvious precaution is to ensure that only sufficient paint for the job in hand is present in the process area at any one time. The bulk storage of paint should be located in a Dangerous Goods Store. Many of the substances used in paints today are also toxic and must be stored and used with extreme care. It is essential with such paint that the correct equipment, protective clothing and procedures are used at all times.

12.8.2 Spraying

A spraying system involves feeding a thin stream of paint from an external reservoir through a tube to a spray gun where it is joined by a stream of compressed air. Alternatively, the paint may be fed from a small container on the gun itself. The pressure atomises the stream of paint, breaking it up into a cloud of fine particles that can be directed on the articles that are being painted. Whilst large articles are treated in a spraying compartment or room, small articles are sprayed in booths which resemble small cabinets that have an open front which are set at a convenient height for working. The process is a hazardous one for three reasons:

(a) the vapours given off during drying combine with the air to form explosive mixtures. These vapours are also given off during the spraying, thus adding to the hazard.

(b) the solid residues of cellulose paint are very highly flammable and are easily ignited even by a frictional spark from a steel-scraping tool during cleaning. Although the spray is directional, thick layers of deposit accumulate on the sides of the booth, on the fan blades and inside extraction ducts. These residues are spontaneously combustible if they come into contact with vegetable oil (for example, if the booth is used first for cellulose and later for linseed oil paints). They may also ignite if allowed to accumulate on a warm surface. The solid residues of the synthetic paints are not however hazardous in this way.

(c) as mentioned earlier, some paints contain toxic and carcinogenic substances, and by converting the paint into a spray it can be absorbed more easily by the operator if he or she is not wearing the correct protection.

Precautions comprise the avoidance of means of ignition and the removal of flammable vapours, plus adequate cleaning to alleviate the hazards of the flammable residues. Regulations exist which should be complied with rigidly. Also, where the paint contains toxic or carcinogenic materials, protective clothing and equipment should be used. Many substances are applied today in the form of spray, including ordinary oil paint, varnishes and water stains. The hazards vary and the essential factor to be considered being the flash points of the solvents and thinners. However, any paint is a little more hazardous in the form of a fine spray with air than it is in its normal liquid form.

12.9   WELDING

12.9.1   Welding is a process of uniting metals by fusing them together while they are locally in a plastic condition. To bring about this condition a very high temperature (about 4000 degrees centigrade) is necessary, and this is obtained either by an oxy-acetylene or similar mixture flame or an electric welding plant. Both welding and cutting requires proper preparation and supervision before, during and after work.

The two forms of welding, gas and electric arc, each have some hazards that are peculiar to the particular form, but fire, explosion and burns as well as toxic fumes and gases are hazards common to both forms. Ultra violet radiation is also another hazard. In the case of gas welding the gases used are highly flammable and in the case of acetylene the mixture can be explosive. In addition, as oxygen is often used to support combustion, this can lead to oxygen enrichment, which can radically change the ignition characteristics of many substances. Electric arc welding equipment has all of the hazards of electrical apparatus, and therefore, high standards of maintenance and repair of the equipment is essential.

12.9.2   The main precautionary measures are:

(a) the welding appliance should not be removed from the workshop area to other parts of the premises without the permission of a designated official

(b) before operations commence, all combustible material in the vicinity should be removed, wetted down or completely covered over with incombustible material. A check should be carried out for any openings or cracks below the working area that may allow sparks to drop through and ignite materials at lower levels. Any found should be covered with an incombustible material.

(c) outside contractors should be given strict instructions as to the procedures to be adopted within the premises. Any hazardous areas should be pointed out to them.

(d) hand extinguishers should be provided near the site of welding or cutting operations and operators should be experienced in the handling of such equipment

(e) when welding or cutting operations are carried out in particularly hazardous areas it is advisable to have a person standing by with a fire extinguisher

(f) a fire extinguisher, preferably of the dry powder or vaporising liquid type, should be carried on the welding trolley. Where sprinklers are installed check that the control valve(s) is open and the system is operational before commencing welding or cutting.

(g) leaking tubing, badly fitting valves and regulators and loose connections on the welding equipment are all sources of danger and the cause of many fires. Regular maintenance of equipment is essential (see below).

(h) empty drums which have contained flammable liquids should not be stored in the vicinity of welding or cutting operations. If such containers are to be welded or cut they should be thoroughly de-gassed, preferably by the application of steam, before commencing to weld or cut.

(i) welding should only be carried out when the 'hot working' procedure has been implemented. (See *Figures 12.2 and 12.3* for examples of 'hot work' permits).

(j) adequate ventilation of the welding site is essential and environmental monitoring as well as hearing protection may be necessary

(k) employees who weld should be fitted with and should wear the appropriate face masks and protective clothing so as to minimise the ingestion of the harmful products of welding and brazing.

12.9.3   Maintenance of welding equipment

All welding equipment should be kept clean, in good working order and should be regularly inspected. Rubber hose should be colour coded – red for acetylene and black for oxygen and should be checked for cuts, cracks, burns and worn parts. Copper alloys with a high copper content react with acetylene to form an explosive compound (cuprous acetylide) and tubing of these metals should not be used for acetylene.

Figure 12.2

CUTTING AND WELDING PERMIT

Date _____ Bldg. _____

Floor _____ Area _____

Work to be done _____

_____

Time started _____

Permit expires _____

THE FOLLOWING PRECAUTIOUS HAVE BEEN OBSERVED:

☐ Sprinkler protection in service

☐ Flammable and combustible materials removed 50 ft. (15m.) from area

☐ All hazardous operations discontinued

☐ Floor and wall openings within 50 ft. (15m.) covered

☐ Adequate portable extinguishers at work site

☐ Noncombustible covers provided

☐ Cutting and welding equipment in good condition

☐ Fire watch provided

Location of nearest fire alarm box _____

_____

Fire Dept. phone no. _____

_____
(supervisor's signature)

_____
(welder's signature)

Time work completed _____

Area checked after completion of job by _____

Date _____

ZVK 64-1 4-74 25M SETS   PRINTED IN U.S.A.

A Hot Work Permit

Figure 12.3

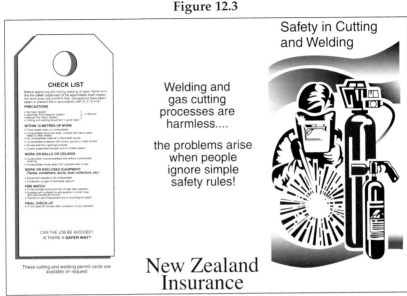

A Hot Work Permit

12.10 VENTILATION

12.10.1 Ventilation must be considered from two aspects, favourable and unfavourable. In rooms in which flammable gases or vapours accumulate (such as Spray Booths in which paints with a low flash point are used) it is necessary to have adequate ventilation. In a battery room containing a number of batteries which are charged from time to time adequate ventilation is essential because the process gives off oxygen and hydrogen and these produce an explosive atmosphere. A celluloid store must also be ventilated, as should a store for vegetable fibres.

12.10.2 These are examples of the favourable aspect of ventilation.

Neutral ventilation by means of an open window may be all that is needed to reduce the percentage of flammable vapour in the air to a harmless level. However, this is not always reliable, windows will be closed in bad weather and it may be necessary to install artificial ventilation to regulate the supply of fresh air.

Artificial ventilation has made great advances as buildings have increased in size. Today's large buildings can be ventilated with clean, pure air without a single window or door being open provided that the airconditioning equipment has been properly installed. Such ventilation or air-conditioning plants are elaborate, and a large air-conditioned building is full of ducts, with electric motor-driven fans with wiring and accessories. However, such plants can expose the occupants of the buildings to considerable hazard in the form of the 'sick building syndrome'. To help prevent this it is essential that the equipment is properly maintained and the cleanliness of the water in the cooling system be checked on a regular basis.

12.10.3 Even though the purpose of ventilation may be to rid the atmosphere of flammable gases or vapours (the favourable aspect), the installation itself may have an inherent hazard (the unfavourable aspect). This is because a ventilation system needs to have ducts to carry the moving air around the building. Air that is forced into, or drawn out of a building by power-fans will provide a fire with a plentiful supply of oxygen. In addition, ducts will pass horizontally and vertically through a building, and if vertical, they are almost certain to act as floor openings. A shaft for heated air or for ventilating purposes ranks as a hazardous feature unless it is totally enclosed in brick, stone, cement or concrete. Whether protected by proper enclosure or not the shaft will provide easy access for a fire, sparks or smoke from one part of the building to another. In practice, however, most ventilation ducts are made of sheet metal. Wooden ducts of any kind are very hazardous and present a very real hazard. Their use should, therefore, not be permitted.

12.10.4 Oil, metal dust, carbonaceous matter and fluff, where they are present in the air current, will be deposited on the inside of ducts. Even if the maintenance staff are aware of this (which they should be) it may be difficult to gain access to the deposit for cleaning. A spark, or perhaps some local heating or even self-heating, may start a fire which would spread rapidly through the duct, perhaps escaping to and involving another part of the building. Ducts liable to such deposits therefore should be fitted with cleaning doors at regular intervals. Fans and ducts in paint-spraying rooms should be accessible for cleaning because of the solid residues that are combustible.

12.10.5 Proper ventilation of flammable liquid stores helps to prevent the formation of flammable mixtures of the vapour with air. For the heavier than air vapours (e.g. acetone, alcohol, ether, benzol, petrol and carbon disulphide) the ventilation should be at floor level. Sufficient ventilation should be provided in all situations to remove or dilute the flammable gas or vapour so that the concentration in the store should never rise above approximately 25% of the lower flammability limit of the gas.

13

PROACTIVE FIRE EXTINGUISHMENT METHODS

13.1 FIRE EXTINGUISHMENT SCENARIOS

13.1.1 (a) it is important to extinguish fire as soon as possible but particularly, if a large loss is to be avoided, before flashover. Of course, in some cases where very high value heat sensitive goods or equipment are concerned (e.g. com-puters and micro-electronics) a much earlier application fire control is essential. **The Tetrahedron of Fire** (see *Figure 3.5*) and the **Law of Conservation of Energy** (which states energy is neither created nor destroyed – it is simply turned from one form of energy to another) provide the clues to all fire extinguishment scenarios.

Fires can be extinguished by upsetting the reaction path in the flame zone. This can be done in any of the following ways, but in practice, usually a combination of methods is used.

(i)   **fuel** – Remove the fuel from the flame zone and the fire goes out. Examples: fire breaks; turning off gas or liquid fuels, blanketing fuel with a vapour barrier (e.g. foam)

(ii)   **oxygen** – Remove (very unusual), restrict or dilute the oxygen in the flame zone to (generally) below 16% and the fire will be extinguished. Examples: dilution by inert gas such as Carbon Dioxide, (CO_2) or steam; closing down air intakes; limiting the openings in a building; breaking the air up into bubbles (high expansion foam); dropping a lid on the fuel or smothering with a blanket.

Note: Some fuels e.g. explosives contain their own oxygen supply in the form of oxygen rich compounds.

(iii)   **chain reaction** – Interfering with the chain reaction by means of chemicals can prevent it going to completion and thus, releasing the stored heat of the fuel. The chain reaction is changed to produce

287

alternative products that have high levels of stored energy, with the result that insufficient heat is released to sustain the fire. Examples: The action of halons and dry powder.

(iv)   **heat** – Probably the easiest of the four ingredients to remove, and once removed is a real stopper, (whereas with oxygen dilution for example, the inert gas may disperse and if the other factors are still present, re-ignition will occur). Of course, to some extent cooling removes fuel by stopping the release of flammable vapours into the flame zone. Example: Cooling with water, providing a radiation shield (e.g. with dry powder), venting hot gases from a building (more a "slowing down" technique).

(b)   As mentioned earlier, often a combination of effects are used to achieve extinguishment. For example, dry powder has the effect of interfering with the chain reaction, diluting the air around the flame zone, shielding the fuel surface from radiated heat and to some extent, acting as a blanket across the top of the fuel to separate the fuel from the flame zone.

13.1.2   Extinguishants and the Mechanism by Which They Work

Water

(a)   the most common of all extinguishants, water, owes its effectiveness principally to its very high latent heat of vapourisation. That is to say, although water in the liquid form increases its temperature uniformly as heat is added, at boiling point (100 degrees centigrade) a great deal of energy is absorbed to convert it to its vapour phase (commonly but incorrectly described as steam) but without a corresponding increase in temperature i.e. the heat is hidden or latent heat associated with vapourisation. Although this feature is common with all liquids, water is unique because of the size of its latent heat of vapourisation. (A similar but much less marked effect occurs when ice melts – the latent heat of fusion.) *Figure 13.1* illustrates this and gives values in calories for each gram of water.

Figure 13.1

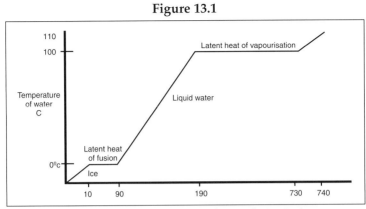

Value in Calories for each Gram of Water during Fusion

(b)   other advantages of water are:

(i) it is cheap and generally in abundant supply

(ii) the vapourised water from the fire has some oxygen dilution effect

(iii) it can be readily pumped and piped

(iv) it is safe, clean and non-corrosive if dried off after the fire

(v) it will dissolve the acid gases released by burning plastics and thus prevent corrosion

(vi) when turned to a high pressure fog it is extremely effective on fires involving high flashpoint liquids (e.g. fuel oils).

(c)   a few (comparatively insignificant) disadvantages are:

(i) water which is not turned to steam by the fire can damage property beyond the area of the fire (prompt salvage work can mitigate this)

(ii) it is a conductor of electricity (but see below)

(iii) it is not very effective on low flashpoint liquid (e.g. petrol) fires

(iv) if applied wrongly to any fire involving a liquid it can cause the fire to spread

(v) it is generally ineffective on fires involving combustible metals (as are most common extinguishants).

13.1.3   Water and Electricity

(a)   a great deal of concern exists about the use of water on fires involving live electrical equipment. Electricity itself does not burn. Where electricity is involved in fire it merely provides the heat side of the Fire Tetrahedron. Yet fires involving electricity are often thought of as needing a different or special extinguishing agent, and there is a common belief that water is most unsuitable. From the point of view of extinguishing the fire and minimising the loss, nothing could be further from the truth. An electrical fire is really just a fire involving ordinary combustibles in which the initial heat was provided by the electric current. Water is the best extinguishant of ordinary combustibles and may also achieve the following additional beneficial effect where electrical equipment is involved:

> (i)   cause a short circuit protective device to operate (e.g. fuse, circuit breaker) thus removing the source of heat
>
> (ii) quench or cool an electric arc if that is the cause of the fire
>
> (iii) immediately cool any electrical equipment (which is particularly susceptible to overheating – especially electronic circuits)
>
> (iv) immediately wash the equipment and remove contaminated products. If plastic PVC insulation has been burning, Hydrochloric acid is produced from hydrogen chloride gas and this is very corrosive.

(b)   in fact, it is common where a high degree of protection of electrical areas is required, that automatic sprinklers or other automatic water spray systems are installed and used. Where water is being applied by hand, such as from extinguishers, hose reels or fire brigade hoses – there is one additional consideration other than loss control. That is the question of the safety of the operator. (This, of course, does not arise with a sprinkler system.) However, the exact nature of the danger is seldom well understood.

(c)   there is a very real danger that the operator will provide a **conducting path** for electrical current to earth. If that happens, he would experience an electrical shock in the following way. If a live wire is touched to earth (the ground) or to anything which conducts electricity in contact with earth, then an electrical current will flow. Some things (e.g. plastic insulation) do not conduct electricity, other materials (e.g. copper, steel, the human body) do. Hence, the human body if it is connected to a live wire can become part of the conducting path.

Water, if it is completely pure, does not conduct electricity. However, it is rarely completely pure as it usually contains dissolved gases, impurities and minerals that generally make it conductive to some extent. The potential danger to the operator is that a solid water stream from his hose or extinguisher will provide a conducting path between the live wire and the operator who, if he is in good contact with the earth or earthed metal, will suffer a shock.

(d)   in practice, this frequently does not occur because:

   (i)   most hose streams are not in fact a solid stream of water, but are a broken series of drops. Even the solid, big volume hose streams produced by the fire brigade hoses break up within a few metres of leaving the nozzle.

   (ii) where, because of broken streams or low impurities, the water stream is relatively non-conducting, i.e. it has high resistance, big voltages would be required

   (iii) circuit breakers or fuses should have already cut off the power

   (iv) the operator may be insulated from earth by footwear.

Of course, for the operator who must make an immediate decision, these things cannot be scientifically evaluated and hence there is a strong tendency to play safe by completely discouraging the application of water by hand.

(e)   conclusion:

   (i)   water is a good extinguishant for electrical equipment involved in fire

   (ii) Operators applying water by hand to electrical equipment, should always act as though it is still alive. They should stand well back and use a spraying action.

13.1.4   Foam

(a)   most easily thought of as a mass of bubbles, usually of air, foam principally extinguishes fire by separating the fuel from the flame zone. Obviously the bubble walls (formed by the foam compound) must be sufficiently strong not to be broken down by heat. The application of foam to a flammable liquid (on which it must float) requires considerable skill otherwise the foam will dive beneath the liquid and then float up with the fuel on top.

(b)   there are however, some modern developments that may see foam become a more popular extinguishant, certainly in specialist applications such as crash fire fighting.

A quick summary of foam types is as follows:

(i)   **conventional:** In which the foam compound expands in the ratio of 4 to 1 to 20 to 1. This type is becoming increasingly obsolete.

(ii) **high expansion:** In this the foam compounds resemble detergents and expansion ratios of 1,000 to 1 are not uncommon. The resultant foam is very light and can be directed through nylon "socks" so as to fill an entire room such as a basement or cellar

(iii) **aqueous Film Forming (AFFF):** The resultant foam is a mass of bubbles and acts like a blanket which spreads across the top of a flammable liquid. Usually added to water at about 3%, it is now very commonly used as a first attack by crash fire vehicles. It is particularly effective at preventing re-ignition.

(c)   foam extinguishes a fire by forming a blanket on the surface of a burning liquid. The foam blanket remains in position for sufficient time to prevent re-ignition and to allow the liquid to cool. Foam extinguishers are, therefore, especially suitable for dealing with fires in which a liquid has been overheated in a process.

Examples include: Oil quench tanks, oil-fired boilers (where a sill is provided) and frying ranges.

13.1.5   BCF and BTM

(a)   these are the modern day equivalent of carbon tetrachloride, which is a highly poisonous extinguising compound. BCF and BTM are examples of the family of vapourising liquids known as the **Halons** or **Halogenated Hydrocarbons**. **Halogens** are a group of chemical elements of which the common ones are Fluorine, Chlorine, Bromine and Iodine, which all have similar properties, although only the first three are important in a fire extinguishing context

Hydrocarbons are compounds containing only hydrogen and carbon which include the paraffins, olefins and the acetylenes and which range from **gases** – Methane, Ethylene, Acetylene, through **liquids** – Hexane, to **solids** – Greases. They provide the building blocks for plastics and many other materials. Generally these compounds are all high energy fuels.

In a halon compound one or more of the hydrogen atoms of a hydrocarbon are replaced by one or more halogens, and the resultant compound is often a very effective extinguishant.

For example BCF (Bromochlorodifluoromethane) is really a modified form of methane. BTM (Bromotrifluoro-methane) is a slightly different modification of methane.

(b)   both extinguish a fire by interfering with the chain reaction in which their action can be thought of as leading the **chain carriers** (the chemical message boys of the reaction) off on a false errand. With a liquid fuel they extinguish quickly and, providing there is no reapplication of heat, completely. However, in a class A fire, re-ignition is likely because the solid fuel holds its heat and once the BCF/BTM has dispersed, the chain reaction will be re-established. Unfortunately those selling BCF/BTM tend to overlook this significant limitation when they claim their product as a **general purpose** extinguishant. It is not.

(d)   The advantages of BCF/BTM are:

(i)   comparatively clean and non-corrosive

(ii) limited toxicity (at worst, a mild headache compared with "carbontetrachloride" which at best disables the liver and at worst, causes death)

(iii) very quick flame knock-down

(iv) non-conductive.

and the disadvantages are:

(i)   fairly expensive

(ii) very little cooling effect

(iii) by-products after application to the fire can be corrosive

(iv) causes degeneration of the ozone layer.

Halons have a similar range of useful applications to carbon dioxide extinguishers but an important application was for dealing with fires in petrol and oil-driven engines as well as computer rooms.

Because these compounds destroy the Ozone layer they are being phased out progressively throughout the world. However they are very effective in extinguishing certain types of fire and are frequently used as the main fire fighting agent in enclosed areas which contain sensitive electronic equipment such as computers. As a consequence an intensive search is being undertaken to find alternatives to these compounds. At the present time FE-25 (Pentafluoroethane) is being developed to replace Halon 1301 and FE-232 (Dichlorotrifluoroethane) is being developed to replace Halon 1211. Neither contain bromine and therefore FE-25 which also does not contain any chlorine has a zero ozone depletion potential but FE-232 which does has a very low ozone depletion potential of 0.02. Both are more expensive than the compounds that it is proposed they replace.

A possible replacement for halons which is now becoming available is the Water Mist which utilise very small volumes of water kept under very high pressure which is released when a fire is detected by an independent detection device.

13.1.6   Dry Powder

(a)   there are a number of different types of dry powder which have special uses, such as those that are suitable for fighting fires involving:

(i)   flammable liquids and gases

(ii) combustible metals;

as well as those that are suitable for other types of fires. However it is important not to mix the different types of powder together.

(b)   dry powder is generally the best type of extinguisher for dealing with fires in flammable liquids. In extinguishing the flames over the liquid, dry powder acts more rapidly than foam and is particularly suitable for dealing with fires which may spread to surrounding materials before a complete foam blanket could be formed over the burning liquid. These extinguishers deal more effectively with large areas of burning liquid than other extinguishers of comparable size. They are effective too on fires in free flowing liquids, especially where the liquid spills and spreads over a fairly large area. Dry powder is a non-conductor of electricity and can safely be used on fires where there is a risk of electric shock.

(c)   dry powders are however hard to clean up after a fire and the use of them in say, a textile factory, would make the cost of salvage of machines after a fire a very expensive business.

13.1.7   Carbon Dioxide

(a)   a common but over-rated extinguishant. Its principal extinguishing action is by oxygen dilution. It is most ineffective at preventing re-ignition and, generally, is quite useless on Class A fires. Indeed, the high velocity gas discharge from carbon dioxide extinguishers can blow burning material (e.g. paper from a waste paper basket) around and spread the fire.

(b)   it has some application in gas flooding systems, particularly on board ships and perhaps inside the cabinets of computers as an alternative to Halon

(c)   Carbon dioxide, by extinguishing the flames over the liquid, acts more rapidly than foam and is more suitable for dealing with fires which may spread to surrounding materials before a complete foam blanket can be formed over the burning liquid. Like dry powder it is a non-conductor of electricity.

Carbon dioxide extinguishers are suitable for dealing with small fires involving escaping liquids on both horizontal and vertical surfaces. They are also suitable where the over-riding factor is to avoid damage or contamination by dry powder deposits or foam. Examples of risks where they are especially suitable include: coating and spreading machines, delicate laboratory equipment.

Work is under way to find a less injurious flooding agent and there are indications that FE-13(tm) (trifluoroethane which has a zero ozone depletion potential) may be a suitable alternative to both carbon dioxide and halons although it will probably be considerably more expensive. Another alternative to both halon and carbon dioxide is Inergen which is a mixture of Nitrogen, Argon and Carbon Dioxide which is able to reduce the level of oxygen to 15%, a concentration that will support life but not combustion.

13.2 FIRST AID FIRE-FIGHTING EQUIPMENT

13.2.1   Hand held fire extinguishers and hose reels are referred to as First Aid fire fighting equipment. The supply of extinguishant in extinguishers is limited and such extinguishers can only be used on very small fires during the early stages of ignition. However hose reels may be connected to an unlimited water supply and certainly have a better fire fighting capability than most other First Aid extinguishers for this reason. However, they cannot deliver the volume of water required to fight the larger fires.

13.2.2   All fire extinguishers consist of:

(a) a container

(b) an extinguishing agent

(c) an expellant to eject the extinguishing agent

(d) a hose or nozzle to direct the extinguishing agent at the fire.

In addition, it must be remembered that the expellant rises to the top of the extinguisher in the operating position. Therefore, if the hose or nozzle is also situated at the top of the extinguisher in the normal operating position, it is essential that a siphon be fitted inside the body of the extinguisher in order that all of the extinguishant be ejected.

13.2.3   Siting of Extinguishers.

Extinguishers for general protection should be as near as possible to exits or on staircase landings. They should be positioned within 30 m of one another. However where large undivided floor areas necessitate positioning appliances away from exits or outer walls, they should be installed on escape routes. Wherever the are placed extinguishers should be in conspicuous positions accessible for immediate use which are clearly marked and visible from some distance away.

In buildings where there are perhaps hose reels, fire buckets, fire blankets, fire alarm call points and fire instruction notices as well as portable extinguishers, it is advantageous to group the equipment and notices together at fire points. However, where there are major flammable liquid and electrical equipment risks, the appropriate extinguishing equipment should be installed close to these risks.

13.2.4 Servicing

All First Aid extinguishers deteriorate over time and it is, therefore, essential that all extinguishers should be serviced annually by a reputable fire protection contractor and the date of the last service marked on the extinguisher. In addition, employees should be given regular training in the use of this type of extinguisher.

13.2.5 Types of First Aid Appliances

(a)   **water type appliances**

(i)   Water Gas Pressure Extinguishers

A cartridge of gas is contained inside the body of the extinguisher and the pressure released into the body of the extinguisher expels the water through a short hose line.

(ii)   Soda Acid Extinguishers

The chemical reaction between an acid and an alkaline is used in this extinguisher. A solution of Bicarbonate of Soda is held in the body of the extinguisher, separated from a quantity of sulphuric acid held in a glass container. In operation, the container is either smashed or a loose fitting plug is removed by turning the extinguisher over and the chemical reaction takes place. In the process, carbon dioxide is formed and the pressure expels the solution, sulphate of soda, as a watery extinguishant.

(iii)   Hose Reels

These vary from country to country but generally consist of 20 m to 45 m lengths of 15 mm or 20 mm diameter Hydraulic hose, permanently fitted to the building's water supply. The criteria for assessing the value of the hose reel are:

- it should produce a 6 to 10 m jet
- the nozzle should reach within 6 metres of all parts of the area that is to be protected
- it should be able to produce a flow of 24 litres/minute for at least 30 minutes.

(iv)   Bucket Pumps

These are not used in the UK but in a number of other countries consist of a 10 or 20 litre tank with a double acting pump and hose. The advantage of such units is that the discharge, unlike that of an extinguisher, is controllable. In addition, such units can be refilled by a second person while the operator is fighting the fire. A 20 litre bucket pump may protect up to 500 m^2.

(b)   **special risk extinguishers**

In some situations water may not be considered an appropriate extinguishant for a special risk. In such instances it is permissible to use additional special risk appliances, or an agreed number of special risk appliances in place of water type appliances. Special risk extinguishers are as follows:

(i) Foam

(ii) Dry Powder

(iii) Carbon Dioxide

(iv) Halons – although these are now generally being phased out.

13.3   FIRE SERVICE

13.3.1 Should a fire progress beyond the stage where it can be controlled by first aid appliances then a major fire fighting effort will usually be required to bring the fire under control. For this reason, and to avoid the spread of fire to surrounding buildings the fire brigades were established to protect property and lives from the threat of fire. To aid the fire brigade, towns and cities large enough to warrant a towns main water supply, install fire hydrants on the water mains for fire-fighting purposes. Hydrants are normally sited in the ground 100m apart, clearly marked and protected from traffic by a steel cover.

13.3.2 Fire Brigades in cities and large towns are permanently manned; whilst in smaller towns a mixture of permanent and volunteer members of the brigade may be normal. In some countries but not in the UK country towns that do not warrant permanent manning, usually make use of volunteers – enthusiastic men and women who provide a valuable service in many such towns. In addition to these public fire brigades, there are a number of private fire brigades situated at remote industrial complexes, which are beyond the effective response time of the nearest public fire brigade.

13.3.3   Private Fire Brigades

(a)   for a private fire brigade to be effective the following criteria should be met:

(i)   a stored water supply of at least 455 m3 (or 100,000 gallons) should be available

(ii) a hydrant main of not less than 100 mm diameter, with sufficient hydrants to ensure that all portions of the site or building are within reach of a 10 m jet of water from the end of a 25 m hose length

(iii) a means of pressurising the hydrant main either by gravity or using a pump. If the latter is used, the power source that drives the pump must be independent of mains electricity, e.g. a diesel engine.

(iv) at each hydrant a 25 m length of hose and branch should be kept in a marked cabinet or better still on the brigade's mobile appliance

(v) a well-drilled private fire brigade organisation should be available.

(b)   in some countries a well organised private fire brigade may also be required to fulfil the following:

(i)   it should have a fire station within the complex

(ii) it should have a siren, with alarm switches throughout the works and surrounding neighbourhood

(iii) it should have a fire chief and at least seven other firemen, drawn from the ranks of employees living adjacent to the complex

(iv) it should have a fire tender capable of carrying hose branches, axes, breathing apparatus and ladders

(v) it should have adequate protective clothing for the firemen

(vi) it should carry out a weekly drill and a monthly wet practice. The wet practice should be held in a different place each month, without prior notice to firemen.

13.4 AUTOMATIC FIRE DETECTION INSTALLATIONS

13.4.1   The next level of protection in the fire protection of a building is the installation of an automatic fire detection system. This consists of fire detectors and manual call points positioned in zones throughout a building. These are wired to control and indicating equipment that shows the location of the alarm call and actuates audible alarm sounders. A reliable power supply is provided including an emergency supply. The most effective systems are those which are also connected to the fire brigade or to a central fire alarm. This type of device is ideal for raising the alarm so that people may be evacuated, but detection devices have limited value in protecting property.

13.4.2   In some countries such as New Zealand and Australia automatic fire detection systems are generally acceptable subject to the following criteria:

(i)   premises are no more than 8 km from a permanently manned fire brigade or 3.5 km from a volunteer station

(ii) an adequate supply of water for fire-fighting purposes should be available on the premises

(iii) the occupancy of the building is a suitable one

(iv) first aid fire-fighting appliances are installed throughout the building.

Fire detectors are designed to detect one or more of the three characteristics of a fire; **smoke, heat** or **flame**. Of these the smoke detector is the first to detect a fire well before any sprinkler would operate. The next detectors to operate are the heat detectors and followed by the flame detectors, again some time before a sprinkler would operate. No one type of detector is the most suitable for all applications and the final choice has to depend on individual circumstances.

13.4.3   Factors Affecting Choice

The system chosen should have detectors which are suited to the conditions and which will provide the earliest reliable warning in those conditions. A detector has to discriminate between a fire and the normal environment existing within a building. Each type of detector responds at a different rate to the different kinds of fire. Therefore it may be necessary to install a combination of the various types of detector. The likely fire behaviour of the contents of each part of the building, the processes taking place and the design of the building, must be considered as well as the susceptibility of the contents to heat, smoke and water damage. A recent development has been the very early smoke detection apparatus (VESDA) which is able to detect a problem and raise the alarm before ignition actually occurs.

(a)   **heat detectors**

These are suitable for use in most buildings and in general they have a greater resistance to adverse environmental conditions than other types of detector. Where fires can occur in which heat is generated rapidly, but with little smoke, they may give a faster detection of fire than a smoke detector. Fixed temperature heat detectors are not suitable in cold stores where ambient temperatures are abnormally low. Combined fixed temperature and rate-of-rise detectors should be avoided if rapid changes in ambient temperature are likely.

(b)   **smoke detectors**

These give the earliest warning for most types of fire in which the early smouldering stages of the fire produce considerable quantities of smoke:

(i) **Ionization detectors** respond most quickly to smoke containing small particles, such as those produced by clean burning wood fires. They may show a less rapid response to smouldering fires involving polymers.

(ii) **Optical beam-type smoke detectors** are probably most suitable for protecting tall compartments, cable tunnels and open areas. They respond to an integrated change in smoke density or temperature over the path length of the beam and respond best to optically dense smoke but less well to smoke containing small particles. They are not suitable for installation where blower heaters or processes producing waste heat could cause thermal turbulence.

Both types of smoke detectors respond sufficiently well to most fires to be generally useful. However, neither ionization nor optical detectors detect fires from materials such as alcohol which do not produce smoke particles. Also, false alarms may be caused by smoke and other fumes, dusts, fibres and steam produced by normal processes and activities, or by vehicle engines.

13.4.4 Types of Circuits

Normally, only fire detection systems that operate on the closed circuit principle are acceptable. Under the closed circuit principle the detection circuit must be charged either with an electrical current for electrical systems or air pressure for pneumatic systems. Operation of the detector has the same effect as opening a closed switch, i.e. the power is no longer there, or the air pressure is released in the case of a pneumatic system. Loss of energy to operate an alarm is referred to as fail safe, consequently, high standards of battery maintenance or air tightness are essential. See *Figure 13.2* for an example of a detector.

Figure 13.2

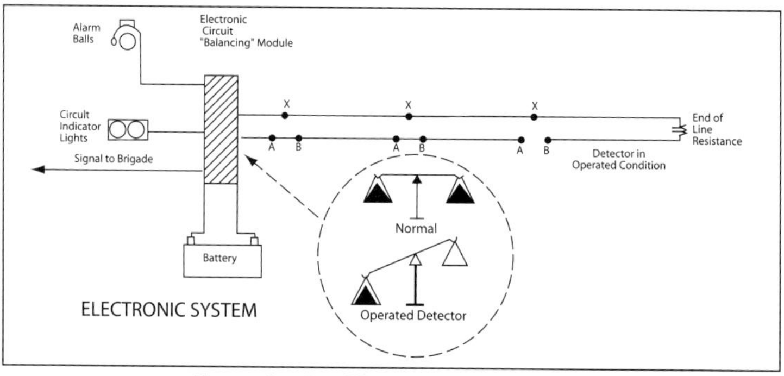

Example of an Electronic Fire Detector

13.5 MISCELLANEOUS ALARMS

13.5.1 Evacuation Alarms

Manual evacuation alarms are usually required by law in any building in which people work, or which is visited by members of the public. They normally consist of a circuit that includes bells or hooters and switches protected by glass. This glass has to be broken and the switch activated to sound the alarm warning people to leave the building. These systems are rarely connected to the fire brigade, and they are used to provide a warning to evacuate the building for a wide range of emergencies such as fire, release of toxic or asphyxiant gas or an incipient explosion.

13.6 AUTOMATIC FIRE-FIGHTING

13.6.1   The installation of an automatic sprinkler system in a building gives that building the ultimate safeguard from fire because the operation of a sprinkler is automatic and fire-fighting starts immediately the fire is detected. Whilst it may not completely extinguish a fire, if it is properly designed it will contain the fire to the area of initial outbreak. The advantages of an automatic sprinkler system are:

(i)   it provides the equivalent of 1 fireman per 10 square metres of floor area for 24 hours every day of the year

(ii) by-laws governing building construction may be applied in a less stringent manner but the building still achieves code compliance

(iii) continuity of business and jobs is guaranteed

(iv) the lives of people in the building including any that are disabled are better protected. As a consequence the owner and occupier of the premises are likely to be complying fully with the appropriate health and safety legislation or regulations

(v)   water damage from firefighting is reduced. A standard sprinkler operating at 5 bar delivers about 180 litres of water per minute, whereas a 65mm hose operating at the same pressure delivers over 1000 litres per minute

(vi) fire damage and loss are dramatically reduced. Most fires can be controlled by relatively few sprinklers as a sprinkler delivers water to the seat of the fire in a way in which a hose stream often cannot. In addition many hose streams are required to fight a fire that is out of control.

(vii) tax and insurance premium relief may be available

(viii) it will significantly influence how contingency planning for the building will be developed and maintained

(ix) it may act as a loss mitigation tool that is very cost effective in helping cope with potentially catastrophic releases of hazardous chemicals into the workplace.

An automatic sprinkler system consists of pipes and heat

operated valves **(sprinkler heads)** by means of which a fire is automatically detected, the alarm given and water delivered to the seat of the fire. A fire is thereby able to be extinguished or kept under control until the fire brigade arrives.

13.6.2 Sprinkler Heads

A sprinkler head is a heat sensitive valve that opens, releasing water as a spray when its heat sensitive element reaches a specific temperature. The orifice size of the head (10, 15 or 20 mm) is determined by the risk to be protected. The water distribution pattern of the head depends on the type of deflector used. *Figure 13.3* shows the various components of a sprinkler head.

Figure 13.3

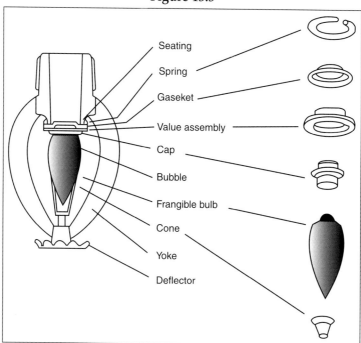

Seating

Spring

Gaseket

Value assembly

Cap

Bubble

Frangible bulb

Cone

Yoke

Deflector

Example of an Electronic Fire Detector

Method of Operation – 2 basic types

(a)   **Frangible bulb** – the sealed glass bulb contains liquid and a small gas bubble which accommodate small changes in the volume of the liquid due to temperature changes. Very high temperatures however cause the liquid to expand sufficiently to absorb the bubble.

The resultant increase in pressure fractures the bulb, allowing water to escape from the head. (See *Figure 13.4*)

Fig. 13.4

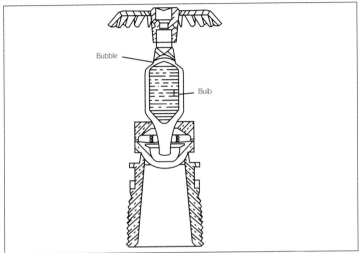

Footnote: The Grinnell Quartzoid, Issue D, glass-bulb automatic sprinkler. The operating temperature is regulated by adjusting the amount of liquid and the size of the bubble when the bulb is sealed.

(b)   **Fusible link** – heat melts the solder allowing the levers of cantilever types to move or the strut of strut types to part letting water escape. The solders used are alloys of tin, lead, cadmium, bismuth and antimony. (See *Figure 13.5*)

Figure 13.5

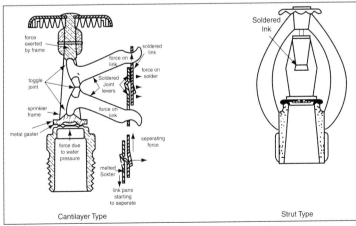

The Melting of Metals Activate the Sprinkler System

13.6.3 Distribution Patterns

The design of the deflector determines the spray pattern of the sprinkler head. Whilst there are many different types of deflectors for a variety of special purposes, it is important to understand the differences between the three in most common use:

(a) **conventional**

Conventional sprinklers produce a spherical discharge pattern with some of the water being thrown up towards the ceiling. (See *Figure 13.6*)

Figure 13.6

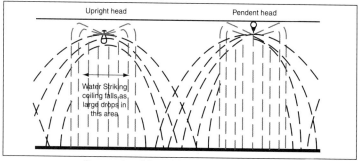

Conventional Sprinklers Discharge Pattern

(b) **spray**

Spray sprinklers produce a hemispherical discharge below the sprinkler with little or no water reaching the ceiling. (See *Figure 13.7*)

Figure 13.7

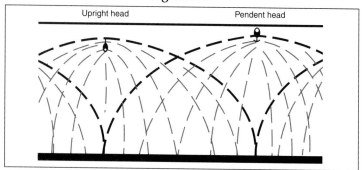

Spray Sprinklers Discharge Pattern

(c)   **sidewall**

Sidewall sprinklers are sited close to a wall and deflect most of the water away from the wall. (See *Figure 13.8*)

Figure 13.8

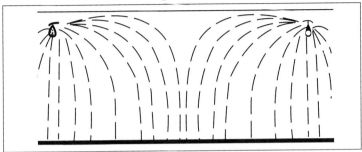

Sidewall Sprinklers Display Pattern

13.6.4   A sprinkler installation may be:

(a)   **wet pipe** – with all pipes leading from the water supply through the various controlling valves on to the sprinkler heads permanently filled with water under pressure. This is the type of system that is in most common use.

(b)   **dry pipe** – with the pipes above the installation control valves charged with compressed air under sufficient pressure to prevent the entry of water. On operation of a sprinkler head the compressed air escapes first and the water follows. Dry pipe installations are necessary where there is danger of the water in the pipes freezing at any time during the year, e.g. in freezing chambers, cool stores or cold rooms or where temperatures above 70 degrees centigrade may be encountered.

(c)   **alternative wet and dry** – operated as wet pipe installations in the summer and dry pipe installations in the winter. The dry pipe valve is latched open during the summer when the system is wet.

(d)   **tail end alternate or tail end dry** – basically wet pipe installations where the portion of the system that is liable to freeze is dry or alternate wet and dry. (See *Figure 13.9*).

Figure 13.9

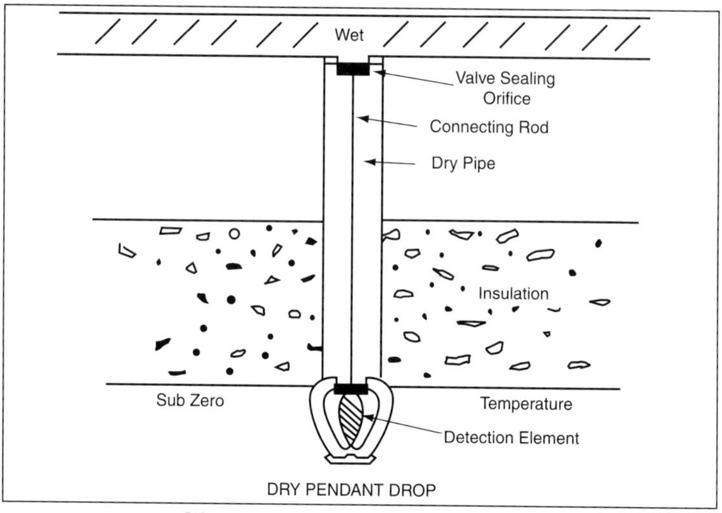

DRY PENDANT DROP

Wet or Dry, Wet and Dry Installations

(e)   **pre-action**, where a dry pipe installation is combined with an independent system of heat or smoke detectors installed in the same areas as the sprinklers. Normally heat or smoke detectors will operate before the sprinklers and a pre-action valve opens to allow water to flow into the sprinkler pipework before the first sprinkler head operates. In a re-cycling system heat detectors are used which re-close the pre-action valve if air temperatures fall, and re-open if the air temperature rises. This prevents further water discharge and thus limits water damage.

13.6.5   There have been a number of developments affecting sprinkler systems in the USA during the last few years, some of which are now beginning to make an appearance in other countries.

These include:

(a) **the Early Suppression Fast Response (ESFR) heads** which activate at a lower temperature than the traditional forms of sprinkler heads. As a consequence, they therefore start fighting the fire more quickly, and have been used in the States in conjunction with plastic piping in private dwellings in addition to other situations.

(b) **the large drop sprinklers** which produce very large drops of water and are as a consequence much more effective at extinguishing the very hot type of fire, such as that involving high stacked goods.

(c) **the Extra Large Orifice (ELO) sprinklers** which deliver much greater quantities of water and as a consequence are very useful in those situations in which much greater quantities of water are necessary to extinguish any fire that may start, such as the very hot fire, or one that is seated deep within a stack of goods.

13.6.6 Sprinkler Rules

Most countries have a comprehensive set of rules governing the installation of sprinklers which not only detail the integral parts of an acceptable installation but also the rules for designing a suitable distribution taking into account its occupation. The rules which also cover the requirements of the water supply which usually cover the following features:

(a) the type of occupancy to be protected determines the type of sprinkler system that should be fitted. In other words, the density of water which the sprinkler system should discharge (its **design discharge density**) is geared to the hazard of the occupancy. The greater the hazard, the more water that is required.

(b) the sprinkler system should provide the design density of water specified for the hazard, at the hydraulically most unfavourable location in the protected premises, i.e. the most onerous point, taking into account pipe size, distance and height from the valves at which tests are conducted to prove the water supplies.

(c) apart from providing minimum pressures, the water supply should also be proved capable of providing the specified flow at the specified pressures for a specified minimum time.

13.6.7 Storage

The other key factor that affects the hazard classification of occupancy is storage. Both the combustibility of the storage and the height to which it is stacked have a pronounced effect on sprinkler design. The sprinkler rules classify most goods into a number of categories of combustibility and normally specify the maximum height to which goods in each category can be stored and still be adequately protected by an Ordinary Hazard System or its equivalent. Above that height an Extra High Hazard System or its equivalent is required but the actual density of water discharge will again depend on the category and height.

Examples of typical Ordinary Hazard Limits are:

Category I   up to 4 m: Carpets, Clothing, Groceries

Category II   up to 3 m: Chipboard, Lino, Wood Furniture, Rolled Paper (horizontal storage)

Category III   up to 2.1 m: Celluloid, Rubber Goods, Rolled Paper (vertical storage)

Category IV   up to 1.2 m: Off-cuts of foam, plastic and foamed rubber

As will be appreciated from the above, sprinkler systems in storage occupancies are tailor-made to suit the hazard. However, if the hazard increases (e.g. higher stacking, more combustible goods) beyond that for which the system was designed, the fire will invariably beat the sprinkler system. The sprinkler rules therefore normally require warning signs to be hung from the roof of storage areas to warn storemen not to exceed the design heights of the sprinkler system. It is also advisable to periodically review the sprinkler system to check that it continues to be suitable for the current occupation and storage.

13.6.8   Water Supplies

Water supplies to sprinkler systems are categorised as primary and secondary. A primary water supply must be 100% reliable and able to work under the most trying circumstances.

Water supplies normally acceptable as a primary source are:

- a towns main

- an elevated tank

- an automatic-starting electric motor or diesel engine-driven pump

In some countries a pressure tank may also be acceptable.

Any one of the above may be used as a secondary water supply and in addition, an approved automatic-starting electric motor-driven pump may be used as a secondary water supply. Sprinkler systems are usually classified in terms of their water supply – for example:

(a) duplicate or Class A Two independent water supplies

(b) superior or Class B Two towns main water supplies with independent sources

(c) single or Class C A single approved water supply

13.6.9   The sprinkler rules in most countries specify the precautions to follow when a sprinkler system is shut down for servicing. For example whenever a sprinkler system is taken out of action the following steps should be taken:

(a) advise Insurer

(b) advise Fire Brigade

(c) carry out any alterations and repairs during normal working hours

(d) check that there is no indication of fire before draining the system

(e) prohibit smoking, cutting and welding operations during the shutdown

(f) during the shutdown First Aid Fire-Fighting appliances should be readily available and trained personnel should be on stand by ready to respond immediately to an outbreak of fire

(g) a special check should be made after the shutdown to ensure that all valves are correctly re-opened.

13.6.10 Protection of Special Risks

Fixed manual fire protection systems are installed to assist manual firefighting to protect some special risks. Some of these types of systems are:

drenchers

These consist of an array of pipework erected on the face of a wall and connected to the town's water supply through a valve that is normally kept closed. In the event of a fire in an adjacent building, the valve is manually opened and water is sprayed, via outlets, over the windows and doors in the wall to keep them cool. Similar to water spray projectors.

gas flooding

Where large ovens are used for drying purposes and there is a likelihood of fire, pipework with openings are placed in the oven connected to a stored supply of gas carbon dioxide or a vapourising liquid, such as Halon or one of its new replacement compounds. A valve controlling this gas is sited adjacent to the working position of the operator of the ovens, where it can be quickly operated if required.

foam

In situations where hot oil dip baths are used for metal treatment or similar, a foam generator may be permanently sited adjacent to the bath outlets over the bath. The operator simply activates the generator if required.

water spray

Electrical transformers and gas storage tanks can be protected by pipework fitted with spray nozzles connected to a water supply through a manually/automatically operated valve. Spray nozzles are purpose built to give a variety of directed water spray patterns between 30 and 180 degrees. These systems are used primarily to cool the equipment and to prevent an adjacent fire from destroying or damaging it. Spray projectors can also be used on contained oil fires, because the combination of oil and water under pressure forms an emulsion that is cooler than the boiling oil. Where emulsification takes place it prevents re-ignition but it is not the primary mechanism for extinguishment.

fixed fire mains

These are installed in high rise buildings and/or oil tanks. In high rise buildings they save the fire brigade laying hoses vertically up the height of the building. They should be charged with water (wet riser), have an outlet with fire brigade hose couplings on each floor and should be sited in a fire resistant stairwell. In oil tank farms there is usually a pipe with an outlet into the top of each tank which runs back to a fire control point from where the brigade can pump water into the pipe. Such a system usually incorporates a fixed foam generator.

13.6.11 Processing Risks

(a)   **heat treatment of metals**

Automatic sprinklers with a high pressure water supply should be installed to protect the quench tank operation and the system should be extended at least 6 m in all directions beyond the tank. Sprinklers should also be installed throughout the heat treating department to cover overflows, leaks in oil distribution or hydraulic systems and any other combustibles including the building itself. Sprinkler water may cause oils heated above 100 degrees centigrade to boil over but they will protect the building and equipment against serious fire damage and will extinguish the oil fire on the floor and in the tank. Fixed automatic carbon dioxide or dry powder systems set to operate at a lower temperature than the sprinklers may be necessary in addition to sprinkler protection where the value of the machine or its importance in the production line warrants the additional expenditure.

(b)   **salt baths**

Dry clean sand is the most suitable material to extinguish fires involving nitrate or cyanide salts. The sand can also be used to dam the flow of molten salt but it should never be thrown into the salt bath itself. Dry powder extinguishers can be used for fires involving nitrate salts but not on cyanide salts. Water, foam, carbon dioxide or vapourising liquid should not be used.

(c)   **flammable liquids**

When a large volume of oil, tar, varnish, resin, benzene, alcohol, ether, acetone, or similar flammable spirits is on fire it is almost useless attempting to extinguish the blaze with water without specialised equipment. If water is used, a sheet of blazing liquid may float and spread on the surface of the water, and the fire zone thus be extended. Where these substances are stored, special first aid fire appliances should be provided in the shape of pails of sand, ashes, fine earth or special chemical extinguishers.

(d)   **aircraft within hangars and similar**

A deluge system is used in very high hazard areas where the prime objective is to protect the structure e.g. aircraft hangars. Such systems use enormous quantities of water as the heads open at once, deluging the area with water

(e)   **electronic equipment (computers) switch gear and similar equipment**

It is normal to use gas flooding to protect computer suites from fire. These systems make use of smoke detectors to sense a fire in its earliest stages. Two detectors with different levels of sensitivity are normally used. The first sounds the alarm to evacuate personnel from the area and the second releases the gas into the protected area, whilst at the same time shutting down the air conditioning system and closing the fire dampers in the ducting.

The most commonly used gas in these systems until recently was Halon; much less common was the use of carbon dioxide (CO_2). However neither of these systems are an adequate substitute for a sprinkler system and sprinklers should be installed in computer suites. There is now considerable evidence to show that salvage from water damaged electronic equipment is better than that from gas flooded environments.

13.6.12 Selection of the appropriate Fire Detection or Extinguishing System

The choice of the most appropriate system will depend on a number of factors including occupation, value at risk, the dependency on the processes, materials used etc., and on the amount of money able to be spent on the system. If cost was not an issue every commercial property should be fitted with not only an evacuation alarm but also smoke detectors and sprinklers. Certainly smoke alarms should be fitted to all private dwellings and whenever possible so should sprinklers. Usually however a choice has to be made as to which system is to be fitted so as to provide the most cost effective solution in the particular circumstances and the chart below provides a guide for doing this. (See *Figure 13.10*).

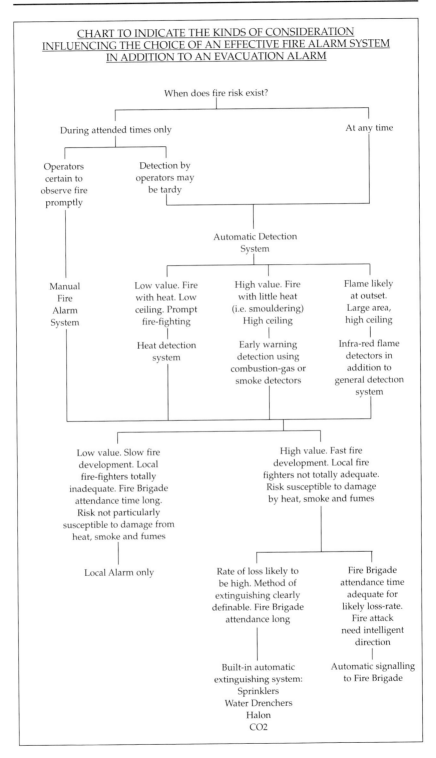

CHART TO INDICATE THE KINDS OF CONSIDERATION
INFLUENCING THE CHOICE OF AN EFFECTIVE FIRE ALARM SYSTEM
IN ADDITION TO AN EVACUATION ALARM

When does fire risk exist?

During attended times only

At any time

Operators certain to observe fire promptly

Detection by operators may be tardy

Automatic Detection System

Manual Fire Alarm System

Low value. Fire with heat. Low ceiling. Prompt fire-fighting

High value. Fire with little heat (i.e. smouldering) High ceiling

Flame likely at outset. Large area, high ceiling

Heat detection system

Early warning detection using combustion-gas or smoke detectors

Infra-red flame detectors in addition to general detection system

Low value. Slow fire development. Local fire-fighters totally inadequate. Fire Brigade attendance time long. Risk not particularly susceptible to damage from heat, smoke and fumes

High value. Fast fire development. Local fire fighters not totally adequate. Risk susceptible to damage by heat, smoke and fumes

Local Alarm only

Rate of loss likely to be high. Method of extinguishing clearly definable. Fire Brigade attendance long

Fire Brigade attendance time adequate for likely loss-rate. Fire attack need intelligent direction

Built-in automatic extinguishing system: Sprinklers Water Drenchers Halon CO_2

Automatic signalling to Fire Brigade

315

14

SALVAGE, REHABILITATION, WASTE AND CONTINGENCY PLANNING

14.1   SALVAGE

14.1.1   An important element in loss reduction is doing things that can minimise the ensuing losses once a loss-producing event has occurred. A quick response by people who have been trained in salvage work, whether it is in the form of first aid for personal injuries or the protection of damaged plant etc. to prevent further damage, can dramatically cut losses.

14.1.2   With much of the plant and equipment used in today's offices and factories it is essential that the corrosion initiated by the products of burning plastics and water (mainly hydrochloric acid) is stopped and the items cleaned of all traces of such substances. Electronic equipment, such as computers, is particularly prone to this type of damage and washing with distilled water has been found to be particularly effective in cleaning electronic equipment of the products of combustion.

14.1.3   The salvage action will vary from peril to peril but having the following planning and training is common for handling most loss producing events:

(a) a plan to deal with the loss

(b) people trained to respond quickly and correctly to the loss

(c) the proper salvage equipment and supplies.

14.2   REHABILITATION

14.2.1   Like salvage, rehabilitation is an important element in loss reduction where personal injury is involved. The quicker a person is able to recover from an injury the faster they are able to return to their optimum level of productivity and income earning capability. The return to full health is however not only in the best interests of the injured person but also the employer because:

(a) the work skills that the injured person has are again put to good productive use

(b) the disruption caused by having to cover for the work done by the injured person will cease.

14.2.2 Whilst rehabilitation must be supervised by qualified medical personnel, considerable benefit may be gained from involving the organisation for whom the injured person works. This is particularly true where the organisation employs a nurse or an occupational health professional. The nurse in the work situation is ideally placed to co-ordinate the rehabilitation of an individual. As a professionally trained medical worker the nurse can communicate with the doctors in the hospital or general practice who are initially concerned with the patient's rehabilitation, at the same time working in the factory environment he or she is familiar with job requirements and can communicate with factory management. The nurse is thus able to ensure that rehabilitation proceeds step by step with both the medical profession and the organisation's management being equally aware of the patient's progress.

14.2.3 Repair of damaged building and equipment is another area that can have a significant effect on the cost of loss. With many losses involving damage to property a further, often very much larger loss occurs because of the resultant interruption of the organisation's operations. Therefore, the quicker the repairs can be started and completed the lower the cost of the business interruption loss and therefore the overall cost of the loss.

14.3   THE HANDLING OF WASTE

14.3.1 Many countries have enacted legislation or regulations governing virtually all aspects of waste and reference should be made to these in order to obtain details that apply in a particular country. Virtually every process produces some form of waste, all of which, under certain conditions, can be instrumental in causing loss. The waste itself of course represents a loss, but what is usually of greater concern is the hazards of the physical and chemical form of the waste material. These can range through the many different types of materials that are used in industry.

14.3.2 Whilst most wastes can be disposed of without any significant problems there are, however, a number of substances where extra special care is required. These substances are dangerous or toxic for human beings or are extremely flammable such as those listed below in *Table 14.1*

Table 14.1

SUBSTANCES WHICH MAY CONSTITUTE SPECIAL WASTES
Acid and alkalis
Antimony and antimony compounds
Arsenic compounds
Asbestos (all forms)
Barium compounds
Beryllium and beryllium compounds
Biocides and phytopharmaceutical substances
Boron compounds
Cadmium and cadmium compounds
Copper compounds
Heterocydic organic compounds containing oxygen, nitrogen or sulphur
Hexavalent chromium compounds
Hydrocarbons and their oxygen, nitrogen and sulphur compounds
Inorganic halogen-containing compounds
Inorganic cyanides
Inorganic sulphur-containing compounds
Laboratory chemicals
Lead compounds
Mercury compounds
Nickel and nickel compounds excluding inert polymeric materials
Peroxides, chlorates, perchlorates and oxides
Pharmaceutical and veterinary compounds
Phosphorus and its compounds
Selenium and selenium compounds
Silver compounds
Tarry materials from refining and tar residues from distilling
Tellurium and tellurium compounds
Thallium and thallium compounds
Vanadium compounds
Zinc compounds

This list however is not exhaustive and new substances are being added each day. In addition, the regulations in each country may include different materials and it is, therefore, necessary to regularly check these in order to keep up to date.

14.4   WASTE DISPOSAL

14.4.1 With most manufacturing risks the number of machines provides a fair measure of fire hazard. This measure is appropriate where the machines themselves may cause a fire or where they create readily combustible waste or where they create conditions favouring fire. Woodworking machinery is an example of the accumulation of fire risk in direct proportion to the number of machines. All these machines produce waste, some making much more than others. Moreover, some machines create waste which is more readily combustible, especially when it is in the form of light shavings such as are produced from planing machines and spindle moulders.

14.4.2   One of the signs of a well managed factory has been said to be the regular or routine clearance and disposal of waste, and a good manager will readily appreciate the hazards which arise from undesirable accumulations of manufacturing waste. In factories in which combustible litter is created by the processes and warehouses in which such accumulations are likely to be found on the floors there should be arrangements for all waste and refuse to be cleared away at regular intervals. This should be removed as soon as possible from the building and safely disposed of in an environmentally appropriate way. Ideally, the workplace should be cleaned as the work continues so that litter is never allowed to build up. For example:

(a) in clothing factories it is important that clippings, cuttings, waste paper and refuse of every description be swept up each day when work ceases, deposited in bags or bins and removed from the factory at least once a week.

(b) in saw mills and joinery works, all sawdust, shavings and other refuse should be removed daily out of the building, and all oily and greasy waste and cloths should be kept in metal receptacles and removed outside the building every night. Most woodworking risks of any size have cyclone system of waste extraction which collects sawdust and shavings wastes and when it is produced by each machine and transports it away from the working area to a storage point outside the building.

(c) in motor garages, all oily and dirty waste and greasy cleaning cloths should be kept in metal receptacles and removed from the premises at least once a week, if not on a daily basis

(d) the printing industry generates large quantities of paper waste that should not be allowed to accumulate. Whilst it is preferable for this to be extracted automatically to a separate building, all paper waste should be removed daily and floors should be swept at the end of each shift with waste removed to a separate storage area. Rags used for cleaning machines and types become contaminated with flammable spirits and ink or varnish and may spontaneously combust if stored for any length of time. They should be placed in metal bins with self-closing lids and taken out of the building at the end of each shift. If not sent away for cleaning they should be burnt in an approved incinerator.

14.4.3   In fact, the floor sweepings, solid waste, rags and other trade waste on every production plant should be placed in proper metal receptacles with covers. The contents of these receptacles should be safely deposited outside of the building each night, so that they may be regularly disposed of in a safe manner. Many different kinds of dust are produced as a result of industrial processes. All are a form of waste that should be removed regularly and not allowed to accumulate. Regular cleaning of all places where it might lodge and collect and the installation of automatic dust extraction plant at the point of its production are essential in helping to minimise the risks of personal injury, fire and explosion that may be involved.

14.4.4   Disposal of Drums etc. that Contained Toxic Materials

Thoroughly scrub out the open drum, flush and wash again until as much as possible of the poison has been removed. It is essential that extreme care must be taken in disposing of the waste produced. If it is possible to break the hazardous material down in a safe way this should be done and to be sure that the drums are not re-used, the sides and bottom should be perforated before discarding. In any event empty drums of this type should be safely discarded in accordance with the regulations governing their disposal. It should be noted that rain water may rinse traces of poison out of a drum into the soil or the drainage streams, where the poison could eventually reach animals or humans. Perform all operations involved in the disposal of these types of drum with extreme care and with thoroughness.

14.4.5   Disposal of Salts used in Salt Baths

Empty salt bags should be thoroughly washed out with water before disposal. Waste nitrate salt must not be disposed of indiscriminately as an explosion could result if the salt is burned with carbonaceous material.

14.5   MANAGEMENT OF WASTE STRATEGIES

14.5.1   If waste is not disposed of in an appropriate way it will end up polluting the environment. Most countries today have legislation in place that is aimed at not only preventing pollution but also penalising any serious offenders. All waste in effect constitutes loss to the organisation. Furthermore the legal climate in most countries is weighted against the unwise disposal of waste. It is therefore sound economic sense for an organisation to spend time on minimising waste as far as possible and in ensuring that any that remains is properly disposed in the most appropriate manner for the particular substance.

This may be achieved by one or more of the following :

(a) reusing

(b) recycling

(c) reducing the waste be it gas, solid or liquid.

A reduction in the amount of waste represents a saving for the firm's bottom line.

14.5.2   Management should pro-actively manage the waste that their organisation is producing because waste represents loss. The following are a number of strategies that are useful in reducing and disposing of waste that is produced:

Waste Prevention -
Product substitution
Non production of material

Source Reduction -
Product formulation
Process modification
Equipment redesign

Recycling -
Solvent recovery
Spent solution recovery
Waste oil-refining

Treatment of waste -
Thermal destruction
    incineration
    wet air oxidation

Chemical destruction -
chemical oxidation
chemical reduction
absorption

Physical -
filtration
evaporation
condensation
freeze crystallisation

Biological -
aerobic
anaerobic

Disposal of waste -
Landfill
Residuals
Repository

These have been listed in decreasing order of effectiveness in reducing waste. In addition, the emphasis on technology decreases as we move down the list.

14.6   CONTINGENCY PLANNING

14.6.1 Contingency Plans, Emergency Plans, Crisis Management Plans and Business Continuity Planning are different names for an essential objective of managing risk, ensuring the survival of the business. All risk management should begin with the identification of risk and then proceed on to doing something about the risks that have been identified i.e. controlling them in some way.

This will invariably involve reducing the probability that a loss will occur or the severity of any loss that may occur or both. Whilst the former may go some way to reducing the likelihood of loss neither reducing the probability of loss nor its severity is ever likely to eliminate loss totally. Nor is it certain that the control measures will always work as expected. Therefore it is prudent for every organisation to have in place contingency plans that will not only reinforce the risk and loss control measures taken but more importantly act as a further means of limiting the consequences of loss in the event of a major loss occurring.

14.6.3   The contingency plan cannot provide a selection of possible solutions that would solve all of the myriad of problems created by a disaster. Rather it should provide the framework in which the organisation's management may work in the abnormal conditions created by a disaster to manage its effects and to bring about the organisation's recovery from its effects. Using the Business Continuity Plan for the particular type of disaster the management should be able to marshal the organisation's skills, knowledge, manpower and other resources to resolve all of the problems created by the disaster.

14.6.4   Every organisation should prepare plans for preventing and coping with actual or potentially severe loss situations covering both salvage operations and plans for carrying on the business of the organisation following the occurrence of a major loss. Contingency planning involves the following three elements:

(a) **the Disaster Plan** which is essentially preventative or if these measures fail the first line of defence. It should cover:

(i) **Loss prevention and control** This element is concerned with identifying and assessing all of the major hazards on an on-going basis and implementing risk and loss control measures prior to the occurrence of any incident. Under normal conditions loss prevention and control measures should be implemented over time as appropriate when the funds are available.

(ii) **Emergency Plan** that sets out in broad terms the management structures, procedures and resources that may be used to handle a major emergency once it has occurred. The Plan details measures to counter the immediate effects of the major loss incident by saving life, limiting damage and bringing the situation under control as quickly as possible.

(b) **the Crisis Management Plan** is complementary to the Disaster Plan and focuses on reducing the impact of the emergency by getting the business back into operation as quickly as possible. In this phase of Contingency Planning regaining the confidence of customers and employees is as important as replacing or repairing the damage.

For any set of contingency plans to be fully effective these three elements must be integrated as a co-ordinated flow of action is essential. See *Figure 14.1*.

Figure 14.1

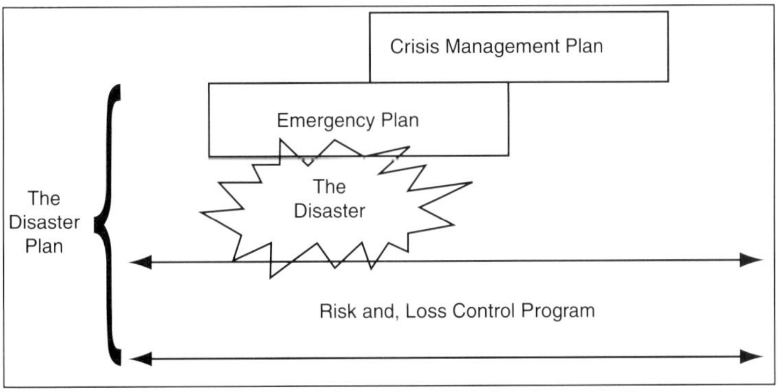

The Three Elements of an Integrated Contingency Plan

14.6.5   The Disaster Plan

The Disaster Plan must be designed with the needs of the individual organisation in mind. It should take account of:

(a) disasters which might affect any organisation e.g. serious fire, flood, windstorm, earthquake and other emergencies brought about by severe natural forces

(b) disasters which may arise from the nature of the operations carried out by the organisation. These may range from explosion or the release of toxic or other harmful material to the need to recall products which have been shown to be, or are potentially, harmful.

(c) disasters which occur elsewhere, but which could still affect the organisation in a potentially catastrophic manner. Explosion, pollution, interruption of supplies, services, communications, access or distribution channels, epidemics and political risks may all come into this category.

The range of threats that have to be considered may seem so great that planning for them appears to be almost impossible. There are, however, two factors that substantially reduce the difficulty involved.

Firstly hazard identification and risk assessment if properly carried out will quickly enable the maximum threats to be established. Secondly because the plan is concerned with consequences not causes and because the effects of disasters with widely different causes are frequently broadly the same, different types of disaster may be grouped together for analysis.

14.6.6   The Crisis Management or Recovery Plan

The Crisis Management or Recovery Plan starts with a situation that has been dictated by the disaster, and using in-depth understanding of how the organisation operates, plots the path back to normal operations in a quick and effective manner. Pre-incident central co-ordination and research, and total involvement of all management are essential in the creation of a recovery plan.

Remember it is often not a question of if a disaster will strike the organisation, but when!

Contingency Plans form the safety net for the organisation. Whilst they cannot guarantee survival they can increase the chances of a speedy return to normal operations.

14.6.7   The success of salvage operations (and under this heading would fall the minimisation of both personal injuries and property damage) depends upon people trained to deal with emergencies and the necessary equipment being available at all times. There is little point in having first aid boxes, or the equipment and supplies for stripping down and cleaning smoke or water damaged machinery being available if no one knows what to do and vice versa.

14.6.8   The severity of interruption losses is not necessarily directly proportional to the severity of the property damage. There are many recorded instances of relatively small property losses resulting in prolonged stoppages of production. Therefore, in preparing a Contingency Plan to deal with the major interruptions to the organisation's business the first steps should be to identify:

(a) all potential sources of loss-producing events which may disrupt operations

(b) interdependencies between different parts of the organisation itself; for example, would damage to one process or storage area disrupt all production of one or more of a firm's products?

(c) dependencies upon individual suppliers or customers. The 'Life Lines' projects that many Local Authorities around the world have carried out into the types of disasters and their likely effect on the supply of various services such as power, water etc may be of considerable help in identifying both these dependencies as well as alternative sources of supply

(d) alternative sources of supply or outlets where any of the above dependencies exist

(e) all seasonal factors.

It may be feasible to make some changes immediately that could reduce the potential impact on the business of any incident, such as the duplication of key items of plant or power supplies. Likewise, by holding larger stocks of raw materials and parts, (perhaps distributed between two or more buildings), or by finding another supplier, it may be possible to reduce the vulnerability of the business to a breakdown in supplies from a sole supplier. In every case, management would have to decide whether the extra costs involved are a reasonable price to pay for the reduction in risk. 'Just in Time' systems of supplying materials can create considerable difficulties in the event of a major loss and provision needs to be made to cope with these.

14.6.9 The Contingency Plan should specify the management approach to each of the different types of loss situations, setting out the steps to be followed under various circumstances and assigning responsibilities for various tasks. Many of these steps need to be arranged well in advance of a loss occurring; for example, mutual assistance arrangements may be made with competitors whereby if one suffers a major loss of production facilities others will assist in the manufacture of its product(s).

14.6.10 In addition, both the Disaster and Crisis Management Plans should be tested regularly and updated where shortcomings are found so that the Plans are not only kept in an up-to-date state as possible, but also so that the personnel involved have been trained. It however must be realised that having a plan, even if it is kept up to date and even if people have been fully trained in what to do, will not necessarily result in your being able to cope with the crisis when it occurs. It is essential for those who are drafting or amending the plan to bear in mind that:

(a) the more severe the crisis is, the greater the loss or lack of resources

(b) the plan will not work without people to make it come alive

(c) the effects of stress on both people and the plan will be unpredictable. The plan as a consequence will work in unpredictable ways.

(d) once a crisis strikes, until the organisation is able to and begins to help itself, it cannot help others.

14.6.11 The key to successfully coping with a crisis is a fast response by the organisation, providing of course that it has the necessary skills, equipment and supplies as well as adequate preparations having been made. The actions taken in the first day or so after the crisis has happened have a significant impact in limiting the extent of the ultimate effects of the crisis in the organisation. The actions taken in the period immediately after the occurrence of the crisis is in many instances critical in saving life. In this the efforts of ordinary people who are on the spot and who have access to basic equipment such as lamps, gloves, shovels and crowbars may achieve quite remarkable success in recovering people who are buried and who may otherwise die if left until relief teams reach the area from outside.

14.6.12 One of the most critical factors in coping with a crisis is gaining an understanding of its scale. To achieve this reliable information needs to be gathered in order that the critical decisions are made as quickly as possible after the event. The systems and procedures that should normally swing into place following the occurrence of a crisis should be set up so as to achieve this within a few hours after the event itself. There are however a number of reasons why an organisation or community may delay to make such decisions quickly or make incorrect decisions of which anyone involved in contingency planning should be aware:-

(a) personal differences, red tape, demarcation disputes and uncertainties. All of these exists in virtually every organisation.

(b) the social culture may be such that all decisions are made in a group environment rather than on an individual basis. Making a group decision takes considerably longer because of the time needed to ensure that all members of the group have all of the necessary information and are fully consulted.

(c) a lack of the necessary information on which to make an informed decision.

All of these problems may be overcome by pre-planning as well as by maintaining a flexible approach and by being aware that they may arise particularly in the middle of coping with the crisis.

General Index to Risk Control

D

E

F

H